Parenting in the Digital Age:

A South Sudanese and African Guide

Santino Atem Deng

The publisher wishes to acknowledge and thank Dr. Douglas H. Johnson for his invaluable help and support for Africa World Books and its mission of preserving and promoting African cultural and literary traditions and history. Dr. Johnson and fellow historians have been instrumental in ensuring that African people remain connected to their past and their identity. Africa World Books is proud to carry on this mission.

All rights reserved. It is illegal to reproduce, duplicate or transmit any part of this book in either electronic means or printed format. Recording of this publication is strictly prohibited. No part of this publication may be reproduced, stored in a retrieval system, or transmitted, in any form, or by any means, electronic, mechanical, photocopying, recording or otherwise, without the prior permission of the publishers.

Copyright © 2024 Santino Atem Deng

ISBN: 9781763683983

This book is sold subject to the conditions that it shall not, by way of trade or otherwise, be lent, re-sold, hired out or otherwise circulated without the publisher's prior consent in any form of binding or cover other than in which it is published and without a similar condition including the condition being imposed on the subsequent purchaser.

Cover design, typesetting and layout: Africa World Books
Unit 3, 57 Frobisher St, Osborne Park, WA 6017
P.O. Box 1106 Osborne Park, WA 6916

Table of Contents

About the Author   vii

Chapter One
Preface and Introduction   1

Chapter Two
Navigating Modern Challenges within
the African Context   15

Chapter Three
Parenting in the Diaspora: Upholding Cultural Identity
in a Changing World   43

Chapter Four
Navigating the Complexities of Forced Migration
and Acculturation   53

Chapter Five
Parenting in a Multicultural Society: Balancing Cultural
Preservation and Adapting to New Norms   71

Chapter Six
Acculturational Challenges: Negotiating Between
Tradition and Integrating into the New Environment   89

Chapter Seven
Bridging Generational Divides and Cultivating
Family Harmony   111

Chapter Eight
South Sudanese Youth Identity: Views on Parenting
and Culture   129

Chapter Nine
Promoting Positive Parenting Approaches and Resilience   156

Chapter Ten
Adapting to Change: South Sudanese Family Strategies
in Australia   178

Chapter Eleven
Navigating Challenges and Embracing
Educational Opportunities   218

Chapter Twelve
Parenting in the Digital Age: Balancing Technological
Benefits and Risks for Child Development   239

Chapter Thirteen
Balancing Tradition and Innovation: Parenting in the
Digital Age for African Diaspora Families   260

Chapter Fourteen
Human Development and Wellbeing Amid Migration   280

Chapter Fifteen
Charting the Future: Conclusion and Next Steps   299

References   319

ABOUT THE AUTHOR

Dr. Santino Atem Deng (PhD) is a distinguished leader, scholar, and advocate committed to advancing education, community development, and social justice for South Sudanese and African diaspora communities. As a founder and Chairman of Ramciel University (https://ramcieluniversity.edu.ss/) in South Sudan, Dr. Deng has impacted higher education and continues shaping South Sudanese youth's future. His extensive academic and professional background and his journey as a refugee underscores his dedication to fostering resilience, cultural continuity, and educational excellence.

Personal Background

Dr. Deng's early life is a testament to resilience, a quality that has shaped his character and work. Born in South Sudan during a period of intense civil unrest, he fled Sudan in 1987, traversing Ethiopia and Kenya before finding refuge in New Zealand in 2000 and Australia in 2013. His experiences as a Jesh El-Amer (Red Army) and determination to pursue education amid overwhelming challenges have profoundly shaped his life's work. His father, Justin Deng Anyuon (known as Deng-Matiat), a revered educator, instilled in him a deep commitment to education and community service, a commitment that is the driving force behind his mission today.

Educational Background

Dr. Deng's educational journey is a powerful testament to his resilience and unwavering commitment to learning. Despite the hardships of his early schooling in South Sudan, Ethiopia, and Kenya, he completed his secondary education at St. Patrick College in Wellington, New Zealand.

He earned a Bachelor of Arts in Education from Massey University, a Postgraduate Diploma, and a Master of Education/Counselling from The University of Auckland. In 2016, he completed his PhD in Social Science at Victoria University, Melbourne, with a focus on South Sudanese family dynamics, parenting practices, and the challenges of resettlement in Australia, showcasing his scholarly dedication and commitment to understanding and addressing social issues.

Dr Deng will complete an Executive Master of Public Administration (EMPA) in 2025 through the Australia and New Zealand School of Government (ANZSOG) in partnership with the University of Melbourne (as a conferrer of the degree). This Victorian government-sponsored program, designed for Australian federal, state, and territory government executives, will further strengthen his capacity for leadership and innovation in government public service.

Professional Background

Dr. Deng brings over two decades of diverse experience in education, research, social services and justice, mental health, and community leadership. His roles as an educator/lecturer, counsellor, researcher, and trainer, with a focus on trauma, migration, and family support, have uniquely positioned him to address the complex issues faced by

South Sudanese and African diaspora communities. His extensive work in resettlement, social inclusion, government agencies, parenting practices, and leadership in community programs across Australia and New Zealand has established him as a key advocate for minority groups.

Academic Publications

Dr. Deng's extensive research, which focuses on the challenges and dynamics of South Sudanese families in the context of migration and resettlement, has resulted in some significant publications. These works delve into crucial themes such as family dynamics, parenting practices, acculturation, and the mental health of refugees, offering valuable insights and practical guidance for those working with refugee and migrant populations.

1. **Fitting the Jigsaw: South Sudanese Family Dynamics and Parenting Practices in Australia** (Victoria University, Melbourne). This PhD thesis examines the adaptation challenges of South Sudanese families in Australia, providing insights and nuance into how migration impacts parenting and family structures.

2. **Refugee Resettlement and Parenting in a Different Context** (Journal of Immigrant & Refugee Studies) - Co-authored by Prof Marlowe, this article is a significant collaborative effort that invites the reader to be part of the exploration of the integration of South Sudanese parenting practices with Western norms. It highlights the tensions and adaptations that occur during resettlement, providing valuable insights into this complex process.

3. **Positive Parenting: Integrating Sudanese Traditions and New Zealand Styles of Parenting.** This study evaluates the effectiveness of parenting strategies that blend Sudanese traditions with New Zealand practices, focusing on community-based interventions.

4. **Sleep Difficulties Among South Sudanese Former Refugees Settled in Australia** (Transcultural Psychiatry). Co-authored with colleagues, this paper investigates the impact of trauma and resettlement stress on sleep patterns among South Sudanese refugees, linking mental health challenges to sleep disorders.
5. **South Sudanese Australians: Transnational Kinship During Conflict and Economic Crisis** (Understanding Diaspora Development). Co-authored with colleagues, this Book's chapter discusses the role of transnational networks in maintaining family ties and cultural identity during crises, emphasising the resilience of the South Sudanese diaspora.
6. **South Sudanese youth acculturation and intergenerational challenges:** This article examines the acculturation challenges South Sudanese youth face in Australia, highlighting the tension between traditional values and adapting to a new culture. It emphasises the role of identity struggles, media influence, and inadequate community support, and it recommends balanced integration strategies for better psychological adjustment.

Notable Achievements

Dr. Deng's numerous impactful achievements reflect his deep commitment to social justice and community development. As the Founder and Chairman of Ramciel University, he guides its strategic direction and ensures it meets its educational objectives. His role as an Adjunct Fellow at Victoria University, Melbourne, allows him to continue contributing to academic research in social sciences. His leadership as Chair of the South Sudanese Australian Youth Justice Expert Working Group (EWG) at the Victorian Department of Justice and Community Safety is a testament to his dedication to reducing youth offending and enhancing community safety.

Current Position and Work

Dr. Deng is the Founder and Chairman of Ramciel University, South Sudan, an Adjunct Fellow at Victoria University, Melbourne, and an Honorary Fellow at Deakin University. He also founded the African-Australian Family and Parenting Support Services (AFPSS), which offers comprehensive support services to African-Australian families in Victoria.

In 2022, the Victorian Government appointed Dr Deng to lead the South Sudanese Australian Youth Justice Expert Working Group. This group is focused on identifying and addressing the factors contributing to the overrepresentation of South Sudanese and African youth in the criminal justice system. Dr Deng's work in this role is expected to lead to significant systemic changes, benefiting minority communities across Victoria and Australia.

Personal Philosophy and Motivation

Dr Deng's personal philosophy is deeply rooted in the transformative power of education. Inspired by his father's legacy and his own experiences as a refugee, he views education as a critical tool for overcoming adversity and fostering personal and communal development. His unwavering commitment to empowering young people and parents and preserving cultural identity drives his work, offering hope and guidance for a brighter future.

Community Involvement and Advocacy

Dr. Deng has tirelessly advocated for South Sudanese and African communities both in the diaspora and South Sudan. His leadership in community organisations, such as the SPLM Chapter in New Zealand and Australia, highlights his dedication to social justice and cultural preservation. He has played a key role in lobbying for international support for South Sudan's independence and has been instrumental in educating Western nations about the challenges marginalised groups face.

Dr. Deng's life and work stand as a testament to the power of resilience, education, and community. Through his leadership, research, and advocacy, he has significantly contributed to the well-being and development of South Sudanese and African diaspora communities. His journey from a young refugee to a respected scholar and leader inspires those who strive to make a meaningful impact in their communities.

Dr. Deng's contributions to the field provide valuable insights into the lived experiences of South Sudanese communities in the diaspora and offer practical guidance. His work equips policymakers, researchers, and service providers working with refugee and migrant populations with the necessary tools to navigate the complex challenges faced by these communities, making them feel more prepared and empowered to make a positive impact.

Personal Interests

Dr Deng's dedication to preserving South Sudanese and African culture and traditions is a testament to his commitment to cultural continuity. His active participation in cultural events, mentorship of young people, and contribution to developing educational resources that bridge cultural and generational divides all stem from his personal interests and motivations. His journey from a young refugee to a respected scholar and leader inspires those who strive to make a meaningful impact in their communities.

Acknowledgments

However, I would like to extend my most profound appreciation to the many South Sudanese and African participants in Victoria, Australia, especially those who have volunteered their time to participate in the individual interviews and focus group discussions for my PhD and continue conversation whether in the community and at my professional work for this book. They have generously shared their parenting experiences, challenges, shifts and changes within their family and community life, which testify to their resilience and strength.

I am grateful to my wonderful family for the support they have all given me throughout my research and for their patience and understanding throughout this journey. To my mother, Rosa Adut Deng, who passed away in 2022 before the completion of this book, with a smile on her face and melodious singing, for her care, support and encouragement. I am also grateful to my father, the Late Justin Deng Anyuon, a teacher who taught for half a century and taught many South Sudanese dignitaries for setting the inspiration for the esteemed value of education and the importance of sharing and passing the skills and knowledge from one generation to the next. Thank you, Sir Dad! May your souls continue to rest in eternal peace!

I left home and them behind during the civil wars in Sudan, but they made me feel grounded by that, which helped me overcome the challenges of forced migration and other adversities.

CHAPTER ONE

Preface and Introduction

Preface

Families face unprecedented challenges from migration, globalisation, and technological change in an increasingly interconnected world. While bringing the world closer together, these forces have also fragmented communities, particularly those of South Sudanese and other African families living in the diaspora. The lives of these families encapsulate both the anxieties and possibilities of our time, making their experiences a unique lens through which we can understand modern parenting. "Parenting in the Digital Age: A South Sudanese and African Guide" was written to explore these dynamics and support families striving to navigate the complexities of preserving cultural identity while adapting to new environments.

This book emerged from countless conversations, observations, research, and experiences as a counsellor and community member. It is rooted in the lived experiences of families who have journeyed far from their homelands, often carrying little more than the cultural values, customs, and practices passed down through generations. These families are now tasked with integrating into new cultural landscapes while contending with the realities of migration, acculturation, and digitalisation that have transformed parenting into a complex and often unfamiliar terrain.

As globalisation continues and migration becomes an increasingly common experience, migrants and host societies face profound challenges. These challenges threaten traditional ways of life and cultural identities, making the need for resources like this book all the more urgent. This guide is designed to help South Sudanese and African families preserve their cultural heritage while navigating the new life spaces they now occupy.

This book is intended for anyone who works with or cares for South Sudanese and African families in the diaspora or their home countries. It is a valuable resource for parents, teachers seeking to improve their cultural awareness, community leaders and activists aiming to serve their communities better, policymakers striving to create inclusive societies, and anyone interested in fostering cultural diversity and social inclusion. The ideas and guidance presented here will equip you with the knowledge and tools needed to fulfil your role and confidently support responsible parenting.

Throughout this book, I have endeavoured to provide practical recommendations that address the multidimensional aspects of parenting in the diaspora, including cultural preservation, resilience, wellness, education, and economic stability. Each chapter offers actionable strategies that readers can incorporate into their daily lives to help shape their children's experiences and optimise their development. These steps are designed to empower parents, helping them navigate the complexities of modern parenting with confidence and clarity.

The narratives, case studies, and strategies shared in this book are drawn from the stories of South Sudanese and African families. Their cultural heritage and community networks have provided enduring strength amid adversity. Their ability to endure, transform, and maintain their ancestral worldviews reflects their remarkable resilience, adaptability, and the human capacity to adapt and thrive.

I hope this book offers inspiration, direction, and empowerment, whether you are a parent, teacher, community leader, or policymaker. It aims to equip you with the skills and knowledge necessary to support the social, emotional, and academic success of South Sudanese and African families and anyone who resonates with these experiences. The challenges of migration and technological change are significant. However, these families can successfully navigate their parenting journey with the proper support while fostering a welcoming and inclusive environment.

This book was written with the conviction that cultural cohesion can be preserved in the context of migration and that migrants have the resilience, adaptability, and social capital to build a better world for their children and future generations. I am deeply grateful to the many families and individuals who shared their stories, insights, and wisdom, infusing this book with richness and inspiration. Their voices have made this book possible.

My heartfelt thanks also go to the community members and colleagues who have supported and encouraged me throughout this journey. Your efforts continue to inspire and sustain me.

I hope this book serves as a valuable guide for all who are committed to preserving and supporting South Sudanese/African and other minority families in the diaspora and at home. May we all approach the challenges of modern parenting with confidence, compassion, and a deep sense of commitment to maintaining the cultural values that define who we are. It is my hope that the insights and strategies shared in this book will be a valuable resource in your journey.

How to Read This Book

This book is structured to guide you through the complexities of modern parenting in the context of migration and digitalisation. Each chapter focuses on a specific aspect of the challenges and opportunities that South Sudanese and African families face in the diaspora. Whether you are a parent seeking practical advice, a teacher looking to enhance your cultural awareness, or a policymaker aiming to create inclusive policies, you can navigate the chapters based on your interests and needs.

- For Parents: Each chapter offers actionable strategies and insights tailored to the unique challenges of raising children in a multicultural and technologically advanced environment.
- For Educators and Service Providers: This book provides cultural context and understanding that can enhance interactions with students and clients/customers from South Sudanese and African backgrounds.
- For Community Leaders and Policymakers: The chapters highlight the broader social and cultural dynamics and offer guidance on effectively supporting and empowering these communities.

Feel free to read the book sequentially for a comprehensive understanding or focus on the chapters most relevant to your current needs. Each chapter stands independently, providing valuable insights and strategies that can be applied separately or in conjunction with other chapters.

Introduction

The 21st century presents a unique set of challenges for families across the globe. However, for South Sudanese and other African families living in the diaspora, these challenges are magnified by the complex interplay of migration, urbanisation, and the rapid advancement of technology. While offering unprecedented opportunities, these forces also disrupt long-held traditions and cultural practices that have been the bedrock of African communities for generations.

Migration has always been a defining characteristic of human history, but in recent decades, the scale and impact of migration have reached new heights. For South Sudanese families, migration often involves fleeing conflict, persecution, or economic hardship. The journey from their homeland to a new country is fraught with peril, and the emotional toll of leaving behind everything familiar cannot be overstated. Once in the host country, these families face the daunting task of rebuilding their lives in an unfamiliar environment where the social and cultural norms may differ significantly from what they have known.

In the context of migration, the challenge of cultural preservation becomes paramount. Many South Sudanese parents are acutely aware that their children are growing up in a world vastly different from the one they were raised in. The values, customs, and traditions that were once passed down seamlessly from one generation to the next are now at risk of being lost in the face of new influences. This creates a tension between the desire to maintain cultural identity and the need to adapt to the realities of life in a new country.

Acculturation, or adapting to a new culture while retaining aspects of the original culture, is often a double-edged sword. For children and young people, acculturation can lead to identity confusion as they navigate between the expectations of their parents and the pressures of fitting in with their peers. This tension is particularly pronounced in the diaspora, where the younger generation may feel caught between two worlds: the traditional values of their parents and the modern, often individualistic, values of the host society.

Urbanisation adds another layer of complexity to the lives of these families. Many South Sudanese and African families come from rural or communal settings where life is centred around the extended family and the community. In these environments, parenting is a collective effort, with aunts, uncles, grandparents, and neighbours all playing a role in raising children. However, this communal support system is often absent in urban settings, particularly in Western countries. Families are more isolated, and parents must navigate the challenges of raising children in a fast-paced, competitive, and sometimes alienating environment. The values of individualism and self-reliance that dominate urban life can be at odds with the collectivist values many African families hold dear.

Technology is among the most significant disruptors in South Sudanese and African families' lives today. The digital revolution has transformed nearly every aspect of life, from communication to learning, working, and socialising. For young people, technology offers a gateway to the wider world, providing access to information, entertainment, and social networks that were unimaginable just a few decades ago. However, this access also comes with risks. The internet and social media expose young people to a range of influences that may conflict with their cultural values, and the anonymity of online interactions can lead to behaviours that would be unacceptable in face-to-face interactions.

For parents, the rapid pace of technological change can be overwhelming. Many find themselves struggling to understand the digital world their children inhabit, leading to a generational divide that can strain family relationships. Parents may worry about the impact of screen time on their children's development, the risks of cyberbullying, or the potential for exposure to inappropriate content. At the same time, they may feel ill-equipped to guide their children in the responsible use of technology, especially when they themselves are still learning to navigate this new digital landscape.

Despite these challenges, the experiences of South Sudanese and African families in the diaspora are also marked by resilience, adaptability, and a deep commitment to preserving their cultural heritage. This book is a testament to that resilience. It is a resource for families seeking to maintain their cultural identity while adapting to the demands of life in a new country. It offers practical strategies for navigating modern parenting challenges, from managing technology's impact to fostering resilience and well-being in children.

Each chapter of this book addresses a different aspect of parenting in the digital age, focusing on the unique experiences of South Sudanese and African families. The chapters build on each other, providing a comprehensive guide to the complexities of modern parenting in the diaspora. The narratives and case studies presented in this book are drawn from the real-life experiences of families who have successfully navigated the challenges of migration, urbanisation, and technology. Their stories offer valuable insights into strategies to help other families thrive in a rapidly changing world.

In the following pages, you will find a wealth of information on cultural preservation, resilience, wellness, education, and economic stability. These themes are explored through the lens of African values and traditions, focusing on how these can be maintained and adapted in modern life. The book also provides practical advice on creating a supportive and nurturing environment for children, fostering positive relationships within the family, and navigating parenting challenges in a digital world.

Whether you are a parent, a teacher, a community leader, or a policymaker, this book is designed to provide you with the tools and knowledge you need to support South Sudanese and African families in the diaspora. It is a call to action for all of us to work together to preserve the cultural values that are the foundation of these communities while also embracing the opportunities that come with living in a globalised world. By doing so, we can ensure that the next generation of South Sudanese and African children grow up with a strong sense of identity, a deep connection to their cultural heritage, and the skills they need to succeed in the modern world.

Chapters Summary

Chapter One: Preface and Introduction
This chapter sets the stage for the book by introducing the challenges faced by South Sudanese and African families living in the diaspora due to migration, globalisation, and technological change. It highlights the complex task of preserving cultural identity while adapting to new environments. The chapter provides a roadmap for readers, including parents, educators, and policymakers, to navigate the intricacies of modern parenting within this unique cultural context. The emphasis is on the resilience of these families and their capacity to blend traditional values with modern realities to ensure the successful upbringing of their children in a rapidly changing world.

Chapter Two: Navigating Modern Challenges within the African Context
This chapter delves into the impact of migration and technological advancements on African parenting practices. It examines the balance between preserving traditional African family structures, such as the extended family system and adapting to new societal norms in urbanised and diaspora settings. The chapter also discusses the pressures of acculturation and the challenges South Sudanese families face in

maintaining their cultural identity while integrating into new environments. It emphasises the importance of resilience and cultural preservation in overcoming the hurdles posed by migration and modernity.

Chapter Three: Parenting in the Diaspora: Upholding Cultural Identity in a Changing World

This chapter explores the core values and beliefs that underpin South Sudanese and broader African parenting practices, particularly within the diaspora. It highlights the role of respect, community, and family hierarchy in child-rearing, emphasising the importance of extended family and community support in maintaining cultural continuity. The chapter also addresses the challenges of forced migration and the need for cultural adaptation while preserving traditional values. The role of religious institutions and community organisations in supporting these families is also discussed.

Chapter Four: Navigating the Complexities of Forced Migration and Acculturation

This chapter analyses the migration and acculturation processes experienced by South Sudanese and other African families. It examines the pre-, in-, and post-migration contexts, focusing on the psychological, cultural, and spiritual adjustments required in the host countries. The chapter discusses the traumatic consequences of forced migration and offers strategies for parents to help their children navigate these challenges without losing their cultural essence. The complexities of acculturation, including identity conflicts and the impact on family dynamics, are also explored.

Chapter Five: Parenting in a Multicultural Society: Balancing Cultural Preservation and Adapting to New Norms

This chapter focuses on the delicate balance between preserving cultural heritage and adapting to new cultural norms in a multicultural society. It highlights the importance of cultural practices and rituals in maintaining children's strong sense of identity. The chapter discusses the challenges of confronting discrimination, the role of the community in cultural adaptation, and practical strategies for fostering open communication and resilience within the family. The chapter concludes with practical advice on how to integrate cultural preservation with the demands of modern parenting.

Chapter Six: Acculturational Challenges: Negotiating Between Tradition and Integrating into the New Environment

This chapter delves into the acculturation process, examining how South Sudanese and other African families negotiate between their traditional values and the demands of integrating into a new environment. It discusses the impact of acculturation on family dynamics, including role reversal and the challenges of maintaining authority and discipline in the face of new societal norms. The chapter also addresses the issues of discrimination and prejudice, offering coping strategies and support systems to help families navigate these challenges while preserving their cultural identity.

Chapter Seven: Bridging Generational Divides and Cultivating Family Harmony

This chapter explores the intergenerational conflicts that often arise within South Sudanese and African families in the diaspora. It examines the underlying dynamics of these conflicts, focusing on communication styles and the role of active listening in resolving misunderstandings. The chapter also discusses the challenges of integrating into the host society while maintaining family harmony, offering strategies for bridging generational divides and fostering a sense of unity within the family.

Chapter Eight: South Sudanese Youth Identity: Views on Parenting and Culture

This chapter provides insights into the perspectives of South Sudanese youth on parenting and culture. It explores the tension between traditional values and the influence of the host society, particularly in terms of power, control, and respect within the family. The chapter also addresses the challenges of resettlement and the role of parents in supporting their children's integration into the new society while maintaining cultural pride and identity. It offers strategies for helping youth navigate these challenges and achieve future success.

Chapter Nine: Promoting Positive Parenting Approaches and Resilience

This chapter emphasises the importance of resilience as a foundation for well-being within South Sudanese and African families. It explores the role of collectivism and spirituality in fostering resilience and offers contemporary psychological insights into positive parenting strategies. The chapter provides practical advice on nurturing resilience in children, focusing on developing strong family bonds, cultural pride, and a growth mindset.

Chapter Ten: Adapting to Change: South Sudanese Family Strategies in Australia

This chapter examines the strategies employed by South Sudanese families in Australia to adapt to the challenges of resettlement while maintaining their cultural identity. It discusses the role of community leadership, the blending of South Sudanese and Australian parenting practices, and the importance of recognising and addressing shortcomings in the adaptation process. The chapter also highlights the need for parents to embrace change and act as role models for their children, ensuring the preservation of cultural values while navigating the complexities of life in a new country.

Chapter Eleven: Navigating Challenges and Embracing Educational Opportunities

This chapter focuses on the vital role of education in the lives of South Sudanese and African diaspora families. It discusses these families' educational challenges, including language barriers, discrimination, and limited resource access. The chapter offers strategies for promoting academic success, fostering a growth mindset, and nurturing cultural pride and identity. The critical role of schools and educators in supporting the educational aspirations of these families is also emphasised.

Chapter Twelve: Parenting in the Digital Age: Balancing Technological Benefits and Risks for Child Development

This chapter explores the impact of technology on modern family dynamics, particularly within South Sudanese and African families. It discusses the benefits and risks of technology in parenting, including its influence on family communication, the potential for exposure to inappropriate content, and the challenges of managing screen time. The chapter offers specific strategies for fostering digital literacy, responsible online behaviour, and integrating technology into everyday family life in a balanced and healthy way, such as setting clear rules for screen time and discussing online safety.

Chapter Thirteen: Balancing Tradition and Innovation: Parenting in the Digital Age for South Sudanese Families

This chapter continues the discussion on the impact of technology on contemporary parenting dynamics. It examines the challenges and risks associated with technology use, particularly in maintaining traditional values within a rapidly changing digital landscape. The chapter offers practical advice on harmonising technology with cultural values, fostering healthy technology habits within the family, and navigating the evolving intersection of technology and parenting.

Chapter Fourteen: Human Development and Wellbeing Amid Migration

This chapter provides an overview of the stages of human development within the context of migration, focusing on the challenges faced by South Sudanese and African diaspora families. It discusses the importance of access to healthcare services, mental and emotional health, social wellbeing, and economic stability. The chapter emphasises the role of culture and resilience in promoting human development and offers strategies for ensuring the overall wellbeing of individuals and families amid migration challenges.

Chapter Fifteen: Charting the Future: Conclusion and Next Steps

The final chapter reflects on the book's core themes and offers insights for the future. It discusses the importance of building resilience, balancing acculturation with cultural preservation, and empowering families through education. The chapter concludes with actionable strategies for fostering mental and emotional wellbeing, promoting cultural continuity, and cultivating hope and resilience for future generations of South Sudanese and African diaspora families.

These summaries capture the essence of each chapter, highlighting the key themes and providing a clear understanding of the book's content.

CHAPTER TWO

Navigating Modern Challenges within the African Context

Introduction

A delicate balance between tradition and the ever-changing realities of modern life marks parenting in the 21st century. In the African context, this balance becomes even more complex due to migration, technological advancement, and the pressures of adapting to new societal norms. The chapter delves into the intricate journey of South Sudanese and other African families as they grapple with the dual challenge of preserving cultural identity while embracing the demands of a rapidly evolving global environment.

Rooted in communal values and a deep sense of familial interconnectedness, African parenting has long been guided by the extended family, where child-rearing responsibilities are shared among parents, grandparents, aunts, uncles, and even the broader community. However, migration, urbanisation, and the influence of technology have reshaped these traditional roles. Parents in the diaspora, particularly those from South Sudan and other African countries, are tasked with navigating not only the cultural dissonance that arises from living in a new environment but also the pressures of raising children in a world vastly different from their own upbringing.

For South Sudanese families, the transition is especially poignant. Many have fled conflict, endured displacement, and now find themselves in a new cultural landscape where societal norms, values, and expectations differ from their homeland. The trauma of war, coupled with the challenges of integration into a foreign society, has created a parenting environment where old traditions meet modern realities head-on. Parents face the difficult task of maintaining cultural values while adjusting to the influences of technology, Western ideologies, and the individualistic nature of their new surroundings.

This chapter explores the evolving role of African parents in these shifting contexts, examining how migration, urbanisation, and technology impact family dynamics. It offers insights into how parents can successfully blend traditional African values with modern approaches to parenting, ensuring that their children grow up with a strong sense of identity, resilience, and the ability to thrive in a globalised digital age.

The African Family: Balancing Tradition in a Rapidly Changing World

African society boasts a rich and diverse cultural heritage, with unique family structures and parental roles. The African family, often extended, comprises parents, children, and a network of relatives, including grandparents, siblings, and their children. This extended family serves as a social network and plays a crucial role in child-rearing, with parental responsibilities shared within the community.

Traditional African Family Systems: Foundations and Evolutions

Individual identity remains embedded in family and community. In much of sub-Saharan Africa, development has historically centred around the extended family, which remains the central unit of social organisation. It reflects a focus on communal living, which informs parenting attitudes. There is a strong sense of communal responsibility and togetherness related to child-rearing. In many of these cultures, a child's upbringing is a collective rather than an individual enterprise involving parents, other relatives and community members. Although a child might live in one family, he or she draws on multiple sources of wisdom and life lessons, which in turn roots the individual in family and community.

A premium is placed on the extended family or, as it is often referred to, 'the family'. The extended family socialises and raises children. Elders are respected, and cultural values, rules of conduct, and wisdom are often transmitted to the younger generation. Family gatherings are a critical part of social life. Children are socialised by their families into the importance of their community, respect for their elders, and the value of 'collective responsibility'. It is also the strength of the community on which family members can rely for a level of support and as a platform for their lives.

Extended Family's Role in Raising Children

Even adults who were not involved in the day-to-day childcare become deeply invested in a child's education, discipline and moral guidance, which can include everything from selecting their partner to advising them. Many children grow up mentored by grandparents, aunts, and uncles across Africa and beyond, and it is this extended family involvement that makes children grow up with a context that genuinely reflects the example of multiple family members. This diversity in the child's life during infancy directly contributes to the child's social and cognitive development into adulthood, highlighting the strength of collective responsibility in traditional African families.

In communities like the Maasai in Kenya and Tanzania, elders play a significant role in socialisation. They pass down cultural heritage to children through teaching rituals, conduct, and stories from the past. This transmission of cultural knowledge reinforces the idea that a child is not solely raised by parents but by the entire community, thereby preserving cultural identity and a sense of belonging.

Urbanisation and Its Impact on Family Structures

Urbanisation and modernisation have indeed altered the family structure among Africans. An increasing number of Africans are migrating to urban areas in pursuit of economic opportunities, leading to the formation of nuclear families. The nuclear family is gradually replacing the extended family system. While communal support was once a cornerstone of African society, it is becoming less common due to these changes. However, it is essential to note the resilience of African families in adapting to these shifts.

However, urban living increasingly necessitates smaller families, primarily parents and young children. While this may alleviate the burden of family responsibilities on parents, the lack of support from extended family among urbanites may place more stress on parents as they balance work and family demands. Furthermore, the physical distance from extended families means that culture and the old ways risk being forgotten. This underscores the importance of preserving traditional African values in the face of urbanisation and migration.

The demands of time in modern urban settings, where people work long hours and often do not work with neighbours or are susceptible to isolation, affect the maintenance of their cultural practices as they raise children here in the Diaspora. This requires a new approach and methodology in parenting: the spirit and essence of the communal approach remain alive, even in a nuclear family structure.

Urbanisation's Transformative Effects Across African Nations
One can infer this in many other African countries; for instance, in Nigeria, one such shift is the movement of young families to villages and subsequent migration to metropolitan areas, which are more home to cities such as Lagos and Abuja. This has been helped by road improvement and ease of transportation, thereby eroding family support and nurturing by parents. Parents have suddenly become isolated and made to depend on their children. The balance is suddenly tilted toward childcare by third parties such as schools, daycare centres, and crèches. In Ghana, too, urbanisation has prompted a similar erosion of family values through the movement of parents away from villages and close proximities, leading to smaller nuclear families, with attendant loss of traditional nurture. Thus, children miss out on the best traditional cultural education by extension families. The parents find themselves pulled on both sides, juggling work and family priorities to maintain professional commitments and career advancement.

However, we observed that, in some urban regions of South Africa, for example, these new nuclear family formations have also occurred at the same time as a weakening of traditional practices, like the extent of communal gatherings and collective child-rearing, which have enabled the passing on of traditional values in the past. With the weakening of these traditional supports, parents have been forced to find alternative ways to guarantee that their children grow up with strong cultural identities.

The Impact of Migration on Parenting

Migration within and outside Africa is now one of the defining demographic features of the world, as far as I am aware. For many families on the continent, and especially in conflict-ridden areas such as South Sudan, migration does not involve a decision but is a necessity. War, poverty and political instability may result in migration. The family will move to another part of the continent or outside the country to find safety and a better life.

Evolving Migration Patterns in Africa

Over the past few decades, millions of Africans have been on the move, driven by war, economic hardship, and environmental degradation. As of 2024, the International Organization for Migration (IOM) estimates that over 281 million people globally live outside their home countries, making up approximately 3.6% of the world's population (Serraglio & Adaawen, 2023). This includes both voluntary and displaced people, such as refugees, asylum seekers, and those displaced due to conflict, natural disasters, or economic challenges.

Africa faces significant migration and internal displacement challenges. By 2024, the number of internally displaced persons (IDPs) on the continent is estimated to exceed 30 million, primarily due to ongoing conflicts, violence, and climate-related disasters. Countries such as the Democratic Republic of Congo, Somalia, Ethiopia, and South Sudan are among the most severely affected. Regarding international migration, around 40 million Africans are estimated to live outside their country of birth, with key migration routes leading to Europe, the Middle East, and other African nations. Economic opportunities, political instability, and environmental factors remain the primary drivers of migration within and beyond the continent (Serraglio & Adaawen, 2023).

This mass movement has caused significant disruptions in family life, often separating family members across borders. For instance, due to the prolonged civil conflict in South Sudan, millions of people have been displaced both domestically and internationally. Many South Sudanese parents and children have fled to neighbouring countries such as Uganda, Kenya, and Ethiopia, as well as farther afield to nations like Australia, the United States, Europe, and Canada. Forced migration adds complexity to parenting, as families must navigate the challenges of displacement on top of the developmental and cultural shifts they encounter in new environments.

The Impacts of Forced Migration on Family Dynamics

Families separated by conflict or economic causes often suffer from separation between family members. The impact of this separation on parents and children is psychologically and emotionally severe, causing guilt feelings, anxiety and a sense of helplessness among parents and a sense of abandonment, loss, insecurity and possibly intergenerational psychological trauma in children.

For example, in refugee camps across Africa, countless displaced families have trouble maintaining close relationships in overcrowded, somehow impersonal conditions. Trouble with privacy, conversation space, and a certain measure of mutual respect can exert significant pressure on family relations and the parenting process. Parents, too, might have trouble giving children the emotional security they need. Secondly, the displacement experience toughens gender norms: in most cases, women are the ones who adopt the breadwinner role, and in most camps and settlements, this lacks the support system of a broader family or partner.

Parenting Challenges in the New Environment

These challenges confront families that migrate to countries outside Africa, especially since parents must adapt to a new cultural environment. They must also assist their children to navigate the challenges of growing up in a foreign country, which often involves the tensions of holding on to cultural identity and being part of the host society. For example, South Sudanese families in Australia have had to adjust to many social norms and values that differ significantly from anything in their culture of origin. For parents, there are particularly tenuous tensions between sticking to traditional parenting approaches and adopting more individualistic and permissive approaches in the host public. These tensions can lead to family conflicts where children exposed to more of the host culture at school and among peers may reject values and norms.

This tension of acculturation often means that, over time, there may be significant distrust and a divide between generations of parents and children out of step with each other. The younger generation, often adapting faster to a new culture, may feel alienated from their parents' perspectives and struggle to communicate with them. Being out of step on the family foundation may lead children to seek guidance outside their parents and within the stature of friends – where harmful influence could be present instead of a healthy, resilient drive.

South Sudanese Families in the Global Diaspora

The challenges that South Sudanese families in the diaspora face shed light on the realities of parenting in migration settings. For instance, many South Sudanese parents in the US have grappled with expectations of raising children to be more independent and expressive, often against the grain of the more social and disciplined upbringing they received in South Sudan.

One woman, a South Sudanese mother of seven living in Melbourne, said she was frustrated because she could barely impose her values on her children, even as an authoritative figure. She cannot seriously talk to people because Australia is a land full of rights and freedoms. How can you enforce respect for elders or community responsibility in such a society? All she could do was build cultural pride and a sense of identity in them.

Similarly for Australians, South Sudanese families have had to deal with the added barriers of racism and a history of shameful systemic discrimination and police racialisation, all of which combine to make acculturation more difficult. Parents defend culture while working with their children and against a society they feel does not understand or accept them. These are the challenges that South Sudanese parents go through for their children in order for them to be raised with dignity and pride.

Preserving Cultural Values and Identity in the New Environment

Culturally, sustainability in a foreign land takes effort and resilience. Some African parents try to replicate their home environment in the diaspora (homing in) while remaining open to new influences (homing out), using different strategies that may include:

1. Safeguarding Against Cultural Loss: If our children do not hear the language at home, they may lose that ability. By keeping the language alive at home, there is the hope to delay the current trend of obscure tongues falling out of use. For many communities, language is a primary gateway to culture; it is difficult to imagine an Irish person disconnected from Irish culture, a Mexican person unbothered by Mexican style, or a Yoruba person who does not adore fried plantains. Loss of language means loss of culture. Protecting against forgetting is the most important reason.
2. Preserving Cultural Practices and Traditions: Cultural practices

such as traditional food, music, dance, rituals, religious holidays, and celebrations as part of everyday cultural life help children appreciate and identify with their ethnic background and can promote community connectedness.

3. Cultural Celebrations and Traditions: Celebrating holidays and ethnic events within the community reinforces cultural practices and can help children realise continuity.
4. Community: Kinship and attachment to other families from the same community can be essential sources of support for parents and children alike. Community events, community-based ethnic or cultural associations, and religious institutions are places where cultural identity can be sustained.
5. Balancing Tradition and Modernity with Precision: Parents are expected to maintain a separate cultural identity but should also adapt to and embrace some of the positive aspects of the host culture to ensure that their children also learn to live in both worlds and develop flexibility and resilience along the way.

South Sudanese's Journey: War, Forced Migration, and Independence

Exploring those problems in the diaspora must begin with the homeland's history, which was shaped by war and displacement and unfolded toward an independent South Sudan in 2011 (Johnson, 2016).

The First Sudanese Civil War (1955-1972)

In a nutshell, the First Sudanese Civil War set the stage for South Sudan's tortured history. The war sought to resolve long-standing tensions between northern, predominantly Arab and Muslim governments and the southern regions, which were home to many diverse

African ethnic groups that often had different religious and cultural practices. Efforts by the South to gain greater autonomy resulted in a protracted conflict temporarily resolved by the Addis Ababa Agreement made in 1972. However, the persisting issues of political exclusion, the relative distribution of resources, and cultural marginalisation reignited tensions that led to the Second Sudanese Civil War (1983-2005).

The Second Sudanese Civil War (1983-2005)
This second Civil War was one of the bloodiest and deadliest African wars. It broadly defined the preceding two decades of interethnic violence with massive destruction and forcible displacement. More than 2 million human lives were lost, and more than 4 million displaced – a diaspora forming much of today's South Sudanese identity. The war affected the social fabric of the South Sudanese people, shaping who South Sudanese are today. It also transformed families in a way that affected parenting practices, impacting different aspects of child-rearing, from education to child labour (Deng, 2016a).

Specifically, the Comprehensive Peace Agreement (CPA) 2005, a post-war agreement that ended the Second Sudanese Civil War and laid the groundwork for the South's independence (negotiated with international support), was crucial in pushing the threshold for peace. This agreement is what enabled the referendum to be held in 2011 and, through that, paved the way for South Sudan's independence. However, the struggle over power in the new political landscape has revealed more challenges, culminating in a relapse of conflict in 2013. This has further fragmented the new country, with more than 3 million people displaced.

Challenges and Success of South Sudanese Families in the Diaspora

South Sudanese families, having endured war and displacement, have seen their generational flows and family patterns shift both within and outside their homeland. This displacement has significantly altered the role of families and parenting strategies. In the diaspora, South Sudanese families confront unique challenges, including adapting to new cultures, overcoming language barriers, navigating professional discrimination, and learning to thrive as immigrants within their host countries' economic, social, and legal frameworks. Their ability to survive in the diaspora and maintain their cultural roots and languages is genuinely inspiring.

As a result, a South Sudanese diaspora could be found worldwide, particularly in Australia, the United States, Canada and Europe. Memories of a homeland and a resilience honed through struggle have accompanied many South Sudanese who fled the conflict with them. Their stories are of survival as much as they are a labour of peace, the recreation of stability elsewhere while connections remain with home.

These communities contribute significantly to their host countries, enriching them with their diverse culture, resilience, and determination. The South Sudanese Diaspora is characterised by resilience, determination, and excellence, particularly in sports and academia. These accounts are a testament to the excellence of the South Sudanese people and a source of great pride for future generations. Their positive contributions are ample reasons for us to be even prouder and offer our support.

The Bright Stars: Celebrating Basketball Triumphs

Perhaps the most impressive sporting achievement in South Sudan's short history is that of the country's national basketball team, the

South Sudan Men's National Basketball Team, known as the 'Bright Stars'. In 2023, the Bright Stars became the first South Sudanese team to qualify for the FIBA Basketball World Cup, albeit late because North African teams did not qualify in time. The qualification for the world's largest team sport event after the Olympics resulted from an almost impossible run through the African qualifiers. Under the Basketball Africa League, a partnership between the International Basketball Federation and the National Basketball Association, South Sudanese basketball debuted at the Olympics in 2024. We are running out of superlatives for this country and its impressive sporting achievements, securing more milestones for the youngest nation in the world. The team is a squad of diasporic young talent, many from Australia, signalling the global impact of the South Sudanese diaspora and spotlighting the nation on the world sporting stage.

Their success is proof of the prowess, perseverance, and dedication of South Sudanese players and coaches, who overcame formidable personal and collective obstacles to represent their nation globally. It has raised the pride of all of South Sudan's diaspora communities worldwide.

The project benefitted from the massive success of the NBA's most famous South Sudanese star, Luol Deng, a renowned philanthropist famed for his role as a cultural ambassador from South Sudan. Born in what is now South Sudan but forced to flee with his family to the civil war in the then Sudan, Deng settled in the United Kingdom, where he enjoyed a stellar career as an NBA basketball player (playing a total of 10 seasons for London, Chicago, Miami and Los Angeles). However, his most extraordinary efforts were on the basketball court and trying to bring peace and development to South Sudan.

Through his Luol Deng Foundation, he has created educational opportunities and provided healthcare and sports programmes for young people across South Sudan and the UK. The story of Deng's escape to England also highlights how diaspora becomes a crucial part of the narrative for many graduates from the newest country on the planet. Deng might not have known anyone in the UK when he arrived in 2001, but he was soon in demand on the basketball court.

Academic Excellence and Broader Contributions
Meanwhile, the South Sudanese diaspora has also seen it thrive internationally. In education, law, anthropology, history and other disciplines, numerous examples of women and men have done well against the odds of displacement and disorientation, limited language access, resources and the like. However, there have always been highly educated South Sudanese who prioritise education, the classroom and the library because they desire to expand and amplify their voices and those of others. Our intellectual gifts and resilience as a people have made us worthy of attention. Such stories can be a source of inspiration and motivation for South Sudanese everywhere. They reveal how schooling can transform lives.

In this way, their academic awards inspire many future generations by demonstrating society's abiding commitment to learning and forging ahead. With each additional medical or engineering degree awarded, and each social science or humanities monograph published, our scholars are not only contributing to the body of knowledge in their professional fields but also breaking ground and defying stereotypes. Looking back at these accomplishments, a young South Sudanese person can be inspired to achieve even greater heights. The struggle is well worth it; a young South Sudanese person can accomplish the seemingly impossible: striving to be extraordinary rather than average.

Resilience and Strength of the South Sudanese Diaspora

Their success stories go beyond individual accomplishments and encompass the South Sudanese diaspora's collective strength, resilience and potential. A newfound reputation for hard work and success is central to identifying what it is that the South Sudanese do better, like many other diasporic communities. South Sudan is a young diaspora, and much of the work remains. According to Brown: 'South Sudanese in the diaspora are some of the most talented and hardworking people you will ever meet. They are ready to work hard for the things they want to succeed at.

It is a source of pride and inspiration when these athletes and scholars' perseverance achieves success. Lives marked by relentless dedication and refusal to be confined by their circumstances act as role models and a key to better opportunities for future generations. The mere sight of a South Sudanese participating in a world-class platform makes us reconsider generalisations, stereotypes and prejudices. This is a powerful way to show the world that difficulties faced by members of the diaspora or the motherland can be overcome. South Sudanese can fully participate in the world scenario if we remain committed and support one another on the journey. Their achievements exemplify this, and again, we can be proud. It shows the individual's potential and suggests a brighter, more promising future for the South Sudanese and the greater African community anywhere in the world.

The Role of Technology in Modern Parenting

In the digital age, technology can be integrated into almost every aspect of parenting and parenthood. Today, smartphones, tablets, social media, educational/parenting apps, instant messaging/e-mail, and much more are available to support parenting and foster communication between parents and children in unprecedented ways.

Technology allows instant access to information (parenting advice, developmental milestones, parenting blogs, parental communities of people facing the same challenges or difficulties, and so on). It also provides educational resources and tools to assist in a child's education from an early age. However, technological developments also bring significant challenges.

The ubiquitous use of technology in childhood could potentially pose children at risk of exposure to inappropriate content and cyberbullying, and the risk of internet addiction use of the Internet will keep children online for long hours together. This may lead to a situation when it becomes difficult to differentiate between healthy use and overuse, requiring parents to monitor their child's activities on the Internet more closely. Modern parents must balance the benefits of technology that can enhance their child's life against the risks associated with a child's exposure to the online world. However, this requires them to set clear boundaries, teach the children how to behave responsibly online and remain aware of the changing nature of online risk.

Furthermore, technology has changed the dynamics of family interactions, sometimes creating a rift in one's family where screens become the primary form of communication. It is now more critical than ever for parents to keep an eye on technology usage in their homes as their children look more to them than any other source as a model for using technology in their lives. It is possible to find the right solutions to these challenges by adopting technology to increase opportunities for learning and connection while setting limits to protect children from harm. This era of parenting with technology is a double-edged sword that, when handled with thoughtful care, can significantly enrich the parenting experience – and raise digital natives in this ever-more digitised world.

Technology in Contemporary African Households

In the past decade, the accuracy of their predictions suffered, in no small part, because of the immense penetration of technology in African households, where mobile phones and internet access are omnipresent even in rural communities. That technological revolution has changed the playing field for parenting now that children have global reference points quite at odds with African parameters. For example, some parents in Kenya and Nigeria use technological resources like smartphones and the Internet to monitor their children's behaviour, communicate with them and access resources to help them Learn. However, the speed at which technology evolves has forced parents to wrestle with what the latest trends in the market bring and the possibility of their children getting themselves into danger while using other digital platforms.

The Risks and Opportunities of Technology in Parenting

Nowadays, technology can help us be better parents. Parents can access information about child development, child health, and education by browsing the internet. They can also join social apps or websites to make friends with other parents, share their experiences, and seek help and advice from others. Educational apps and websites are created for children to learn or practice new skills interactively.

However, these are also opportunities with risks attached. Children can be exposed to violence or pornography or inappropriate sexual or social interactions through the internet; social media can have detrimental effects on self-esteem or children's mental health more broadly when it is used to focus unrealistically on portrayals of reality or body image.

Moreover, there is an intensification of opportunities for children to get addicted to increasingly deeper exploitations of technology for leisure and play, social, entertainment, and academic purposes through the domination of gadgetry, which in turn leads to the loss of physical activity, interpersonal contact, and academic accomplishments.

Managing and Safeguarding Children's Technology Use

In order to make the most of the benefits of technology and to minimise its risks, parents need to adopt active strategies for regulating their children's use of technology. Possible strategies include the fact that it is helpful to set clear expectations in addition to modelling tech use. In other words, you must set limits: 'All screen time occurs only between the time you get back from school and dinner', 'We only use smartphones when we are at home.' 'Technology should not come between us and schoolwork.'

Monitor content: enlist internet-monitoring tools to track the content that children are seeing. For example, buffering website access can prevent children from seeing online porn; constant review of apps downloaded may also reveal risks; in-depth social-media monitoring could also help prevent sexting if children are on such platforms. The following strategies might help parents and children mitigate, manage and safeguard technology use:

- Engaging in offline activities: Encourage kids to participate in physical activities, hobbies, and activities that do not involve staring at a bright screen or checking their phones. This will help them find more ways to occupy their time and avoid excessive screen time while also contributing to their overall development.
- Engaging in positive modelling: Try to practice what you preach. Parents can model healthy use of technology by being aware of their own screen time, turning it off, and spending personal time with their children offline. Children are more likely to follow rules and guidelines when their parents exhibit and grasp those same behaviours.

Digital Literacy and Online Safety

Digital literacy can differ from analogue literacy, but specific life-saving skills often must be learned on the go. Fortunately, most parents in Africa these days understand the importance of shoring up their children's digital lives. This means things like sharing meaningfully but carefully. Digital security teaches kids how to be safe online; engaging strangers is not an option these days, as verifying trust and considering online privacy.

Across many African countries, there is a welcome raft of efforts to improve digital literacy with school-based and community-based schemes. Programmes, such as the 'One Laptop per Child' project in Rwanda, are shining examples of how schoolchildren can access digital devices and learn about technology etiquette. Other African countries follow similar paths, ensuring that the next generation of citizens can be aware of and mindful of the opportunities and challenges of an Artificial Intelligence (AI) age.

Parenting Styles and Cultural Identity

Because parenting styles draw on and reflect cultural identity, it is unsurprising that contemporary global cultures emphasise some aspects of parenting more notably than others. For instance, parenting in Africa is often marked by ideas of respect for authority, communal values, and social cohesion.

Varied Parenting Styles within African Cultures

Authoritarian, authoritative, permissive, and uninvolved are the general classifications of parenting styles, albeit to varying degrees (Berry, 1997; Deng, 2016b). They represent divergent cultural values regarding child-rearing.

1. Authoritarian Parenting: This style entails high demands and

low responsiveness. Parents use this style when they are highly controlling and demanding and expect their children to do what they are told unquestioningly. Parents in many parts of Africa tend to adopt this parenting style because it is thought to instil discipline and respect for authority. However, although this parenting style might result in obedient children, it also tends to result in low levels of happiness and self-esteem.

2. Authoritative Parenting. Parents in this style practice high demands with high responsiveness. In other words, they set clear expectations and rules but are also very supportive and nurturing. This type of parent is considered balanced as it blends discipline with warmth, resulting in high levels of compliance and independence. In many African communities where family structure and relationship cohesion are valued and respected, Authoritative Parenting is usually considered ideal.

3. Permissive Parenting: Permissive parents tend to be indulgent and lenient, rarely making decisions for their children and allowing them to determine their own choices with minimal guidance. This style is the least common among traditional African and other cultures. However, it is becoming more popular, thanks largely to the influence of Western practices in more urban and diaspora families, both on the continent and abroad. Permissive parenting can lead to problems of self-regulation and authority, as children lack the constraints to develop self-discipline.

4. Uninvolved parenting: Uninvolved parents are unresponsive and detached, spending little time with their children and offering little guidance or support. This parenting style tends to be associated with poor outcomes, including low self-esteem and poor social skills. It is hardly present in African cultures, characterised by communal child-rearing values.

The Influence of Cultural Identity on Parenting Approaches: This area of study is ripe for further exploration, as it has the potential to provide valuable insights into the complex interplay between cultural identity and parenting practices.

The relationship between parenting styles and cultural identity highlights the embeddedness of parenting strategies in sociocultural contexts. In African contexts, where values of communal living and respect for elders are dominant lifestyle norms, assumptions about child-rearing often follow suit (Deng, 2016a). Children's interests are subordinated to the communities, and respect for authority is paramount. This ethos is instilled through high levels of parental monitoring, incremental modelling of good behaviour, and socialisation on the obligations of community membership.

Authoritarian vs. Authoritative Parenting

While African cultures value both authoritarian and authoritative styles of parenting, they do lead to different outcomes. Authoritarian parenting, characterised by a firm and strict interpretation of rules that must be obeyed without question, leads to high levels of compliance in children. However, this style of parenting can also stifle creativity and autonomy. On the other hand, authoritative parenting, which provides a high degree of structure and support, tends to produce children who are more likely to be highly self-confident, socially skilled, and competent at independent thought, offering a promising approach to child-rearing (Berry, 1997).

Another study of different families worldwide showed that the children of authoritative parents had better self-esteem and higher academic achievement than those of authoritarian parents. This is a testament to the importance of discipline, warmth, and encouragement in properly raising a child.

Blending Traditional and Modern Parenting Practices

As African societies modernise, young women and men as parents or future parents grow increasingly committed to adapting modern ideas, practices and expectations to traditional parental values and styles. In other words, as cultures elsewhere strive to 'indigenise' the attachment approach, the hybrid parenting of African parents reflects a compromise between 'tradition' and 'modernity' in novel ways. In contemporary times, parents seek to pare down inherited problems and unhelpful 'traditions' in their childrearing practices, even as they purposively maintain those heritage elements that they believe benefit their children. This deliberate preservation of cultural identity in parenting practices is a testament to heritage value in a new environment.

For example, many African parents in the diaspora are moving toward an Authoritative style, combining the respect and discipline of International-Traditional Parenting with the care and openness of Modern Parenting. This way, kids can benefit from a culture-rich childhood and simultaneously reduce behavioural problems.

In the case of South Sudanese communities living in Africa and the diaspora, it is pretty clear that there can be a happy confluence between traditional and modern forms of parenting. In South Sudan, raising children is a communal endeavour, extending far beyond the immediate family and involving a network of older siblings, aunts, uncles and more. Once in the diaspora, however, parents often have a direct hand in the day-to-day child-rearing of their children as they face the double challenge of raising children in a new cultural environment.

In some cases, South Sudanese parents in the diaspora strive to be more communicative with their children: 'Even when he is not listening, you still have to talk to him' and also less harsh in their discipline, reflecting the influence of more culture. At the same time, many strive to maintain their cultural identity by teaching their children their home language and traditional values.

Disproportionate Representation of Young South Sudanese and African Australians in the Justice System

The overrepresentation of South Sudanese and other young African men in the criminal justice system in Australia is not just a significant issue but an urgent one. It is a troubling consequence of the diaspora population. This overrepresentation is a statistic and a critical marker of systemic problems these communities face in 'settling in' their new lives in this country. It is a symptom of deeper issues that urgently need to be addressed. These deeper issues elaborate on the systemic problems such as social, relational, and communicative troubles arising from the conterminous vicissitudes of migration, settlement, acculturation, and systemic discrimination.

Many of these young men live in social, economic, relational, and cultural poverty that is tied up with their migrant histories and their parents' and families' experiences of re-settling in a new country, a country that most have scarce knowledge of, feel totally alienated from, internalise negative perceptions about, and feel criminalised in, and where they experience multiple forms of exclusion and disenfranchisement.

There are also socio-economic factors: many African families, including those from South Sudan, often encounter difficulties such as unemployment, housing problems, and limited access to education and social services, leaving them feeling socially isolated and impoverished. These challenges may also increase the risk of developing a criminal lifestyle, especially for young people who often do not fit in either to a new culture or the old and who experience identity conflict that may lead them to feel disenfranchised and alienated.

Excessive Policing of African Australians

Over-policing, racial profiling by law enforcement agencies and discrimination in other contexts contribute to the over-representation of young South Sudanese Australians and Africans in the criminal justice system. In particular, young Africans reported being subjected to discriminatory policing, in which youths are disproportionately stopped and searched even for minor offences and suspected deviant behaviour, itself a product of discriminatory thinking and stereotypes (Deng, 2016b; Pittaway & Dantas, 2024). We know that under-policing disproportionately affects African Americans; for instance, the same thinking applies to discriminatory policing of African neighbourhoods in Australia.

Discriminatory police conduct has far-reaching implications for the community's relationship with law enforcement. However, systemic changes can restore the acceptability of future interventions to dismantle the forces driving overrepresentation. The societal stakes of such overrepresentation cannot be overemphasised beyond personal social support needs. It compromises one's mental health, social cohesion, and life prospects and those of one's wider community. A systemic solution is long overdue to address these challenges, and the impact of such changes can bring hope for a better future.

Substance Abuse and Mental Health Challenges

It is essential to recognise that a complex interaction of drug and alcohol abuse and mental health issues disproportionately contributes to the overrepresentation of young South Sudanese and other African Australians in the criminal justice system. Many South Sudanese Australians, especially the youth, are socioeconomically disadvantaged and live in communities where cultural dislocation and systemic discrimination are overworked constraints to their development.

These often lead to substance abuse and mental health issues, and ultimately involvement in criminal activities, either directly with offences related to substance use or indirectly with behaviours generated from untreated mental health conditions. Some of these young people are also vulnerable and most often lured into crimes by criminal syndicates as they use them to go and steal cars and other valuables for them in return for different drugs or money.

Compounding this effect is the absence of culturally appropriate mental health and substance abuse services for South Sudanese Australians, making it difficult for those with these issues to receive the necessary help and prolonging their presence in the criminal justice system. The lack of appropriate services, especially for struggling parents adjusting to their new parenting practices, is a significant issue. Most African families come from collectivist cultures, where support is drawn from extended family members and the community, and having a substitute is paramount and significant in their new environment.

Socio-Economic Challenges in the Resettlement Process
Research shows that socio-economic disadvantage is a significant factor in this overrepresentation. Refugee families are often struggling with the realities of settlement, such as high unemployment, language barriers, and limited social support. When combined with economic strains and isolation, the opportunities for offending naturally increase, particularly for youth struggling with acculturation and identity, which is often confusing as they struggle to make sense of their origin (parents) and the newly adapted culture.

Acculturation Stress and Intergenerational Conflict
Acculturation stress and intergenerational conflict further compound the problem. Owing to the cultural gap between parents and children,

issues that arise in the family or within the larger African community can lead to misunderstandings or disagreements, fuelling youth involvement in antisocial behaviour and criminal activity (Deng, 2016a, 2016b). Systemic racism in the form of discriminatory laws and policies, along with police and local law enforcement agencies that show racial bias (racial profiling), further leads to the overrepresentation of African communities in the criminal justice system and repeated cycles of reoffending that keep African communities marginalised.

Overcoming these challenges

Nevertheless, solutions to this overrepresentation will not be simple. They will likely need to encompass community-level collaborations, grassroots policy advocacy, and systemic support services to work within the context of these communities and families. The importance of these collaborations cannot be overstated, as they empower the community to take an active role in addressing these issues. Supportive progress needs to be made by enlightening parents about how to help their children navigate acculturation stumbling blocks, fostering adequate communication with their children, and enabling culturally sensitive, evidence-based interventions for at-risk youth.

Conclusion

In navigating the evolving landscape of modern parenting, particularly within the African context, parents face a unique set of challenges shaped by migration, urbanisation, and the pervasive influence of technology. For South Sudanese and other African families, the journey of raising children in a foreign land involves balancing the preservation of cultural identity with the demands of adapting to new societal norms and expectations. This delicate balancing act is both a challenge and an opportunity, offering parents the chance to blend the strength of their traditional values with the advantages of modernity.

As explored throughout this chapter, African parenting has historically thrived on communal support, extended family networks, and shared responsibility in child-rearing. However, the realities of migration, urbanisation, and the digital age have altered this dynamic, often leaving parents feeling isolated in their parenting roles. Nevertheless, despite these changes, African families continue to demonstrate resilience, creativity, and adaptability in their approach to parenting. Drawing on their rich cultural heritage and embracing new methods, they find ways to provide their children with a strong sense of identity while equipping them with the tools needed to succeed in the modern world.

Technology, though a source of both opportunity and challenge, plays a crucial role in modern parenting. It has reshaped how children learn, communicate, and engage with the world while posing risks that parents must carefully navigate. The responsibility of guiding children through the digital landscape requires a delicate balance of supervision, education, and trust. Like all parents today, African parents must embrace technology's benefits while safeguarding their children from its potential dangers.

Ultimately, the experiences of South Sudanese and African families in navigating these modern challenges highlight the enduring strength of cultural identity and community, even in the face of significant upheaval. Through their resilience, these families find new ways to integrate tradition and modernity, ensuring their children can thrive in an increasingly complex world. As African parents continue to evolve their parenting strategies, they remain grounded in the values that have long defined their communities, such as family, respect, and collective responsibility, while adapting to the realities of a globalised digital age.

This chapter underscores the importance of maintaining this balance, offering a path forward that honours tradition and progress. By nurturing their children within this framework, African parents can raise a generation equipped to face the future with confidence, resilience, and a deep-rooted sense of identity.

CHAPTER THREE

Parenting in the Diaspora: Upholding Cultural Identity in a Changing World

Introduction

Parenting in the diaspora is a nuanced and multifaceted journey, particularly for South Sudanese and other African families who must contend with the complexities of upholding their rich cultural identity while adapting to the ever-evolving realities of life in foreign lands. Traditional South Sudanese parenting is deeply rooted in communal values, respect for elders, and structured family hierarchy values that have been passed down through generations, defining the core of childrearing practices. These ideals foster a sense of belonging, responsibility, and respect that permeates family life and community interactions.

However, migration, exile, and the challenges of resettlement disrupt this established framework, as families are confronted with the realities of new societal norms, unfamiliar legal systems, and shifting expectations about parenting in multicultural societies. The experience of displacement brings both the necessity to preserve cultural traditions and the imperative to adapt to the demands of the host country's new social, educational, and legal structures.

In this chapter, we explore how South Sudanese families navigate the tension between maintaining their cultural heritage and meeting the practical challenges of parenting in the diaspora. We examine the enduring values that shape traditional African parenting, such as respect for elders, collective responsibility, and the importance of oral traditions, while also considering the new dynamics introduced by migration, war, and exile. By focusing on how South Sudanese parents in the diaspora reconcile these competing pressures, this chapter provides insight into the resilience and adaptability required to raise children who thrive in their cultural communities and the broader global society.

Enduring Beliefs and Core Values

In South Sudanese and greater African contexts, parenting emerges from traditional ideological frameworks that prioritise deference and hierarchy within the family and community (Deng, 2016a). These are fundamental values and principles and are not incidental practicalities. They appear in the texture of everyday life, affecting who can speak and to whom. They counsel and criticise, provide pleasures and punishments, and expect deference and respect in return. They make and maintain appearances of dignity and despair and form a foundation on which parents raise children.

Respect: A Cornerstone of African Societies

Children are often expected to obey their elders and approach them with a deep sense of deference. A central component of respect is the moral and social contract that glued and held African societies together upon which interaction among family members and throughout the community is based. This complex and nuanced contract celebrated individuals for their capacity for peace and fraternity. As such, men and women are often held accountable for upholding their end of the bargain to show patience, listen carefully, and encourage the smooth flow of life and civility for all. Adherence to this social contract is fostered and learned early in life, as children are expected to obey their elders and approach them with a deep sense of deference. The young learnt this through their cultural rituals and practices, their physical interactions within the households, and the guidance of their elders.

Children are taught, by body language, what is expected of them. When welcoming elders, they bow or curtsy, keep quiet while listening to story accounts and participate actively in community activities. In South Sudanese households, for instance, it is customary for children to kneel while serving elders food, ensuring they do not sit higher than the elders. This physical posture may have been an 'act', but it embodied the respect and humility for the elder's wisdom and authority.

The Community's Role in Raising Children

Community, which is also one of the pillars of African ways of raising children, reflects the community nature of African societies. The notion that 'it takes a village to raise a child' is not just a cliché. It is a reality in some African cultures. This dyadic and communal involvement in raising children means that the raising of children is not the sole responsibility of their biological parents. Instead, this task falls to a broad spectrum of adults ranging from grandparents to other neighbours who accept a child as their own and nurture and guide them with a wide variety of viewpoints that may differ from those of the parents themselves. These culturally rich and communal thought patterns instil a sense of belonging and support that teaches the child that although the nuclear family may be widening, the extended family/community remains responsible for their upbringing.

Family Structure and Hierarchical Roles

Family hierarchy is another central tenet of African parenting that places everybody in their appropriate spot to ensure order and discipline within the family structure. While fathers occupy the top spot on the parenting hierarchy, they are obeyed as the heads of their families. Fathers are the decision-makers and breadwinners of the family, and every household member is expected to respect and honour their decisions. In this scheme, mothers are the day-to-day leaders or caregivers. They are responsible for ensuring that all the children's needs or demands are met and that the family is healthy and safe. This role makes them the pillars of the well-being of the whole family. Something similar is said of older siblings, who are considered the ancillary caretakers in many households; they are to watch out for and care for younger siblings and help their own mothers in whatever way they can. All that order and discipline is par for the course. Still, the hierarchy of people within the family, like everything else in the African parenting scheme, seems to ensure that the household runs efficiently. Each family member's individual abilities and interests work to serve the family as a whole.

Oral Traditions: Pillars of Cultural Transmission

Oral traditions play a crucial role in African child-rearing, as they form the foundation for the cultural instruction of children. These traditions are abundant with stories, proverbs, songs, and rituals encompassing experiences and perspectives passed down from generation to generation. Storytelling is a common form of other relatives and elders telling stories to their children, using narratives to teach them moral life lessons and share historical information and expectations of their social roles. Oral transmission is not just the favoured mode of entertainment in African childhoods but also an essential tool for teaching and learning. Most children learn about their history, absorb societal expectations and develop pride in their identity through oral transmission of such significant cultural knowledge.

Collective Responsibility in Child-Rearing

In traditional African parenting, children are community property. Moreover, their upbringing is usually an affair of the whole community, where aunts, uncles, neighbours, village members and the entire community participate in raising the child. Until an alternative system for taking collective responsibility (such as communal property and upbringing) does away with poverty and inequalities, African approaches to parenting are unlikely to thrive. The collective approach to upbringing ensures that every dimension of a child's development is accommodated. No individual perspective is ever dominant. Everyone expresses their views and contributes their roles towards the overall upbringing of the child. The community, in turn, plays the role of a safety net, stepping in when something goes wrong in a family. This mutual care says: 'We are all part of the family.'

Parenting in Exile: South Sudanese Families Amid Forced Migration

South Sudanese parental practices are firmly rooted in history, particularly the heady history of South Sudan (and Sudan) and the impact of long periods of war and emigration on current parenting practices. Today, one has to trace the long tail that led to today's existence and interpret what came before it. This could be the key to better understanding the logic of South Sudanese parenting.

Civil Wars and Migration: Their Detrimental Effects on Family Structures

The two civil wars fought in Sudan between 1955 and 2005 profoundly destabilised traditional ways of life. The First Sudanese Civil War (1955-1972) and the Second Sudanese Civil War (1983-2005) displaced people, killed many others and caused vast social changes as many families fled to neighbouring countries or further afield, including Australia, Europe and North America. People were forced out of their country to refugee camps, and others were resettled in other countries. The experience in refugee camps or foreign countries brought about new challenges that required the adaption of parenting.

Adapting Parenting Practices in the Diaspora

The war, loss and trauma experienced by adults are used as the backbone of how they discipline, educate and raise their children. There is often an intense focus on how children develop resilience and survival skills reflective of their families' hardships through these childhood losses. Parenting is also marked by cultural blending, mainly as refugees migrate from South Sudan to several different nations, absorbing host-country practices while preserving the cultural practices from home to form a hybrid, significantly when they raise their children in the diaspora. For instance, South Sudanese raising their children in Western countries may use aspects of the host culture to guide their educational and disciplinary practices while maintaining the core values they adopted as children.

Preserving Cultural Heritage Amid Change

They were daily practices through which parents transmitted the history of the community and conservative social values to the younger generation. Many South Sudanese and other African parents today persist in these practices, with a similar objective of transmitting cultural heritage and conservative social values to their children. Parents' continuing interest in storytelling, initiation rituals, and other cultural practices are testaments to the desire to inform younger generations about their past and the value of their identity as a cultural group. The intergenerational transfer of value-laden knowledge remains a central concern. This means that children are well-educated about their origins and are proud of their heritage and cultural background.

The Role of Extended Family and Community in Child-Rearing

South Sudanese and most African cultures have an extended family and community where child-rearing is a group activity. The third pillar of our community is the extended family, which includes but is not limited to grandparents, aunts, uncles, and cousins. A child is raised in this extended family. They embody close emotional support, character guidance, and practical assistance to the parents. This way, a child is made to feel that no one is alone in the world.

Grandparents: Keepers of Cultural Wisdom and Knowledge

In many families, grandparents are a vital source of primary care: caring for children while their parents work and have other responsibilities. Grandparents are also a source of cultural knowledge, sharing stories, traditions and values to help shape the child's identity and development, vital throughout childhood and youth and beyond. Grandparents can also be wise and experienced guides and mentors to their grandchildren and their grandchildren's parents who face new challenges associated with modern parenting.

The Extended Family: Aunts, Uncles, and the Wider Community

The extended family members, including Aunts and uncles, contribute by adding another layer of support to the family system. They functionally extend the mentorship structure in which the parents provide childcare, discipline, and education. For instance, Aunts may take on the role of a secondary caregiver, providing emotional support and guidance to the children. On the other hand, uncles may serve as role models, teaching the children about traditional values and customs. This tells the children that they are born into and part of this collective. It also tells them who belongs within this collective and who does not. This extension of family support outside the immediate caregivers to the larger community at large is a universal phenomenon that can be seen across the globe, be it in collectivist East Asian societies or outdoor schooling in Sweden, where the neighbourhood serves as an extension of the family, with each person acting as an extra parent for the child, thereby plugging in more sources of example and role-modelling into their lives.

Furthermore, within the extended family system comprising various kinships of the broader family structure, community members such as neighbours, teachers, and religious personnel also play a significant part in the upbringing of children. They provide discipline, corrective pressure, and mentorship to children, thereby adding another layer to their social and moral upbringing.

The Influence of Religious Institutions and Community Organizations

This is why religious institutions play such a vital role in African life. Churches, mosques, and other places of worship are often as many places of community as religious spirituality. Within them, we find longstanding cultural traditions sustaining themselves both past and present through our rites of passage, outdoor activities, summer camps, etc. Religious elders offer spiritual wisdom to guide us throughout our lives and clarify our moral truths, as well as an accompaniment that helps enforce our familial values and lingering watchdogs of everyday social behaviours. Community organisations also play essential roles in family support. Local associations, religious groups and cultural organisations in places such as South Sudan offer programs and resources that parents can incorporate into their childrearing adventures.

Conclusion

Parenting in the diaspora is a delicate balance between preserving the values, customs, and traditions that define South Sudanese and African heritage and adapting to the rapidly shifting demands of modern life in a foreign context. Throughout the migration journey, whether shaped by war, displacement, or the search for better opportunities, South Sudanese parents have had to reconcile their rich cultural heritage with the pressures of integrating into multicultural societies. This process involves not only adapting to new legal, educational, and social frameworks but also passing on core values such as respect for elders, communal responsibility, and the importance of family hierarchy.

Despite the profound disruptions that migration and exile impose, South Sudanese families demonstrate remarkable resilience in maintaining key aspects of their cultural identity. They can nurture a sense of identity and belonging in their children by instilling the importance of respect, communal child-rearing, and the power of oral traditions. These principles, which have sustained African societies for generations, continue to play a pivotal role in shaping children's moral, social, and emotional development in the diaspora. Their ability to adapt and thrive in a new environment while holding onto their cultural heritage is truly inspiring.

However, this journey is not without challenges. The need to adjust parenting practices to fit the host country's legal, social, and educational norms often leads to tension, especially when these norms conflict with traditional values. Parents must continually negotiate between preserving cultural integrity and enabling their children to succeed in an increasingly globalised world. In this context, South Sudanese parents in the diaspora demonstrate remarkable adaptability, finding ways to blend traditional values with contemporary practices to raise children who can navigate both their cultural heritage and the demands of modern society.

Ultimately, the experiences of South Sudanese families in the diaspora underscore the enduring strength of cultural traditions even in the face of significant change. By fostering a strong sense of cultural identity, they ensure that their children are prepared to thrive in their new environment and deeply connected to their roots. In this way, South Sudanese parents and many African parents in similar circumstances provide a powerful example of how cultural resilience and adaptability can coexist, ensuring that future generations remain proud bearers of their rich heritage while confidently navigating the complexities of the globalised world.

CHAPTER FOUR

Navigating the Complexities of Forced Migration and Acculturation

Introduction

For South Sudanese and other African migrants, migration is far more than a geographical relocation. It is a profound upheaval that touches every facet of life: cultural, emotional, social, and spiritual. While the decision to migrate is often driven by pressing push factors like conflict, political instability, and environmental degradation or pull factors promising better opportunities, the migration process itself is laden with challenges. The journey does not end upon reaching a new destination; instead, it extends into the complex dynamics of acculturation, where the struggle to maintain one's cultural identity while adapting to a new environment becomes a daily reality.

This chapter explores the intertwined phenomena of migration and acculturation, particularly from the perspective of South Sudanese and African migrant families. I will examine these families' pre- and post-migration experiences, investigating the psychological and social tolls migration exerts and how these pressures influence parenting practices and family structures (De Haas et al., 2019). Migration is a dynamic transition that can be likened to a 'coming of age' process of navigating between two worlds, each with unique expectations and norms. The chapter will also highlight the resilience of migrant parents, who are tasked with guiding their children through this turbulent journey while striving to preserve their cultural roots.

The discussion will address the emotional, psychological, and practical challenges of forced displacement, the trauma from pre-migration experiences, and the intricacies of settling into a new society. Additionally, the chapter will explore how acculturation shapes the parenting styles of South Sudanese and other African families, focusing on the balancing act between upholding traditional values and integrating into the host culture. Through a critical lens, we will unpack the impact of acculturation on family dynamics and provide strategies for parents to navigate these complexities while fostering a strong sense of cultural identity in their children.

By addressing these multifaceted issues, this chapter offers actionable insights for migrant families as they cope with the realities of forced migration and acculturation. The aim is not only to understand the challenges faced but also to propose practical solutions for overcoming them, ensuring that parents and children alike can thrive despite the inherent difficulties of their migration journey.

The Multifaceted Challenges of Forced Migration

Migration is rarely straightforward, and most people who move are fleeing the country, whether due to conflict or economic hardship. South Sudanese are no exception. For decades, ongoing conflict or the fear of conflict has spurred many South Sudanese to migrate (Deng, 2016a). Of course, no one chooses to emigrate lightly. Different families weigh up the risks of the migration journey for themselves, their children and their community when deciding to leave. They examine the dangers and deprivations of migration on the one hand and the dangers and deprivations of remaining in a conflict zone. This section examines the stages of the migration journey, from leaving home to the journey into transit and ultimately to settling in the new country.

The Lasting Impact of Pre-Migration Experiences
The things they experienced before migration have massive emotional inertia and shape their parenting strategies. With their roots dried up and pulled out from under them, the terrors, skirmishes and outright horrors of war: the loss of friends, colleagues and relatives; the bombed-out buildings; the theft and loss of their homes, life savings and livelihoods; the displacement once more from their communities, loved ones and belongings they did not think they would ever have to leave behind again. South Sudanese parents also show remarkable resilience, and we should be grateful each time we have a chance to meet with them. These violent pasts leave deep emotional scars and generate feelings that shape their parenting strategies and the many survivors' ways of coping with the challenges of forced migration (Bürgin et al., 2022).

For example, some parents might have witnessed violence or experienced it in their lives in their country of origin, fearing that they could lose their child in the unfamiliar and potentially hostile environment of a Western country. Whereas this attitude might be born out of concern for the child, it can also manifest as helicopter parenting, where concern for safety and security becomes the overwhelming priority in children's development. Strict rules and boundaries are enforced to avoid exposure to danger; tension might arise between parents and children as the latter adapt to the cultures of the new country.

In addition, the psychological consequences of pre-migration trauma are likely to derive from multiple sources that may include anxiety, depression and post-traumatic stress disorder (PTSD). Both the parents and the whole family may experience these syndromes. The children may feel the tension and anxiety of their parents, so the children may develop similar symptoms. For instance, after a childhood trauma such as displacement, the kid may express insecurity in general, fear of impending catastrophe, and may have difficulty interacting with others. Parents must handle these emotional challenges to provide their children a stable and normal atmosphere.

The Hardships of Forced Displacement
Many South Sudanese families were uprooted, displaced within their own country or left for other parts of the world. It is likely that, one way or another, they have lost their home, community and way of life. For many, displacement means a lifelong feeling of being out of place and adrift. For families living in refugee camps or urban parts of foreign countries, the harms of displacement are compounded by life within a foreign country, with limited resources, overpopulated living conditions, perpetual uncertainty about the future and more. At such refugee camps, there might be no adequate shelter, food, health or education and, in combination with perceived potential threats from strangers and other anxieties that families might share, families are thrown into a cauldron of stress that places great strain on their normal functioning, leading to strangulated parenting.

Children can also become displaced. Fathers often feel the need to migrate elsewhere for employment or to escape military service, or they are killed in combat. Parents face the stresses of separation from their children or serving as their only parent. Children can be born in refugee camps, undergoing some of the most life-altering changes possible. They are then subject to a process of 'refinement' where the most vulnerable are separated. This results in children being far from home, perhaps in different countries, and away from their family members.

For those lucky enough to be close to parents or siblings, the responsibility of caring for a younger child can shift to the eldest, with potentially drastic consequences for their emotional development. Many children I have met have had a complicated experience of intergenerational living, shuttling between families. Being uprooted from my integration into a third culture resonates most personally. Being in a second culture means being in another country that is not your home yet retaining the home language or culture.

Nevertheless, even in urban settings, displaced families struggle: if they are not confined to giant refugee camps, they might still be exposed to superior physical resources but nonetheless confronted by equally formidable obstacles that come with navigating a new social and economic reality in a city they are trying to find footing in such as language barriers, unemployment and social isolation, for instance, a South Sudanese family resettled in a city in a foreign country. Those stresses alone can be a tremendous obstacle to a parent's ability to provide their children with the stability, time and emotional space they need to flourish.

Acculturation: Navigating Between Two Worlds

Acculturation, the adaptation and adjustment to a new cultural environment, is the main challenge for South Sudanese, generally African, families in the diaspora. Understanding the concept is critical as it involves navigating the complexity of adjusting to a new culture while maintaining one's cultural identity (Berry, 1997). The process is far from linear. There is constant retuning and negotiation as families find a balance between the culture they grew up with and the expectations of the host culture. This balance is not just a goal but a necessity for successful acculturation. It's the key to maintaining one's cultural identity in a new environment (See Table 1 below). This section explores the consequential effects of acculturation on family structures and parenting dynamics and the challenges and opportunities acculturation brings.

Table 1: Acculturation Categories

#	Category	Processes and impacts
1	Assimilation	It occurs when individuals adopt the cultural norms of a dominant or host culture over their original culture.
2	Separation	Separation occurs when individuals reject the dominant or host culture to preserve their culture of origin. It often facilitates the creation of ethnic enclaves.
3	Marginalisation	It takes place when individuals reject both original and dominant host cultures.
4	Integration	It occurs when individuals can adapt to the cultural norms of the dominant or host culture while preserving an aspect of their original culture. This process is often synonymous with biculturalism.

Examples of acculturation influences are demographic variables, which include education, age, marital status, gender, personality characteristics, motivations, and socio-cognitive factors. Scholars studied how immigrant youth adapted to and acculturated to their new environment as indicated in the above acculturation categories and devised four options for acculturation profiles (Berry, 1997, 2017; Deng, 2016a, 2016b).

1. Integration (oriented towards original heritage and new national culture).
2. Ethnic (oriented toward original culture only).
3. National (oriented toward new national culture only); and
4. Diffuse (orientation is ambivalent or marginalised).

If we compare these categories against psychological and sociocultural adaptation, then those categories that we label as more integrated should give people the best psychological and sociocultural outcomes; those who are more diffuse give people the worst outcomes; and those who are ethnic and national you will hope, still give people better outcomes than being diffuse but not as good as integrating. This implied that we ought to encourage young people, for example, to have at least some sense that they are not eradicating their spiritual heritage and are clinging to some sense of who they are culturally, but also to lose the diffuse tendencies and establish and create a sense of inclusion into the wider society, this was one of the key arguments that kept recurring throughout this book.

The Impact of Acculturation on Parenting Practices

Acculturation not only changes parenting behaviour due to parental adjustments and adaptations but also requires it. Parents must adapt to the expectations and norms of the host country while trying to retain as much of their traditional practices as possible. These challenges are especially demanding for South Sudanese parents, who often oscillate between the communal, hierarchical mode of African parenting and the far more individualistic, egalitarian parenting style in the West. Finding the right balance is crucial for successful acculturation.

Although parenting practices in many Western societies value open, nonconfrontational communication and autonomy for children, emphasising mutual respect between parent and child, these practices can be contrasted with more authoritarian styles, such as respect for parental authority and demand obedience that is valued in South Sudanese and other African parenting cultures. Parents also transfer some traditional aspects of parenting to their children. As parents acculturate, their parenting practices can change, leading to shifting parent-child relationships.

For example, a South Sudanese parent living in Australia may encourage her child to speak up, share his views, and participate in family decision-making because she resonates with the more egalitarian values of the host culture. However, her endeavour to embrace the host culture may be in tension with her desire to 'stay true' to her cultural ideals that emphasise parental authority and discipline. The child may also find herself inconsistently nodding along with his peers when they complain about their parents being overbearing or harsh.

Acculturation effects may also differ by migration stage and variation in integration with the host society. For families migrating early on in a child's life, acculturation challenges will typically be greater because they are still trying to figure out their new environment's cultural norms and expectations. With time, as they become more integrated into the host society (or return to their country of origin), they will find a way to find a hybrid approach to parenting, combining elements from their culture of origin with the new cultural norms they are exposed to in their new context.

Acculturation and Intergenerational Challenges

One of the most significant aspects of acculturation is intergenerational differences between parents and children, as children who are more exposed to the host culture because of school, social media, and their peers tend to acculturate more quickly than their parents. This generational gap can create conflict within the family unit; children may adopt cultural practices and values that their parents do not share and may reject that their parents uphold, such as speaking their native language or participating in cultural rituals. This resistance can strike at the core of parents' sense of self, as they feel their cultural heritage is eroding. On the other hand, children may think that they must resist their parents' traditions and ways in order to better assimilate with their peers.

Generation-based variances in acculturation can also lead to divergent perspectives on how to relate to authority and instances of discipline. In many African cultures, children are taught to respect and obey their elders unquestioningly. In Western cultures, children are less often encouraged to acquiesce to the will and whims of their elders but to participate fully as equals in decision-making. Even in more pluralistic Western cultures, this can lead to a clash of expectations between parents and children, especially as children evolve their own social consciousness in an effort to resist blindly toeing the line of their parents' demands in public and an attempt to accord equal respect to individuals from their peers' culture.

Imagine an otherwise polite young person defying their parents' directive. In the culture they inherited, this would appear disrespectful. However, as most young people raised in Western cultures have felt entitled to express their opinions and challenge authority when appropriate, they might feel doubly emboldened to do so, seeing this as necessary to assert their individuality and sense of independence. With this internalised obligation to voice a dissenting perspective, a young man might say 'No' to his/her mother/father so firmly.

The Influence of Schools and Social Networks on Acculturation

Immigrant families become part of the broader acculturation process by sending children to school or other social institutions. Often, these institutions are immigrant families' main access points, leading them to a host culture where they will work alongside and experience the lives of the native population for some time. Acculturation can have both positive and negative consequences.

In these instances, school attendance could require children to reconcile increasingly conflicting expectations of conforming to the behaviours and norms of their teachers and classmates, on the one hand, and to their parents, on the other hand. Sometimes, schools support children adapting to life in the host society, providing youth-targeted programs and resources that boost their wellbeing. Sometimes, school might contribute to parent-child conflict, such as when parents feel that their children's cultural values are not being respected at school or if they believe their children are discriminated against or bullied by their classmates.

Schools play a vital role as agents of, but also sites of resistance to, acculturation with an introduction to a new culture, with opportunities to acquire new skills and new friends. They can cause cultural conflict when the school's culture does not align with a family's cultural values. For instance, a South Sudanese child might be asked to be part of activities or lessons that a particular family finds against their religious or cultural norms. The school might see this as an issue of learning, while the family might see the school's expectations as insensitive or culturally ignorant.

In such cases, parents and the school can end up feeling at odds with the child, who literally becomes a target of both parties as they look to reconcile the different cultural expectations. Parents might feel alienated and disrespected by the school's intrusion into what they perceive as their family's cultural norms.

Parents should communicate openly with their children and teachers to navigate these challenges by connecting with the teachers and school administrators to communicate their children's needs and establishing positive communication that preserves parents' cultural values while facilitating changes to respect these cultures. Moreover, encouraging their children to acculturate to the new environment should be prioritised by parents, equipping them with the tools and resources that may be needed, such as following extracurricular activities or encouraging them to find mentors or role models who share some of the students' culture that the student can relate to. Lastly, investing in cultural activities such as rites of passage and other celebrations representing their cultural heritage should also be sought.

Preserving Cultural Values and Identity Amid Acculturations

It can be challenging for parents to maintain their cultural identity in the face of acculturation to other influences and values, and ultimately, it takes deliberate effort and strength to do this, as South Sudanese and African parents are realising. It means creating a home that embodies and communicates cultural values while being open to change and adaptable to other influences. This is particularly important for the children since it helps them navigate their lives effectively between the two cultures, helping them remain resilient in overcoming the complexities of living between cultures.

One effective way to retain cultural identity is through the conservation of language, which is an integral part of cultural identity by encouraging children to speak their native language at home and creating cultural lived experiences such as participating in diverse cultural events and connecting with other families of the same cultural background. Parents can also adopt elements of cultural traditions as normalised routines in their daily lives, such as making traditional foods, celebrating cultural celebrations, and practising religious rituals.

For example, a South Sudanese family living in the United States might try to prepare traditional meals, celebrate South Sudanese holidays, and attend community celebrations of their culture. Such activities can remind the family of their cultural belonging and give children a sense of continuity and tradition.

However, maintaining cultural identity would also entail cultivating cultural pride or helping children feel like they are a substantial part of their culture. For example, parents may try to give their children a strong sense of cultural pride by teaching them about their history and cultural riches. They could help their children feel part of the culture by sharing stories of lives led before the modern world and participating in rituals that are central to the culture. Parents could encourage children to engage with cultural artefacts by listening to music, reading the classics, or learning traditional art like cave painting or pyrography.

In addition, parents can empower their children to embrace their culture through involvement in their community. Having their children take part in community events, such as attending cultural festivals, religious functions, and participating in various social events, will allow children to learn about being bicultural, to feel connected to others who are from a similar background, and can help them develop an appreciation for their cultural identity.

Strategies for Overcoming Migration and Acculturation Challenges

Migration and acculturation represent challenging and complex stressors that require patience, adaptiveness, resilience, and a strong support system. Below are some examples of creative, practical, culturally based approaches that South Sudanese and other African family members can undertake to ease this stressor and maintain their cultural identity.

Building Community Connections and Support Networks

Being involved with a community is more than just a way for families to navigate the challenges of migration and acculturation. It's a path to a profound sense of belonging. A healthy community can provide families practical support, emotional care, and resources for social connectedness, fostering a strong sense of being cared for. Attending and participating in community gathering events such as cultural festivals, religious practices, or other social events affirms cultural identity and allows parents to share their culture with their children. This shared experience helps children feel like they are not alone in facing these challenges. The sense of being part of a community or belonging to something greater instils a deep connection to their culture of origin in children.

For example, many South Sudanese associations host cultural events and meet-ups where families can congregate, celebrate their heritage together, and support one another. Children can also be socialised and exposed to their culture and heritage, cultivate peer relationships with others who share their background and language, and connect to their identity. This kind of community engagement also entails establishing connections with other immigrant families with similar experiences and challenges so that they can come together and support each other.

Balancing Tradition with a New Environment

It would help preserve the identity of one culture but also allow for adaptation to the host society's culture. This involves accepting the positive external contributions of the new culture while integrating them into a centre of core values and practices. It provides children a platform for navigating cultural duality and experiencing itself as a site of adaptability and resilience.

For parents, this aim can be to balance the culture of origin and the host country's culture by creating a home atmosphere that reflects the former but is open to the latter. This can mean, for example, celebrating the host country's holidays or participating in the host country's community activities but continuing to practise cultural traditions and customs. The way that children identify lies at the crux of this matter: their bicultural identity can serve as the platform for them to navigate both cultures and appreciate the best parts.

For example, a South Sudanese family living in Canada might celebrate Canadian holidays such as Thanksgiving while also celebrating the Independence Day of South Sudan. This blending of traditions helps children feel rooted in their cultural past and a new home where many of the children were born and who consider it the only home since most of the children had never been to South Sudan.

Helping Children Cope and Adapt to Acculturation

Supporting children through the acculturation process is about more than just providing resources. It's about fostering open communication and understanding. By talking with their children and encouraging an open dialogue, parents can help their children navigate the inevitable stages of acculturation. This approach not only leads to a closer connection and more trust between parents and children but also empowers children to voice their concerns and feelings. It can also help to prevent conflict in future situations. For instance, a South Sudanese parent might ask their child to talk about what happens at school and their challenges in adjusting to the new cultural environment. Based on this conversation, the parent might provide ideas for how the child might learn to 'surf the changes' without losing their core cultural identity.

Furthermore, parents can help their children adapt to this new environment by providing sources of capital to help them navigate the acculturation process. This may include enrolling their children in language classes, finding mentors to help them acclimate to the culture, and advocating on behalf of their children to school administrators. Parents can help their children navigate acculturation and maintain a sense of cultural identity by providing support and capital. For instance, a South Sudanese parent may enrol their child in an English-as-a-second language (ESL) class to support their acculturation journey but insist they speak the native language at home. This dual-language approach helps mitigate acculturation challenges while remaining rooted in the culture of origin.

Embracing Flexibility and Adaptability in Acculturation

Flexibility and adaptability are helpful family characteristics and essential tools that help families manage migration and acculturation challenges. More flexible parents can better respond to the stressors of migration and acculturation and provide their children with support for their positive adjustment. For instance, a South Sudanese parent willing to educate herself about host norms and values could be better equipped to navigate the complexities of acculturation and, in turn, possibly enable her children to do the same. They could exemplify responding to cultural change with flexibility and adaptively to create an environment conducive to their children's feeling safe, valued and connected to their cultural roots as well as their present lives.

Addressing Mental Health and Trauma Challenges

For children and families who face long journeys to a new place with the potential for trauma along the way, such migration and acculturation have increased emotional and psychological challenges. For migrants and refugees, establishing an accurate, empowering, positive self-narrative can reduce feelings of burnout and facilitate better-coping mechanisms. These are some ways that young refugees and other newly arrived migrants can overcome the barriers to psycho-social wellbeing.

Parents can help their children maintain their psychological wellness by creating a warm, responsive, and protective climate where they can freely express their thoughts and feelings. Counselling or therapy might be a necessary addition to helping children and parents weather the storm of migration and acculturation. For instance, the South Sudanese family might turn to a mental health professional with deep cultural and emotional insight into migration. The therapist can enable the family to make sense of their experience, bolster their resilience, and navigate their acculturation more easily.

Conclusion

Navigating the complexities of forced migration and acculturation is an ongoing journey for South Sudanese and other African families, one that requires resilience, adaptability, and a strong sense of cultural identity. The migration experience, often driven by necessity and shaped by trauma, presents profound challenges to both parents and children. From the emotional scars of pre-migration trauma to the hardships of displacement and the pressures of adjusting to a new cultural environment, families must constantly negotiate between preserving their heritage and adapting to the demands of their host societies.

This chapter has explored how these intertwined forces of migration and acculturation affect family dynamics, parenting practices, and children's development. The emotional inertia of pre-migration experiences profoundly shapes parenting strategies, often resulting in strict, protective behaviours to shield children from perceived threats in their new environment. Simultaneously, acculturation pressures families to conform to new cultural norms, creating tensions between generations and challenging the maintenance of cultural traditions.

Despite these difficulties, South Sudanese and other African families exhibit remarkable resilience. Their ability to adapt while holding onto their cultural roots is central to overcoming acculturation challenges. Parents, in particular, face the dual challenge of guiding their children through an environment that often conflicts with their values while helping them integrate into a new society. This balancing act is not easy, but it is essential for fostering healthy intergenerational relationships and ensuring children can confidently navigate both worlds.

The key to success lies in building community support networks, fostering open communication, and creating a home environment where cultural traditions are upheld while embracing positive elements of the host culture. Schools, social institutions, and peer networks are influential in this process, as they serve as critical contact points for acculturation. Parents must engage with these systems to advocate for their children's needs while respecting and preserving their cultural values.

Eventually, the chapter has demonstrated that acculturation does not have to be a process of cultural loss. Instead, it can be an opportunity for growth and integration, where families learn to navigate between two worlds, merging the best of both cultures. By maintaining a strong cultural identity and embracing the adaptability required for survival in a new environment, South Sudanese and other

African families can raise resilient children rooted in their heritage and equipped to thrive in their multicultural world.

As these families continue to navigate the challenges of forced migration and acculturation, the strategies outlined in this chapter, such as building community connections, fostering cultural pride, and balancing traditional and new values, offer a roadmap for success. With these tools, migrant families can overcome the immediate difficulties they face and create a path forward where their cultural identities are preserved and celebrated, even as they adapt to the complexities of life in a new country.

CHAPTER FIVE

Parenting in a Multicultural Society: Balancing Cultural Preservation and Adapting to New Norms

Introduction

In a rapidly globalising world, migration has become a defining feature of modern societies. For South Sudanese and other African families living in Australia, parenting within this multicultural landscape brings unique challenges. These families face the delicate task of navigating two distinct cultural worlds: preserving the rich heritage of their native cultures while embracing the norms and expectations of their new environments. This balancing act is not merely about maintaining traditions but crafting an identity that harmoniously blends the old with the latest, providing children with a strong sense of self amid ever-changing circumstances.

Parenting in a multicultural society demands a nuanced understanding of cultural preservation and adaptation. It involves deliberate efforts to sustain language, customs, and values passed down through generations while ensuring children develop the flexibility, resilience, and confidence to thrive in a diverse society.

In this chapter, we will explore the complexities of this dual task, offering insights into how parents can foster a deep cultural connection for their children while equipping them with the skills necessary to succeed in an increasingly interconnected world. It will examine the pivotal role of language, cultural practices, and community engagement in this journey and the challenges of cultural adaptation, such as confronting discrimination and fostering resilience. By doing so, this chapter aims to provide a framework for parents to successfully navigate the cultural intricacies of raising children in a multicultural society.

Preserving Cultural Heritage

Cultural preservation is the conscious and deliberate development of methods by which we maintain generational continuity of cultural traditions, values, languages and practices. For South Sudanese, African and all diaspora families, cultural preservation is not merely about retaining a connection to their heritage. It is also about creating a sense of identity, continuity and belonging in a world that can sometimes feel like it is spinning and changing on its axis. Cultural preservation is a form of empowerment, a line of defence creating a platform for children to develop pride in the world and themselves. It enables them to understand better their identity, their place in their cultural community, and their place in the wider world.

The Role of Language in Strengthening Cultural Preservation

Language is a vital component of cultural transmission. The way people communicate with each other becomes the conduit for much of who they are: language is enriched with a people's history, values, and beliefs, but it is also the heart of their worldview. For many South Sudanese and other African families, maintaining their native languages is a top priority. Closely intertwined with ethnic or tribal identity, language provides the primary avenue through which cultural knowledge is transmitted to subsequent generations.

First, the children will develop a sense of connection to their ethnic identity and cultural heritage since their ability to converse in a language native to their family will allow them to interact with extended family members, understand and eventually participate in their cultural traditions, and feel a solid connection to the community. Second, the children's conversational ability in a language Native to their family will help them self-identify with a sense of pride and confidence to succeed in a multicultural society exposed to various languages and cultures.

It takes time to uphold native language fluency away from familiar surroundings. Suppose children attend school and go to the playground with native speakers, watch television and play computer games in the host country's language, and form friendships with native speakers. In that case, they will eventually grow staccato and weak in their native language. Language shifts can further corrode ties between generations. Parents who can no longer speak with their children in a language that captures and represents the shared culture can feel alienated from their children. Language loss often erodes cultural bonds as well, for it is often in language that we find ties to a culture's creative and psycho-cultural structure: its origin stories, poetry, customs, rituals, jokes, tales of bravery and bucking of authority, the wisdom passed through generations.

In addition to speaking their native language at home regularly and consistently, parents can provide books and media (and other resources) in their native language, encourage their children to use the language in their day-to-day conversations, and they can look for programmes or cultural organisations in their communities that provide classes or activities in their native language. By participating in such classes or events, children can engage in activities, meet and connect with peers from a cultural background akin to what they experience at home, and ultimately, reinforce their language skills. Ultimately, this reinforces their cultural identity.

Cultural Practices and Rituals: Foundations of Identity
Cultural practices and rituals are essential for the collective memory of cultural identity. Activities such as traditional ceremonies, religious observances and communal activities embody the cultural values and beliefs that are the lifeblood of a particular culture. Whenever they are enacted in the diaspora, they recall cultural heritage and make it familiar in the lives of children. South Sudanese and other African families are constantly searching for the keys to staying faithful to their culture, even though they face challenges, including lack of support, limited information, and inadequate resources or advice.

Special cultural events, like weddings, funerals and coming of the communities together, provide meaningful markers of cultural continuity. Ceremonies provide a context for many cultural contributions and can facilitate the role of children in sharing their culture with their peers. For instance, a wedding in many African cultures is not just a union of two individuals. The extended family of both the bride and the groom are actively involved. The ceremony spans several days and is carried out by dozens of active community members adjacent to the residence where the wedding is taking place. The event is laden with cultural symbolism, with the rituals passed down through the generations.

Religious rituals also contribute to cultural maintenance because, for many African families, religion is part of their cultural identity. Religious participation provides an ethical framework, an explanation of the world, and a sense of purpose. Religious involvement in rituals of religion and attendance at religious services helps children learn and refine cultural values and feel more identified with their religious community. Going to church or mosque services, observing religious festivals and celebrations, and participating in religious practices at home help children learn their culture and maintain their cultural identity.

When parents continue to foster a specific cultural practice in a diasporic context, they reinvent and adapt it to suit the demands of the new context. For instance, a South Sudanese family living in the United States or Australia can continue celebrating traditional holidays such as Independence or harvest festivals, even if the family lives very far away. Parents can also bring cultural elements into the everyday routine, such as using a specific term of address for elders or engaging in artistic and cultural forms of expression. This can generate a sense of continuity for children, helping them find a sense of belonging in the multicultural world.

Storytelling: A Vital Channel for Cultural Transmission
Telling stories plays a vital role in cultural transmission. In traditional African societies, oral tradition is the primary means of preserving history, traditions, and values from generation to generation. Parents and elders teach the wisdom of preceding generations, use morally laden stories to instil values and teach knowledge to the younger generation. For South Sudanese and African families in the diaspora, storytelling is an essential means of cultural maintenance for transmission from one generation to the next. This practice bolsters children's

pride in their ethnic heritage by telling them family stories about their ancestral home and tales about the courage and daring of their ancestors who helped shape the contours of life today.

To sustain the oral tradition of storytelling, parents may schedule regular sessions to weave folktales, legends and other stories from personal histories into the fabric of their children's lives and educations. These sessions can be formal, for example, during family reunions or celebrations at religious or community centres or informal, at bedtime during automobile rides or between assignments at a work desk. Moreover, children's tales can be expanded upon and improved through multimedia, using books, audio CDs, and films that transmit odysseys through the human mind and heart, passed down from one generation to the next.

Cultural Adaptation and Associated Challenges

Preserving culture is essential for identity and continuity. However, accommodating oneself to the new environment is just as important. Cultural accommodation is the process of adapting to the host's culture and adopting its norms, values, and expectations while maintaining and passing on one's group's cultural identity, values, norms, and expectations within the new society. While challenging, South Sudanese and African families have stepped up to the occasion and navigated the intercultural waters of a multicultural society connected by the continuous flow of different cultural norms and practices.

Balancing Tradition and Modernity

One of the significant tensions of cultural adaptation is maintaining the right balance between tradition and modernity. Parents may struggle to preserve pre-migration traditions and conform to the host society's more individualistic and modern attitudes. Collectivism and individualism are reflected in parenting styles, social norms of interaction, leadership styles, decision hierarchies, ideas about gender, and other aspects of cultural life.

African parenting is often characterised by respect for authority, communitarianism and discipline, which are underpinned by the social and cultural structure of many African societies in which the general welfare of the community is often placed before the individual. In several Western societies, concepts such as autonomy, egalitarianism, open communication, and more authoritarian or permissive parenting styles that encourage verbalisation and assertiveness of children's opinions and ideas to make decisions autonomously are prioritised.

Parents who have been socialised toward a deeply authoritarian style of communication and relationships with others, including their children, might not know how to overcome their fear of losing respect and discipline once they stop tightly controlling the situation by adhering to customary practices. On the other hand, they might realise that to raise children who can function effectively within the rigid individualist, self-reliant framework defining societal values; they must help their children develop the capacities for personal autonomy.

To do so, they must embrace a hybrid approach: they might preserve traditional values (obedience, respect, shame, responsibility) while encouraging children to think for themselves, ask questions and make their own decisions. The cultural identity of the parent can thus be preserved for their children, while the children have the best of both worlds, moving back and forth between the home culture and the host culture. In this way, the children acquire the best of their heritage while developing the skills needed for adaptation and success in increasingly modern, multicultural contexts.

Negotiating Cultural Differences in Social Interactions

Beyond the challenge of cultural adaptation specifically, these families in the diaspora also have to work through the differences that emerge in social interactions with unfamiliar others, especially when more drastic differences affect the formation of relationships. Social mores of greeting, hospitality and interactions are often very different in many contexts between the African and the Western cultures. For example, while in many African areas, it might be ok to greet someone with an embrace, a handshake or a bow, in some countries in the Western world, personal space and privacy are more often held dear, and physical affection is taboo. This can lead to misunderstandings or discomfort between a South Sudanese family in the UK that's accustomed to greeting each other by hugging, versus the British, who might prefer a handshake or just a 'hello'. For example, a South Sudanese family living in the United Kingdom might find their neighbours less inclined to drop by or socially integrate unplanned, a hallmark of life in their homeland. This can alienate the family from a community they might otherwise grow fond of.

Third, parents can inform their children about these differences and remarkable similarities, specifically about the host culture and their own, as well as how the host culture society is similar to, but also uniquely different from, the child's own culture. By becoming culturally competent and sensitive, children acquire empathy towards other cultures and successfully navigate multiple cultural contexts. Fourth, when their children interact with others in the host society, parents can promote and teach them to respect cultural differences and convey the importance of not abandoning their own cultural values and practices to foster positive relationships with others in the host society.

Cultural competence is vital in a multicultural society; it is more than just knowing about other cultures; it also means learning to develop empathy and adaptability, to be flexible and to open our communications by and with culturally and linguistically diverse people. Culturally competent children will be better prepared as they develop relationships with people who seem different, but they can become friends when given the opportunity. Society at large also benefits as it partners with diverse, culturally competent children and youth to become a more harmonious and inclusive community. Moreover, for South Sudanese and African families who are feeling hopeless and powerless, this could be the elixir to bring hope and make them see that their offspring are indeed well-equipped for the future. For children to develop cultural competence, they can be encouraged to learn about other cultures and be introduced to cross-cultural activities to help them practise those skills at a tender age. They can also be encouraged to be open-minded and show respect for other people and their cultures.

Confronting Discrimination and Prejudice

Discrimination and prejudice, for example, are some of the many challenges that some immigrant families face in receiving countries. South Sudanese and, overall, African families often experience racism and xenophobia. There are moments of alienation when we experience this. However, these moments of resilience and strength reinforce the need to preserve our culture. It also gives families purpose in an anti-Black world that justifies why our culture must be kept as our identities and humanity.

They can experience low self-esteem, anger, confusion, and not feeling like they fit in. They also often feel forced, or even pressured, to assimilate and give up parts of their cultural identity to fit in with their peers, thus feeling disconnected from their roots and identity.

Moreover, the family can become the locus of strife as parents strive to maintain their cultural heritage. At the same time, the children feel the pressure to shed their identity or assimilate into the dominant culture in order to avoid being targeted or alienated.

How do parents meet these challenges? Some steps that parents might take include teaching their children about their rights, training them to speak up against injustice in a constructive and nonviolent way, and instilling in them a sense of dignity and self-worth connected to their cultural heritage. Parents can also advocate within the school system and the broader culture to ensure that their children's cultural values are respected and that their children receive appropriate opportunities and resources.

For instance, parents can advocate for inclusive practices in their children's schools, including respectful recognition of cultural diversity and proactive responses to discrimination in its many forms. They can join immigrant community organisations or call on advocacy groups to help change laws to address discrimination (racism, xenophobia) and engage in public activism to foster changes in societal attitudes and policies. Including disempowered and excluded groups is one of the strongest initiatives parents can take to enable an intergroup solidarity perspective in their children. When discrimination is addressed, parents can help their children foster a stronger sense of inclusion, empowerment and resilience.

The Role of Community in Cultural Adaptation

Community serves as a cornerstone of family adaptation: 'Community matters in sustaining families during cultural adaptation. A community member said, "My culture is a crucial foundational and significant aspect of being a family. Understanding my South Sudanese culture, what we stand for, remaining loyal to, and the social networks with others within the community who share similar experiences sustain the family unit." Remaining connected seems to help people adapt to the new environment or country. For example, the community gives a feeling of belonging, identity, togetherness, learning and support. It is also essential in helping the family to navigate adaptation issues. This person explained that "it benefits us by keeping and maintaining the culture, so we do not lose ourselves during the transition to a new society; we have adapted to the new culture. We feel connected and supported as we navigate adaptation issues." It must be acknowledged that families have different needs and may figure out how to address them uniquely. However, the community serves as a crucial foundational and significant aspect of being a family.

Community organisations, churches, synagogues, Mosques and other cultural associations can become essential resources for immigrant families. They can provide everything from language classes and cultural events to counselling and advocacy on labour rights. Families can find cultural allies and fellow travellers adjusting to life in a new country through their activities. For example, South Sudanese community organisations in Australia can provide programmes that provide South Sudanese children with information about their cultural heritage, encourage South Sudanese parents to adjust to the situation of emigration and help them cope with the attitudes of the larger Australian society toward South Sudanese. Engaging in and completing such programs can help families strengthen their cultural identity while gaining the skills and knowledge they need to survive in a new environment.

Community engagement can also address the sense of isolation and alienation that often comes with the migration journey. Families can create new relationships with people experiencing and/or addressing the same challenges they might grapple with in the migrant community as they engage in community activities and events. In turn, this community can be a source of resilience, helping families with cultural adaptation without losing their cultural identity along the way while also feeling less alone and more connected.

Effective Strategies for Cultural Preservation and Adaptation
While this navigating is a normal part of what families do in a climate of cultural sustainability and adaptation, intentionally seeking to avoid unhealthy assimilation requires some clearly intended strategies that purposely support the family in being good stewards of both individual cultural identity and of the more extensive needs of the broader social context. In the following section, I offer some practical ideas for parents who seek to assist their kids in retaining their cultural identity in their new home.

Creating a Culturally Enriched Home Environment
One of the best ways that cultural identity can be preserved for a family is if the home creates a sense of cultural heritage and integrates cultural practices, language and traditions into the family's daily life. Parents can celebrate their culture through holidays and food and integrate artefacts from home and abroad that remind their children of the heritage that keeps them connected as a family. In addition to using food, artefacts, and holidays to preserve cultural heritage, parents could include books, music, and art that reflect the family's heritage. Providing daily access to cultural identity will embed it within the family's life, adding value and recognising the part it plays. Having culture embedded in daily life will help children to feel like their heritage has meaning and pride.

In addition to cultural traditions, parents can provide language-rich environments for their children by speaking their native language around them and giving them opportunities to practise it, such as reading books, listening to music, and watching films or TV programs in the native language. These parental practices help their children maintain connections with their cultural identities.

Participating in Community and Cultural Events
Getting involved in community and cultural events is another key resilience strategy: being involved in a cultural community can enhance one's cultural connectedness and provide support to help families and individuals navigate challenges adapting to a new environment. Parents can encourage their children to get involved in cultural events, local and national holidays, festivals and events, religious services, participation in classes, clubs, recreational groups or organisations, and getting involved in local or national media and their neighbourhood. For some cultures and religions, joining a community group can provide social and religious activities and foster networks for socialisation and marriage opportunities. In engaging with their cultural community, children can learn about their culture and tradition, connect with others like themselves, and develop cultural pride in their identity.

Parents may encourage their children's participation in cultural or secular events and are likely to involve them in community service and volunteer activities that extend cultural values around the importance of helping others and engaging in civic responsibilities. These activities also allow the children to develop adaptive social skills and relationships with their peers and other host community members. For instance, a family could volunteer at a cultural centre to support immigrant families or participate in a community day to clean up the town organised by a local church or mosque. Such activities not only teach children and pass on a strong sense of community service and a commitment to collective responsibility so central to many

African cultures, but they also connect the family to members of their community and forge healthy relationships with others.

Fostering Open Communication and Dialogue

Fostering open communication can help alleviate many challenges during cultural adaptation and preservation. First, parents can encourage their children to share their feelings, thoughts and experiences and consciously listen to their concerns with empathy and understanding. For example, parents can create an open dialogue for their children to respond to the challenges arising from adaptation to the host culture, such as discrimination, peer pressure or cultural differences. If parents can validate their children's feelings during this process, it will enhance their children's confidence and resilience to tackle these challenges successfully.

Parents can also communicate openness in discussing the value of cultural achievements and milestones, such as when a child speaks the native language, attends cultural events, or maintains cultural rituals. Praising children for their attempts to learn the native language or participate in cultural events supports behaviourally and reinforces cultural parts of a child's identity and self-worth. Open communication also allows parents and their children to conceptualise how their cultural identity meshes with their identities in other aspects of their lives, such as their educational and career values, social relationships, and personal beliefs. As part of these conversations, parents normalise experimenting with different cultural identities and seeking feedback from others' perspectives on developing one's identity.

Building Cultural Competence and Resilience

Children who live in a multicultural society need to develop cultural competence (being able to understand and work within two or more different cultural contexts), so parents have to make an effort to teach their children both cultural contexts. Children need to be aware of the differences between the host culture and their own: they need to be taught about the positional styles of both cultures and understand their implications. Parents must teach their children ideational differences (e.g., respect for authority and how physical contact demands differ). They must also teach their children the verbal style of the host culture and how to decipher and interpret the implicit and explicit messages.

By encouraging these habits, parents would be enabling their children to be respectful of cultural differences to understand the different demand characteristics of the social situation that they are involved in (e.g., being accepted as a member of a group or being an outsider), and lastly to know how to adjust their behaviour to reflect the appropriate demands of the context and defend themselves against things that cannot be attributed solely to their own little bodies.

Along with cultural competence, parenting can cultivate resilience in children by teaching them skills to help them address challenges and adversity. For example, parents could facilitate the development of problem-solving skills, encourage them to seek help for their challenges and promote the development of a powerful sense of self-worth and pride in their culture.

For example, because there is consensus among psychologists regarding the importance of modelling a good work ethic for one's children (i.e., setting goals and striving to make them happen), parents can help their child develop resilience by setting goals for the child, persisting through challenges, and discussing how they worked through setbacks. They can also figure out ways to help their children engage in challenging but achievable goals and time limits so the children can feel masterful and develop meaningful life experiences. Finally, they can express support when their child displays resilient behaviour and make sure they feel accepted and understood.

Resilience might be crucial for children who experience discrimination, prejudice, or more significant issues of cultural conflict. Parents may confidently help children overcome such hurdles by teaching resilience and maintaining a strong sense of cultural pride and self-worth.

Leveraging Professional and Community Support
Maintaining and adapting cultural aspects can pose challenges, and families may benefit from culturally informed social-psychological and community services such as counselling, language classes, culture-specific programs and advocacy. For instance, a counsellor who experienced some of the challenges of migration's cultural and emotional consequences may bolster parents in their cultural adaptation challenges by helping them to process and make sense of their experiences, providing support for resilience and facing difficulties with ease.

Secondly, engaging with community organisations and cultural associations can offer families professional support. These organisations can provide a wide range of services, such as language classes and cultural programmes, as well as advocacy and social support. Such connections can help families retain their cultural identity and learn the skills and knowledge they need to thrive in their new context.

Similarly, community resources such as a cultural centre could provide materials to help parents. For example, a workshop at a cultural centre could be offered to help parents navigate some specific challenges related to raising children in a multicultural world: how to preserve specific cultural aspects, how to discipline and encourage older children who are being overly influenced by the broader society, or how to talk to their children about cultural differences in a way that fosters cultural identity and acceptance, not stereotyping of others.

Conclusion

Navigating the intricate path between cultural preservation and adaptation is a profound journey that South Sudanese and other African families undertake in multicultural societies like Australia. This journey is not solely about maintaining traditions or assimilating into a new culture; it is about weaving together the threads of heritage and modernity to create a rich tapestry of identity for the next generation.

Throughout this chapter, we have explored language's pivotal role in maintaining cultural ties, acting as a bridge between generations and a vessel for transmitting values, beliefs, and worldviews. We have delved into the significance of cultural practices and rituals and how they serve as foundations of identity and collective memory, grounding children in their heritage while they navigate new social landscapes. Storytelling emerges as a vital channel for passing down wisdom and fostering a strong sense of belonging and pride in one's roots.

At the same time, we have acknowledged the challenges of cultural adaptation. Balancing tradition with modern societal norms requires flexibility and open-mindedness. Parents often find themselves negotiating cultural differences in social interactions, confronting discrimination and prejudice, and fostering resilience in their children. These challenges, while formidable, also present opportunities for growth, empathy, and the development of a more nuanced cultural competence.

Community emerges as a cornerstone in this journey, and providing support, shared experiences, and a sense of belonging bolsters preservation and adaptation efforts. Families reinforce their cultural identity by engaging with community and cultural events while building bridges to the broader society.

Effective cultural preservation and adaptation strategies revolve around creating a culturally enriched home environment, fostering open communication, and leveraging professional and community support. By intentionally integrating cultural elements into daily life, encouraging dialogue about cultural experiences, and seeking external resources, parents can equip their children with the tools they need to thrive.

Balancing cultural preservation with adaptation is an ongoing, dynamic process. It requires intentionality, resilience, and a holistic approach that values the richness of one's heritage and the opportunities presented by a new cultural context. For South Sudanese and African families, and indeed all families navigating multicultural landscapes, this balance is crucial for nurturing strong, confident individuals who are deeply rooted in their identity yet adaptable and empathetic to the diverse world around them.

By embracing their heritage and the new cultural norms, parents can help their children develop a robust sense of self that honours their roots while empowering them to succeed in a globalised society. This harmonious blending enriches individual families' lives and contributes to the cultural mosaic of the broader community, fostering inclusivity, understanding, and mutual respect.

As we move forward in an increasingly interconnected world, the experiences and strategies discussed in this chapter serve as a valuable guide. They remind us that while the challenges are significant, the rewards of cultivating a strong, adaptable cultural identity are immeasurable for individuals, families, and societies alike.

CHAPTER SIX

Acculturational Challenges: Negotiating Between Tradition and Integrating into the New Environment

Introduction
Acculturation is an intricate and dynamic process in which individuals and families navigate the delicate balance between maintaining their cultural heritage and adapting to a new societal context. For South Sudanese and other African diaspora communities, this journey is particularly challenging, as it involves reconciling the deeply rooted traditions of their homeland with the often-contrasting values, norms, and expectations of their new environment. The acculturation process is far from linear; it is an ongoing negotiation shaped by unique personal experiences, historical contexts, and the cultural landscapes of the home and host countries.

This chapter explores the multifaceted challenges that arise from this cultural balancing act, shedding light on the psychological, social, and emotional hurdles these families face. As South Sudanese families in the diaspora attempt to integrate into new societies, they encounter profound shifts in identity, family dynamics, and community roles. These shifts often create tensions between generations, as children adapt more quickly to the new culture through school and socialisation, while parents struggle to preserve traditional values and practices.

The ongoing tension between tradition and modernity is at the heart of these challenges. For many parents, the fear of losing their cultural identity is palpable as they witness their children adopt aspects of the host culture that may conflict with their own values. Simultaneously, children face the task of developing a bicultural identity, often caught between two worlds and grappling with the pressures of fitting into both.

This chapter delves into the complexities of the acculturation process, examining how families can successfully navigate these challenges. It explores how preserving cultural identity serves as a source of strength and continuity while also emphasising the importance of integration and adaptability in ensuring a family's well-being and success in a multicultural society. By understanding the phases of acculturation, the psychological toll it takes, and the strategies for managing its effects, families can better support each other through this transformative journey, ultimately fostering resilience, pride, and a harmonious balance between tradition and new beginnings.

An Overview of the Acculturation Process

Acculturation is not a singular moment of consolidation but a fluctuating and ongoing process that could occur over several generations (Berry, 1997; Deng, 2016b). It imports continuous adaptation and negotiation of the values, beliefs and ways of life in the culture of origin and the new cultural locale where people and families are settling. The acculturation process for South Sudanese and African families begins well before the arrival of refugees in their new homeland. It commences with the decision to migrate. The decision is often precipitated by multiple push and pull factors: the push to leave is often a combination of drought, conflict, economic deprivation and political uncertainty in the country of origin, while the pull is the promise of security, economic opportunities and better educational prospects in the host country.

The extent to which all these factors operate in one direction or the other depends, of course, on the reasons for migration, the degree to which the conditions back home did not prepare the children, parents and caregivers for the new environment, the degree of cultural difference of the target society in comparison with the one left behind, and the kind of networks of support are available in the host country. The acculturation pathway can be very different depending on whether the migration was voluntary or a flight from persecution, whether the family was or was not middle class, and whether or not they could maintain ties to their cultural community.

Stages of Acculturation

The acculturation process has different phases, presenting distinctive opportunities, threats, and psychological dynamics. Nevertheless, the phases are not clean-cut, and families can shuttle between them.

1. Initial contact and culture shock: When individuals and families first enter the host country, they experience the initial contact phase, which is often a time of excitement, curiosity, and anxiety as families confront a different cultural milieu for the first time. The excitement of arrival in a new country and its promise of shifting horizons is tempered by the reality of cultural norms and language differences and the practicalities of adapting to a new environment.

Culture shock is widespread and is often characterised by a sense of disorientation, frustration and homesickness. The constant demands of assimilation can be overwhelming and alienating as families grapple with the realities of the new culture and try to reconcile them with their lives back home. For example, a family arriving from a rural village in South Sudan might be unprepared for the fast pace and urban density of the cities in some Western countries, where interpersonal encounters, mass transit systems and even the overall city layout are so strikingly different from what they are used to.

Children are usually affected in polarising ways by culture shock; it can take them very literally by the throat in the perception that they do not understand the new social signals and expectations and deprive them of anchor points by allying them neither with their own kind in the host society nor with their original culture. For parents, too, culture shock carries a sense of compound accusation, a feeling that cultural values are being stressed to the point of snapping, and 'social life' has resulted in 'estrangement'. The stress, disorientation and confusion can be very severe.

2. Cultural adjustment and learning: As families start to acclimate, the initial shock gradually subsides, and they learn how to handle the new cultural setting in the cultural adjustment stage. This phase often features a steep learning curve as families grasp the host society's language, social norms, legal structures and daily practices.

Children often lead this stage because language is the most essential integration element. If a child attends school and plays with children in the host language, parents will often learn the new language more quickly through their children than they do in school or adult classes. These dynamics might turn sibling relationships upside down as children increasingly act as language brokers for their parents, translating family affairs and shielding them from the puzzling realities of their new city, state or country. While this can give children a sense of power and responsibility, these dynamics can also burden children, who anticipate their parents' reactions as they adapt to adult responsibilities while they are still children.

Social norms and laws are also important, primarily through scrutinising the social norms and laws; families must determine how the host society views and regulates family life, schooling, parenting, etc. A simple but everyday example could be related to the legal system in the host society. Within different host countries, the manner and the scope under which parents can speak to or discipline their children may differ markedly from the parents' home country. In different host countries, the legal system may classify certain forms of behaviour and discipline as illegal and chargeable offences of specific degrees of seriousness. Some of these 'illegal' parenting behaviours may have caused concern among parents in the home country but not as much legal concern as in the host society. This can be stressful for families to figure out. Parents must learn the rights and responsibilities that apply to citizens in the host society, as well as the services and resources available to them, including healthcare facilities, schools and social services.

3. Cultural integration and identity development: With deeper immersion into the host culture, a family adjusts in practical terms to the new society and begins to explore and develop a bicultural identity. In this stage, the families experience two cultures simultaneously, but it cannot be easy. Inclinations to assimilate can put the family at odds with one another.

Cultural integration also involves families having to negotiate the often-competing values of tradition and modernity as they both preserve cultural practices and adapt to the expectations of the host society. Parents often find this process especially difficult because they feel that they are caught in the 'middle' between wanting to preserve their cultural identity and supporting their children in integrating into the new society. Such tensions might involve whether to allow their children to participate in 'Westernised' activities they associate with the host culture, such as dating, attending parties, or engaging in certain types of entertainment.

One of the most influential and vital ways we integrate into the culture around us is through the formation of identity. It is essential for children and adolescents who are still solidifying their sense of self. So, children growing up with more than one culture are especially likely to develop a 'double consciousness' of cultural whiplash as they simultaneously bounce between the expectations of the world around them and those of their cultural community. This can result in deep feelings of alienation or confusion, especially when children do not see themselves as really belonging to either culture.

4. Cultural adaptation and continuity: This stage involves the subtle but complex ongoing process of adapting to and establishing stability in the new environment while at the same time maintaining connections with and continuing to reflect upon their original culture. It involves a deep and sustained rooting while maintaining and adapting one's original cultural traditions and identity.

Cultural adaptation is not a static process (that is, once adopted, the acculturating individual is forever changed) but rather a dynamic one involving continual negotiation and adaptation; members of families may incorporate novel cultural practices, develop novel social networks, and figure out means of retaining key cultural traditions in their new habitat. This stage also considers that acculturation is a prolonged process; it may become a multigenerational process in which each succeeding generation experiences acculturation differently.

For instance, the first generation can have a dual identity, where one facet is their own culture and traditions, and the other is adopted from their host country. The second generation might have fabricated or integrated multiple layers of identity. The third generation could be confronted with distinctions similar to a legacy of their culture and full inclusion in their host country.

Balancing Tradition with Integration Challenges

The tension between tradition and integration that South Sudanese and other African families experience overseas is one of their most salient and lasting challenges. Balancing cultural continuity and integration requires that many parents make painful and complicated choices about what to keep, what to alter, and what to let go of in terms of cultural practices to support their children's well-being and prosperity in the new environment.

Preserving Cultural Identity

Cultural identity can be understood not only as a collection of practices and beliefs but as the source of an individual's sense of self, belonging and continuity. For South Sudanese and other African diaspora families, the constancy of cultural identity keeps a sense of familiarity and connection to the past, community and ancestry. Cultural identity is central to psychological, social and behavioural development while promoting attachment, socialisation and pride in one's heritage. It is also a crucial source of strength and resilience during acculturation.

For parents, maintaining cultural heritage often involves actively passing on cultural practices, values and history to their children, for example, celebrating cultural holidays and offering up religious prayers and sacrifices; teaching in the native language in the home; and sharing traditionally passed-down activities such as storytelling, music and dance. These practices are not empty acts: they can serve as a way of maintaining an ongoing relationship with one's culture and the next generations. For instance, a South Sudanese family living in Australia might continue to celebrate South Sudanese Independence Day, practise a traditional South Sudanese religion, and ensure that children speak their mother tongue, e.g., Sudanese Arabic, Dinka or Nuer, at home. Such norms help to reinforce a family's cultural identity and offer a sense of continuity, stability and belonging in a new and often foreign environment.

Preserving a cultural identity in a multicultural society can be a struggle. The dynamics are complicated when families deal with challenges, especially when cultural practices and values are at odds with host-society culture. Still, there are examples among South Sudanese and African refugee families of confronting these challenges and developing cultural practices that help their children straddle their two cultures. As highlighted in the previous chapter, studies have shown that children who have developed dual identities are more resilient in navigating their two worlds.

Cultural Differences in Everyday Life

One crucial way these cultural differences often manifest is how South Sudanese, and those from Africa in general, go about their daily lives. For families dealing with acculturation, this can manifest in every social interaction, at school or work, within the family, or otherwise, as misunderstandings or even outright conflict in how things get done. More troubling still is the alienation professionals with a background in Africa often feel.

For instance, in most African cultures, respect is seen as an essential social attitude that guides behaviour at all levels of social interaction. Children are taught to treat their parents, teachers, or other authority figures with respect and to attend to the family's needs, particularly those of the elders in the family. The interests of the community as a whole are considered to take precedence over individual desires. Examples of such practices include bowing or curtsying to elders; listening reverentially to the stories of the elders; engaging in various activities to promote social solidarity; addressing older people, not just by their names, but by their condoned titles, including grandfather, mother, uncle, aunt, etc.

By contrast, in many Western cultures, people value independence, autonomy and self-expression, and children are encouraged to be independent and challenge authority interests and identities. Such emphasis on individualism can generate pressures in family life that arise when parents and children have different expectations of how they should interact with one another and even different expectations of how the roles of family members overlap with other roles within the wider society. For example, a parent from South Sudan can expect his child to be more deferential to elders and prioritise fulfilling family obligations and commitments. On the other hand, the child can feel pressure to fit in with peers who value independence and self-expression. These pressures can create conflicts and miscommunication.

New Educational System Challenges

The educational system is another area where cultural differences can significantly challenge South Sudanese and other African families. However, it is crucial to underscore the remarkable resilience of these families in navigating these challenges. Education is perhaps the most significant factor in facilitating the acculturation process because, as children's exposure to formal education deepens, the values, beliefs and behaviours that they are taught within the classroom will begin to override what they are taught at home. However, the educational system in the host country will also differ from the educational system at home in many ways, and families will have to navigate these differences.

For example, the concept of competitive individualism highlighted in many Western educational systems might be pitted in conflict with a communal ethos that emphasises 'collective responsibility'. This concept is common in many African cultures. It is a collectivist framework in which 'the individual's success is seen as a communal success and their failure deemed to harm the community at large'. In many African cultures, students learn to collaborate, share knowledge and contribute to their society as learners in return for community investment.

Conversely, Western education systems have long focused on individual accomplishment, emphasising achievement as demonstrated through grades, scores, and anything else that heralded a student's ascendancy and ultimately nudged their way into the top of the educational class. Children who were used to learning cooperatively and functioning within a culture of sharing could be thrown off balance by the new emphasis on individualism and competition. Learning in a classroom that encouraged teamwork and where autonomy was carved out and fostered was like apples and oranges, continents apart.

Similarly, the curriculum in the host country may not have courses or content that help to normalise their cultural experiences, knowledge and history, making the new country and school feel like a foreign and strange place. For instance, if a South Sudanese child comes to the classroom not seeing their culture, history or experiences in textbooks, lessons and classroom activities, it will affect their self-esteem. When children begin to feel that they do not belong, are not a part of, or cannot succeed in school, they are often less likely to be engaged in their learning or succeed in the new environment.

Language barriers can be a significant obstacle to the educational system, especially for families new to the host country. Children learning a language cannot always keep up with their peers, and parents who do not speak the language may have trouble communicating with teachers and advocating for a child's needs. All of this can isolate and frustrate parents and children alike as they try to navigate the system.

Parents can overcome these barriers and help their kids by becoming involved in the education process, contacting teachers, joining parent-teacher organisations, volunteering, and offering resources at home to help with learning. They can also find language-support groups, cultural education services and educational programmes to support their kids' learning. For instance, parents can create a home library with books in their native and the host country's languages, or they can encourage their children to participate in cultural events and activities outside of school. Parents can try to make their home a learning environment, encouraging their kids to engage in learning alongside other cultural pursuits.

Family Dynamics and Role Reversal During Acculturation Process

Throughout the acculturation process, families undergo a redefining of their roles and responsibilities in coping with the ongoing process of adapting to the new social environment and the challenge of family members absorbing the stress and pressures of transitioning to a new culture and adapting to a new family structure. When family members experience and respond to acculturation differently, it can produce stress and tension among family members. For example, through the process of acculturation, long-standing roles and responsibilities that parents may have had as heads of their families become reconfigured and reshaped to reflect the demands of the host society. Such changes can be stressful, especially when parents lose their traditional roles or cannot perform their traditional responsibilities at cultural events.

In many African cultures, the father and mother have specific family roles. The father is mostly the provider of anything within and outside the home and also serves as a guard to the family. On the flip side, the mother is the family nurse and tends to take care of the kids and any inheritance. These roles are often grounded in the traditional African and religious setup, which has remained unchanged over the years.

Nevertheless, these family roles can be threatened or transformed in the host country as parents adjust to the new economic, social and cultural environment. For instance, a father who earned the primary income in the home country might need help finding work. As a result, the primary earner role can be challenged, and families can reconfigure financially. In addition, a mother who manages the home and most of the domestic chores in a home country might now find herself working, and the family could need to readjust to new routines and roles.

Such changes can create friction within the family, as parents may feel they are losing the cultural roots and meaning of life they held back home. Acknowledging the emotional challenges parents face in the acculturation process is essential, as this can help the audience empathise with their experiences. Children's relationships with various family members can also be altered, reflecting these changes. For example, children who quickly master the host country's language may become translators or cultural mediators for their parents, as happened in my interviews with parents and young people of South Sudanese/African backgrounds in Melbourne, who saw their roles reverse as they helped their parents adjust to life in their new country. Here, the parent-child relationship shifts as children take on care responsibilities, empowered by their language ability and familiarity with their new environment. It is evident that the older we become, the harder it is to learn a new language, a situation many parents are caught up in.

Because acculturation changes the fabric of a family, one way to survive these stressors is to maintain good communication and mutual support. Remember that acculturation is a shared experience that affects each family member. Parents can also focus on finding resources and support networks that provide them with the guidance and help they need to navigate acculturation challenges, such as community organisations, cultural associations and counselling services.

Belonging and Identity in a Multicultural Society

It is crucial to emphasise the importance of maintaining cultural identity in a multicultural society. This enriches the societal fabric and helps individuals, especially those from South Sudanese and African families, feel a sense of belonging and pride in their heritage. It is a testament to the richness of our society that we can embrace and celebrate diverse cultural identities.

Acculturation manifests itself in an adaptive challenge weighed on the scales of identity and belonging. For South Sudanese and African families, in my view, the practice of trying to 'make it here' signifies the coexistence of fluid notions of identity and belonging and adaptation and assimilation. Supporting the peripherals of their 'home' embodies the challenges of acculturation across broken waters of identity, hope, homeland and belonging, where fear feels like salvation. These are usually brief moments of paralysis for parents who dash into activity across these waters with heartfelt calls to 'be stronger', 'be good', and 'look after your siblings.' My children grew up acculturated multicultural beings who walk between two worldviews. However, it has been a bumpy journey for many, especially young Africans, as their belonging breaks the hope of a home in an unpredictable environment where racial profiling could be dressed up as crime prevention.

For children, acculturation to the dominant society brings the experience of 'double consciousness', a state of mind in which one is aware of and feels obligated to meet the expectations and norms of both the source and dominant societies. The school-age children raised by South Sudanese parents but who attend Western schools experience conflicting messages about appropriate youthfulness in one domain and not in another. Parallel to what children experience in two cultural communities, this ambiguous sense of 'double consciousness' creates an inner conflict as a child pursues the development and expression of unique cultural values at odds with the dominant world of mass culture. Sometimes, these identities can clash with how parents feel if their cultural heritage and community differ significantly from the new cultural context. Parents might experience acculturation tensions or ambivalence within themselves as well.

Parents can create a safe and supportive environment to help their children navigate these challenges, allowing them to explore and express their evolving cultural identity, practice their culture, connect with their community, and explore their cultural and ethnic experiences openly and respectfully. Parenting out of the margins also involves assisting a child in developing as trans (if), fluid (with different formulations), and bicultural individuals able to exist and thrive in different spaces and dimensions. Parents can do this by cultivating the child's awareness and appreciation for the strengths of their cultures. The parent will help their child cultivate an attitude that allows them to embrace their cultural identity as an endless source of wisdom and resilience.

Discrimination and Prejudice

For many South Sudanese and African families, acculturation can include experiences of discrimination and prejudice, which can lead to feelings of alienation, anxiety and frustration and hurt their sense of self, personal growth, cultural identity or sense of belonging. Children who experience discrimination may be at risk of developing low self-esteem and anxiety and also may face challenges in getting along with their peers. They may also face pressure to assimilate into the host culture while abandoning the cultural identity their parents may encourage them to maintain. This creates a tension between values within the family.

Discrimination can manifest through racism, as well as microaggressions and systemic discrimination. Racism can be overt, such as when an individual is subjected to acts of hostility, including name-calling, harassment and physical violence that target them precisely because of their race or ethnicity. Microaggressions, on the other hand, are more insidious and can involve comments, behaviours or attitudes that reflect implicit biases and stereotypes. Systemic discrimination, on the other hand, refers to how institutions, policies and practices shape an unequal and marginalised social world based on race or ethnicity.

For instance, a South Sudanese child may be marginalised at school by teachers or peers due to their race and/or cultural background, with stereotypes being formed about them based on ethnicity, such as 'South Sudanese students are not academically inclined' or 'Black students are more deviant than White ones'. They may feel a sense of loneliness, frustration and disconnection, as well as an erosion of confidence and poor performance at school. To help their children, parents can equip their kids with the resources to respond to the discrimination and stereotyping they face. They can teach them about their rights, motivate them to speak out when other children and adults deny them those rights and cultivate genuine pride in their ethnic heritage.

Parents can also engage in extra community advocacy for their children. This can include working with schools to promote cultural sensitivity and develop culturally responsive curricula, getting involved with community organisations that aid immigrant families, and finding resources that provide guidance and support for confronting discrimination.

Coping Strategies and Support Systems

Successfully navigating acculturation requires resilience, adaptability, and support for South Sudanese/African and other new migrant families. These families need to develop meaningful coping resources and resilience in order to maintain mental-physical health and yield favourable acculturation outcomes.

Resilience as a Coping Mechanism During Acculturation

Resilience is coping with and adapting to stress, challenges and adversity. For an acculturating family, the goal of resilience is often to plan strategies and approaches to increase skills or enhance attitudes to meet the demands and resulting stresses of living in a new and potentially challenging cultural environment. Resilience can be a combination of personal internal resources and external conditions. Resilience can be developed within a family with a particular bent for looking for the glass-half-full and learning to cultivate that optimism, as well as identifying personal goals while working toward growing a source of meaning and purpose on an ongoing basis. Such an optimistic attitude might emphasise the benefits and positive aspects of the new environment rather than focusing on challenges and obstacles that often come up. By developing resilience, South Sudanese/African families can feel empowered and capable of overcoming acculturation challenges.

Families can support resilience by seeking social support and resources and participating in physical, social and emotional activities beneficial to health and wellbeing (e.g., sports, arts, culture, community service, faith-based activities, and positive peer and mentor relationships). For example, families can support children's resilience by creating a warm, loving home environment where children are affirmed for their strengths and accomplishments, heard when they fear being mocked or excluded from social relationships, and challenged to resolve conflicts.

Building a sense of coherence and efficacy, which refers to a child's understanding of their environment, their ability to manage the challenges they face, and their belief in their own competence, could include families setting realistic expectations for children, providing developmentally appropriate opportunities for children to develop and learn new skills and interests, and supporting children in navigating acculturation dilemmas.

Parents can also support their children's resilience outside the home by encouraging them to participate in physical, social, and emotional strengthening activities such as sports teams, art classes, or other community groups. These activities can help generate a sense of purpose, belonging, and identity.

Social Support and Community Networks

Social support and community networks are crucial for acculturation. When people emigrate from their home country, they must establish a new robust support network consisting of family, friends, community organisations and cultural associations, among other support services. This support network is essential for talking about experiences, giving/receiving emotional support, understanding concerns, exchanging practical support, giving/receiving information and helping with daily activities. This plays a crucial role in maintaining wellbeing and a positive acculturation process.

Parents can find social support by participating in community activities, joining mutually aligned cultural or religious groups, and engaging with other immigrant families with whom they share everyday experiences. These connections can become epicentres of social belonging, shared family labour, and kinship, boosting a family's capacity to face the strains associated with the process of acculturation. This sense of belonging is crucial for South Sudanese/African families in the diaspora, as it helps them feel connected and supported in their new cultural environment.

This mutual support can help maintain cultural identity and ethno-cultural and social networks and develop social capital to fare better as global travellers. Furthermore, by drawing resources that support the acculturation process, families can benefit from counselling services and classes to learn the language and culture of the new homeland and adapt based on their individual needs. Such assistance might include cultural education and language classes, immigration and legal support, education and job services, mental health counselling and financial support. For example, families could use these resources to find quality childcare, learn to drive, search for a job, set up a bank account, deal with a lawsuit, cope with grief, and access emergency services, among other things.

Constructive Cultural Identity and Bicultural Competence

Successful acculturation relies upon the ability to develop constructive and positive cultural identity. For South Sudanese and African families, creating a positive cultural identity requires understanding their cultural background's strengths and learning to embrace and value their traditional values. Parents need to instil within their children a balance of cultural identity and the willingness to accept and appreciate cultural differences while maintaining their positive cultural identity. Parents who promote a positive cultural identity teach their children about their culture and heritage, encourage opportunities to participate in their culture, and motivate and allow their children to be proud of their cultural and ethnic identity. Such activities could include celebrating cultural holidays, such as [specific holiday], participating in cultural or religious ceremonies, and participating in other cultural activities, such as storytelling, music or dance.

Helping them learn these would, in turn, help them share their cultural backgrounds and be proud to be who they are with pride. It can also help them cope better and overcome identity confusion or rejection in their new and dominant culture. As discussed in the previous chapter, this is very significant for integration. Those who struggle with identity crises struggle to integrate, especially when they feel rejected by their new culture, particularly after they might have tried to assimilate into and given up their original cultural identity.

On the one side, positive cultural identity is about fostering a healthy sense of belonging to a specific culture. Conversely, bicultural competence is about being competent and comfortable in two cultures. Parents, as the primary influencers in their children's lives, play a crucial role in promoting their children's bicultural competence in several domains. In each domain, the goal for children is to develop the ability to navigate and engage within both cultures with confidence and pride.

Here are three examples of such domains. First, regarding values, a biculturally competent child should understand and respect the things valued by both cultures. For instance, they can learn to appreciate the importance of family in their African culture while also understanding the value of individualism in their new culture. Second, in terms of norms, she should be able to understand and follow the social expectations in both cultures, such as how she should show respect for elders and engage in ceremonial activities in her cultural community and how she should negotiate relationships in the dominant culture and juggle between her peers' interests and those of her parents. Third, regarding practices, a biculturally competent child should be able to switch between the languages used in each culture. For example, they can learn to speak their native language at home and use the dominant language at school or in the community.

The development of bicultural competence requires parents to highlight the strengths of both cultures and to foster in children a sense of their cultural identity as a source of resilience and empowerment. Parents can facilitate this process by ensuring that children participate in events in both cultures: celebrations, restaurants, sports and arts events, exposure to the history and traditions of their cultural heritage, and engagement with friends and peers from both cultures. Promoting a healthy bicultural identity and bicultural competence can enable parents to encourage children's sense of resiliency and equanimity as they tackle the challenges of acculturation and their sense of belonging in both cultures and to society at large.

Conclusion

Acculturation is a complex and evolving process that affects every aspect of life for South Sudanese and other African families in the diaspora. As they navigate the challenges of integrating into a new cultural environment while holding onto the traditions and values of their homeland, these families face significant social, emotional, and psychological pressures. The process involves continuous negotiation, where parents and children must adapt to new norms, customs, and expectations while remaining connected to their cultural roots.

The delicate balance between cultural preservation and adaptation is at the core of this process. Parents strive to protect their children's sense of cultural identity, fearing that adopting foreign norms might dilute or even erase their heritage. Meanwhile, children, immersed in the host culture through school and social interactions, often face the dual challenge of bridging the gap between their parents' traditional values and the demands of their new society. This generational divide can lead to tensions, miscommunications, and sometimes alienation within families, particularly when the expectations of one culture clash with those of the other.

However, the journey of acculturation also presents profound opportunities for growth and resilience. Families that successfully navigate these challenges often emerge with a richer, more nuanced understanding of their cultural identity, informed by their heritage and the new cultural experiences they have embraced. This bicultural identity becomes a source of strength, allowing children to draw on the best of both worlds as they navigate their future in an increasingly globalised society.

The chapter underscores that while acculturation challenges are significant, they are not insurmountable. Families can build a bridge between the past and the future by fostering open communication, mutual understanding, and a willingness to adapt without losing sight of one's cultural core. In doing so, they preserve their cultural legacy and contribute to the multicultural fabric of their new societies, enriching their lives and communities.

In conclusion, acculturation is a transformative process that shapes the identities, relationships, and future trajectories of South Sudanese and other African families in the diaspora. It is a journey filled with challenges and immense personal and collective growth potential. By thoughtfully and intentionally navigating the tensions between tradition and integration, these families can thrive in their new environments while continuing to honour and celebrate the rich cultural heritage that defines them.

CHAPTER SEVEN

Bridging Generational Divides and Cultivating Family Harmony

Introduction
This chapter examines intergenerational conflict's complex and delicate interplay, a universally experienced phenomenon uniquely amplified within diasporic and multicultural contexts. For South Sudanese and other African families navigating life in their host countries, the tensions between upholding traditional values and adapting to new cultural norms are particularly pronounced. These families face the challenge of balancing deeply rooted cultural identities with the evolving realities of their new environments, often creating friction between parents and children. This generational divide is further complicated by differences in worldview, communication styles, and expectations, which frequently lead to misunderstandings and conflicts.

The chapter explores the underlying causes of these conflicts, focusing on the cultural clashes between traditional values and the influences of modernity. It highlights the evolving roles and responsibilities within families and the impact of cultural assimilation on both parents and children. In doing so, it aims to illuminate the forces that strain familial bonds and offers insights into fostering harmony and resilience within the family unit. The goal is to guide families in navigating the cultural dichotomies that give rise to intergenerational tensions, helping them find pathways to understanding and unity.

This chapter delves into the dynamics of generational conflict and offers practical solutions that promote open communication, mutual respect, and empathy. These tools are critical for bridging the gaps between generations, allowing families to preserve their cultural heritage while adapting to the demands of their new social realities. Through a reflective and empathetic lens, the chapter emphasises the importance of adaptability, cultural preservation, and nurturing a cohesive family environment where tradition and modernity can coexist.

As families grapple with these tensions, their resilience and ability to adapt offer potent lessons in how to thrive in a multicultural world. Understanding the roots of intergenerational conflict provides a means to resolve these tensions. It strengthens the bonds that unite families, enabling them to create a harmonious future while honouring their past.

Unpacking Intergenerational Conflict: Core Causes and Underlying Dynamics

Intergenerational conflicts, characterised by differing views, values, and expectations among family members from different generations, can lead to misunderstandings and outright conflict. These conflicts can stem from various sources, including perceived clashes of cultural affiliations, different forms of generational communication, and diverse life experiences. Understanding the emergence and reasons behind these conflicts is crucial for their resolution, empowering families to navigate the cultural dichotomies that often lead to intergenerational conflict.

One of the primary sources of intergenerational conflict in South Sudanese and African diaspora families is this clash between traditional African cultural values and practices and the norms of their host societies. This clash typically lies at the heart of much of the misunderstandings that plague parent-child relationships, as each generation tries to gain purchase on their identity amid a whirlwind of forces that erode and remould what constitutes their identity. The extent of such clashes can be enormous. Parents who grew up in Africa take traditional African values for granted; they may even see them as essential to holding together the fabric of their identity and their ability to sustain a cohesive sense of continuity. You know, the values of respect for your elders, the notion of communal responsibility, adhering to cultural traditions, and so on. These values often include an intense sense of familial and communal solidarity that almost demands subordination and an extreme in-group mentality.

On the other hand, children growing up in immigrant families that have settled in a more multicultural setting may be more exposed to the host society's cultural directions, which are likely to emphasise individualism, autonomy and self-expression. These social cues might lead their worldview to gradually shift toward the values of the host society as they adopt the behaviours, attitudes and values that underpin the norms of the host society. The diverging cultural orientation between them makes up for clashes involving misunderstandings and can turn into power struggles.

For instance, parents might expect their children to participate in rites of passage from traditional culture, show proper and hierarchical respect towards adult family members, and prioritise family activities over personal interests. These expectations are based on the belief that upholding traditional culture can help maintain the family's identity and function as an autonomous unit. In contrast, host-society values might lead children to view parental expectations as limiting or obsolete. For example, children might resist participating in rites of passage, obeying parental authority, or prioritising personal interests and goals over family activities. These resistances might conflict with parental expectations, as parents might experience their children's behaviour as a cultural rejection. In contrast, children might view parents as threatening their personal autonomy and misunderstanding the realities of the host society.

Impact of Communication Styles on Intergenerational Conflict

Generational differences may include variations in how we communicate, which can be miscommunicated due to perceived inappropriateness of tone. Some values, such as 'Ubuntu' in many African cultures, may even encourage us to word our communications in ways that 'show respect and good mannerisms'. 'Ubuntu' is a Nguni Bantu term meaning 'humanity '. It is often translated as 'I am because we are' or 'humanity towards others'. This value for formal and respectful language is often praised for the unity and cohesion it creates. Many parents expect their children to address them respectfully, avoid direct confrontation, and retain traditional forms of address, such as honorifics or deference in body language.

By contrast, younger generations, especially those who grew up in the host country, might favour a more direct, informal and confrontational communication style. They might be more comfortable communicating their opinions openly, challenging authority, and engaging in discussions that involve debate or disagreement. This difference in communication styles might set the stage for conflict. Parents will perceive their children's behaviour as disrespectful and dismissive, while children experience their parents' behaviours as authoritarian and controlling. These misunderstandings can snowball into family conflicts.

Plural language skills can also deepen generation gaps in communication. For diaspora families, children can be fluent in the host society's language well before their parents and thus reverse positions. I have observed many South Sudanese and African families where children became translators and mediators, relieving their parents' anxieties by making them understand what was happening. These children explained what new foods were offered, helped with communication, and played a new role as their father's or mother's informal interpreter. In children, such role reversal can empower youngsters, giving them a sense of responsibility and agency. It can foster new perspectives when they interpret the world for their parents. However, it also builds tension between generations if the parents feel that all authority has been lost or if children feel too burdened by translating and cultural mediation.

Life experiences can also play a role in creating intergenerational conflict. Parents who grew up during times of crisis through war, migration or economic difficulties, for example, may hold different values, having been shaped by their experiences. These values may emphasise survival, resilience and the importance of maintaining one's cultural identity as a source of empowerment and continuity. To these parents, the cultural practices and traditions in which they were socialised are not just symbolic. However, they are potent aids to survival across time and space, crucial to the ongoing survival of the family.

Conversely, as discussed in the previous chapters, children raised in more settled circumstances might have different needs and not fully comprehend or appreciate all their parents went through to create a new home and life for their families. Following this logic, conflicts between parents and children are more likely to arise when the experiences of parents and children are fundamentally different, and two generations have incompatibly different expectations or when children reject the values their parents live by. Imagine, for example, a parent who endured the violence of war and displacement, a precarious journey to resettlement in a new country, and several other arduous struggles that arose as one tries to carve out a new life and future for oneself and one's family. This parent might value security and stability highly and hold on to cultural traditions to retain a sense of self and belonging in his or her new but uncertain surroundings. This parent might expect children to honour traditions and customs and see them as expressing and upholding the integrity and continuity of the family.

Nevertheless, in a more peaceful, diverse environment, a child will likely prefer self-expression, exploration and becoming a full member of wider society. This may also inspire them to have their own goals and ambitions or to pursue goals and ambitions that conflict with traditional cultural expectations. Conflict can erupt when parents feel that their children are abandoning their culture or when children feel that their parents are trying to hold them back from pursuing their dreams.

Pressures of acculturation, blind adherence to culturally alien rules and codes, erosion of cultural identity, and discrimination and racism in the host country make intergenerational conflict much more stressful for South Sudanese and other African families than it is for their white-Western counterparts. Acculturation is the process of adapting to a new culture and its values. For some, especially refugees or immigrants like most of my respondents, acculturation can be pretty stressful. Nevertheless, for South Sudanese and other African families, the stress of acculturation is compounded by their need to stay faithful to multiple ethnic, cultural and religious identities. While parents often value their ethnic culture and want to pass it on to their children, they also want to 'help the children adapt to this new environment and culture'. They have to find ways to encourage them to adopt the rules of the game in the host society, even if these rules contradict their values.

For instance, parents may believe that daughters and sons should carry out gender-specific tasks (e.g., girls mind the house and cook, while boys lead the family), cultivate a sense of cultural-based identity and responsibility, and serve as honourable exemplars of the family's concern for the next generation. However, children who grow up surrounded by more egalitarian gender expectations in the host culture might resist these classifications. As a result, families find themselves in heated arguments over everything from dishwashing chores to career ambitions and spouses. Parents might find their culture crumbling around them, all the while sharing a similar meltdown: 'You don't know how lucky you are to be living in a time when men and women are treated as equal!' 'Us, lucky? Try walking in our shoes. You'll see.' An example of the typical conversations between the old and young generation.

Furthermore, the issue is maintaining cultural identity. Cultural identity offers continuity, meaning, and connection and serves as a source of identity. It reflects cultural values that shape how one perceives, interacts, and relates to the world and people around them. As parents and youth reflected upon in the previous chapters, cultural identity can also be a driving force in reinforcing connections with fellow ethnic groups and serving as a political tool in the fight for social justice. African and South Sudanese parents in the diaspora tend to fear losing their children's cultural identity if their children become excessively assimilated into their new cultural surroundings, inadvertently being shaped by the cultures that surround them with 'foreign' cultural values.

This may lead parents to enforce strict cultural expectations to maintain cultural traditions. For example, parents might require their children to address them and other family members in their original language, to participate in important rituals, and to socialise with members of their cultural community who share the same beliefs and practices. On the one hand, such attitudes and actions are viewed as fundamental to maintaining the family's cultural identity and sustaining children's connection to the broader cultural group.

However, parental efforts can also create friction, as they can impinge on children's sense of autonomy; by raising children with tight boundaries or strong cultural connections, parents could create challenges for their children that spill into the wider social sphere. Some children, for example, might experience unrealistic parental expectations or be asked to choose between their culture and their personal ambitions.

Impact of Systemic Discrimination on Intergenerational Conflict
Systemic discrimination is associated with both racism and immigration status and is common in many immigrant and minority communities, including South Sudanese and African households. This can contribute to intergenerational conflict. It can introduce more points of conflict and stress in the home when parents experience discrimination from employers, housing providers, police, schools, health care workers or in social interactions and stores. These experiences can lead to high frustration and anger, and even feelings of learned helplessness, which the parents pass along to their children, who may themselves experience discrimination in school, among peers or in the community.

Discrimination against either parent or child can create feelings of alienation and marginalisation, fuelling intergenerational conflict.

For example, children who confront racism at school may resent their parents' cultural distinctiveness and adopt a self-definition more consistent with their (often white) peer group. They may resent what they see as unrealistic expectations or feel that they must choose between their cultural identity and their desire to be part of the broader culture. On the other hand, parents who face discrimination may feel that their children fail to grasp the difficulties of their lives. At the same time, children may bristle at what they see as parental interference in their choices or too much cultural pressure. Thus, parents and children are pulled further apart.

Although intergenerational conflict can be challenging and complex, it is also an opportunity for learning, growing and building family relationships. Instead of adding to the chaos, by engaging with empathy, open and respectful communication, and mutual respect, families can pave the way for closeness and provide a home that honours family tradition and modern life. Open and respectful communication is among the most essential strategies for intergenerational conflict. Open communication allows family members to express their feelings, thoughts and concerns and to hear the perspectives of others. It is the key to healthy family relationships, settling disagreements, and strengthening harmonious family bonds.

Active Listening: A Vital Element of Effective Communication
Active listening, which involves fully attending to what the person speaking says without interrupting, judging or trying to correct them, and reflecting on what you have heard with empathy and understanding, can become an essential part of open communication when engaging in intergenerational conflict. When family members can show each other respect by engaging in active listening, it enables a greater understanding of one another's positions and can help to revive

trust. For example, when a child says they are upset about a cultural norm if a parent listens and reflects on what they have heard with empathy and understanding, they can bridge the gap and encourage the child to open up more.

How we express emotions constructively is a third important aspect of normative communication. All emotions are real, and all human beings experience them. However, they can be seen as conflictual if expressed without consideration for boundary respect or the harm they can cause toward others and ourselves. Children can be taught how to express emotions more constructively, for example, by including an 'I … message', such as 'I feel angry when you say that' rather than 'You make me feel angry.' This type of emotional expression focuses on the speaker's state of mind and their experiences as a way of seeking to express emotions while avoiding them being heard as blaming or accusatory. It is interpreted as less potentially defensive and, therefore, more constructive in conversations and negotiations than conflictual in nature.

A willingness to explore other perspectives can also help deal with intergenerational conflict. Although such conflicts are often rooted in generational differences, they can also provide learning opportunities. By modelling curiosity and a willingness to learn from open-minded questioning, parents can encourage their children to be more accepting of other perspectives. For instance, parents can ask their children if they have experienced racial or other biases in the host society. They can also listen attentively to their views on the hurdles in learning and practising their religious, cultural or language traditions in the host society.

Another strategy is balancing continuity and change, especially adapting one's traditions while maintaining loyalty to them and intergenerational bonds. The balancing of continuity and change goes both ways: children need to see that their parents are flexible and willing to change while making the core cultural identity important. Preserving core cultural values is essential for parents in maintaining cultural integrity and ensuring children grow up with families that have not lost essential values. Core cultural values, such as respect for elders, communal responsibility, and spiritual beliefs, are significant for family life, resiliency, and raising children by ensuring their wholesomeness and development of responsibility.

Parents can emphasise the importance of such core values while allowing flexibility for expression. For example, telling children to respect an elder for listening to them, making them sit and talk with them, and considering their opinions honours the core value of respect for elders while allowing flexibility for children to express their opinions and individualism through other means.

Integrating into the Host Society While Navigating Intergenerational Conflict

Maintaining a healthy connection to their cultural tradition and becoming receptive to the ideas and practices of the host society serve as the twine that holds immigrants' psyches together during stressful times. Parents can support their children by encouraging them to take part in academic or social courses in the host country's language while teaching them the culture's social norms and practices, significantly as circumstances in the host society change over time. For instance, parents might encourage their children to take part in extracurricular activities at school, such as being part of a particular sports team or club, but also explain how to manage the limited hours they have based on cultural responsibility obligations, such as not being able to miss family parties or religious ceremonies.

A third strategy involves developing a bicultural identity, which 'permits one to navigate and participate energetically and proudly in the cultures of the homeland and the host or new home. Parents and other adults should envision two cultural values to develop a bicultural identity, help young people discern their strengths, and 'envision their cultural identity as a source of resilience and empowerment'. This could involve celebrating the national and cultural holidays of their heritage and the host societies, participating in cultural and community events, and asking children to take pride in their cultural heritage while embracing what the host society offers.

Family activities, in particular, mobilise positive forces that can alleviate intergenerational conflict. For instance, family activities draw family members together in shared pursuits to spend time together, converse about important topics, and share lasting memories. Family members often hold family rituals and celebrations, for example, daily dinners, weekly outings, birthday celebrations, religious holidays, college graduations or baby showers. Family rituals and celebrations provide continuity and connection to the family's cultural heritage, which can fulfil a cultural need and help families meet the challenges and demands of daily life.

A family can enlist a child in its rituals and celebrations and confer an honorary family tradition on that child to bridge the gap between generations and leverage family identity and pride. A family night where they cook family recipes, tell stories of the family back in their native country or sit and watch a movie provides an activity that invokes cultural identity and a sense of belonging and opens channels for communicating these values. These activities allow the family to unite during ritual ceremonies, sustaining their sense of family identity, pride, togetherness, and strength.

Secondly, family members can engage in cultural and community events promoting belonging. For example, parents can encourage children to attend a local cultural festival with their families, engage in community service projects to share observations and exchange ideas, or participate in religious ceremonies, often through planning and organising the events. These activities generate a sense of shared purpose and mutual support that foster close connections among family members. Importantly, these shared experiences provide families opportunities to observe how one another works through pressure and difficulties, which could cultivate greater confidence in one another's coping abilities and strengthen family bonds.

Sports, arts, outdoor adventures, or any recreational activities could be a way for parents and their children or parents and their young adults to relax and have fun together, which is essential for building close bonding. I believe family members can strengthen family bonds by doing recreational activities because it could benefit parents and their youngsters to participate in recreational activities in which their kids are interested. For instance, if your children like going to the mountains and hiking, you can organise a hiking tour together, which will help them set trust in you and make your child more cooperative. Telling stories about the distant past and looking for curiosities to collect and identify is another way of spending time with your kids together. They engage in an activity they like, which helps them talk about more personal issues. Playing sports as a family or performing a creative activity such as painting or listening to music are as good as the others due to the fact that they could trigger parents and family members to be more connected. Most of you reading this book might have heard some of these ideas about how parents can build stronger relationships with their families beforehand. Remember, children do not come with a manual when they are born, but as parents and caregivers, we must learn along and develop appropriate parenting practices to foster a joyous being.

Parents may want to use external support and resources, which can be helpful if they cannot navigate intergenerational conflict alone or need external support and resources to help their family arrive at practical solutions and maintain better relationships. Again, parents' ought to explore how to leverage the support of external sources such as community organisations, cultural associations, and paid professional services.

For newly arrived refugees or migrants, community organisations and cultural associations offer a good source of external support and resources for families navigating intergenerational conflict. Often, they might offer programmes, workshops and events for families on the topics of 1) cultural preservation, 2) family dynamics, and 3) conflict resolution. They are an excellent resource for parents who can seek out these organisations to learn about their resources, establish relationships with other families they work with and support, and also sign up for the programmes and activities that may facilitate the process of strengthening their family's cultural identity and better managing intergenerational conflict.

Professional services, such as family therapy, counselling or mediation, offer a neutral space where family members can share their concerns, express their differences, and seek solutions in the presence of an experienced third party. A professional with training in working with intergenerational families can help to identify the issues behind the conflicts, improve communication, and develop an action plan to overcome strained relationships and build harmony and understanding between the generations. Parents can choose to access professional services if they feel that their family's conflicts go beyond their capacity to solve alone or if they need additional support in dealing with the dynamics of acculturation and cultural differences.

For example, parents might draw on their experiences with the rest of society by reading books and articles or taking online courses to further their understanding of intergenerational conflict, cultural differences and family relationships. Through these resources, parents can learn more about the challenges of acculturation for the entire family and specific instances of cultural mismatch, for example, how the parent's cultural emphasis on teacher-student respect can impact opportunities for two-way communication between them and their children. As a result, parents' understanding of these trends will increase, and they may be more equipped to develop parenting strategies to navigate intergenerational conflict and foster harmony and understanding. Parents might read a book on cross-cultural parenting, take an online course on family communication or attend a workshop on positive parenting or conflict resolution.

Empathy, a crucial element in parenting, plays a significant role in handling intergenerational conflict and improving family relationships. It involves seeing things from someone else's point of view, being aware of and respecting their feelings, and responding in a caring and considerate way. As parents, we must play a vital role in promoting mutual respect. We can teach our children the value of understanding and empathy in relationships by modelling empathy, prompting perspective and mutual respect.

Children learn to be empathic by observing interactions between their parents, siblings and caregivers. Parents can model empathy by treating others with kindness and respect, listening to children's needs empathically, and responding to conflicts warmly and kindly. For instance, imagine a young person being upset about a cultural responsibility. Parents can model empathy for an adolescent by listening to the child, acknowledging the hardships entailed in the task requested, and asking questions to understand the child's point of view. They can also share personal experiences navigating similar cultural responsibilities, showing they understand and empathise with the child's feelings. Parents can support their children's cultural values by eliciting a plan for the outcome.

Perspective-taking involves seeing things from another person's point of view and understanding how another person may feel or think in a particular situation; we do not or cannot experience ourselves precisely the skill that is important in navigating conflicts and cultural understanding. Parents can ask their children or adolescents to try to imagine what they would feel or think if they were in another person's position, to understand another person's perspective or to think about how someone else might feel, speaking to them differently, or having a different social or cultural background.

For instance, parents can ask their children: 'How would you feel if your grandparents told you that you must attend the baptism of your cousin to whom we all forgot to send a present and that it is insulting?' Alternatively, 'Imagine your grandmother does not like soccer and says that it is a meaningless sport; what would you think or feel?' Prompts such as this can help children understand why another person may think things are essential or open up spaces for them to explore why their values are important to them and to promote empathy or understanding about the importance of another's point of view when faced with cultural differences. Although home is often presented as a protective zone where children are shielded from the harsh realities of the world or 'normalised' for the prevailing culture, it is crucial to create open and respectful spaces for communicating about culture in our homes.

Mutual respect is a powerful parenting tool. It helps break down barriers between people, allowing for greater understanding. Parents can model and support mutual respect within their family. They can outline respectful behaviour clearly, appreciate and acknowledge each family member's strengths and contributions, and be willing to listen to their concerns. Parents can create an open and respectful environment in their homes by establishing rules of engagement for family discourse and demonstrating respect in their interactions.

Conclusion

This chapter has explored intergenerational conflict's complex and multifaceted nature within South Sudanese and other African diaspora families. These families, navigating life in multicultural societies, face unique challenges that stem from the intersection of deeply rooted cultural traditions and the modern values of their host countries. The generational divide, characterised by differing expectations, worldviews, and communication styles, often places parents and children at odds as they try to balance cultural preservation with the demands of integration.

At the heart of these conflicts lies the tension between tradition and adaptation. Parents often seek to uphold the values and practices of their cultural heritage, seeing them as essential to maintaining family cohesion and identity. In contrast, children growing up in a different cultural context may feel the pull of individualism, autonomy, and self-expression, which can clash with parental expectations. This chapter has highlighted how these differing perspectives can lead to misunderstandings and friction within families, with communication breakdowns and misaligned priorities often intensifying the conflict.

Nevertheless, as we have seen, intergenerational conflict is not an insurmountable barrier but rather an opportunity for family growth and transformation. By embracing open communication, mutual respect, and empathy, families can navigate these tensions in ways that foster understanding and resilience. Parents and children can learn from each other, bridging the cultural and generational gaps that may initially seem daunting.

One of the central insights of this chapter is the importance of adaptability in maintaining cultural identity while embracing the realities of life in a new society. Rather than seeing tradition and modernity as opposing forces, families can create a harmonious balance that honours their heritage while allowing for the flexibility needed to thrive in a multicultural world. This balance is essential not only for the well-being of individual family members but also for the strength and unity of the family as a whole.

Ultimately, the chapter underscores that cultivating family harmony is an ongoing process. It requires patience, open-mindedness, and a willingness to engage with the complexities of cultural change. This journey is particularly significant for South Sudanese and African families in the diaspora, as they seek to raise the next generation in a way that respects their roots while equipping their children to navigate the challenges of their new environment.

Fostering intergenerational dialogue, understanding, and collaboration can help families become stronger and more united from these conflicts. In doing so, they preserve their cultural identity and create a new, bicultural identity that reflects the best of both worlds. This journey is not without its difficulties, but it promises deeper family bonds, greater resilience, and a shared vision of the future that honours tradition and change.

CHAPTER EIGHT

South Sudanese Youth Identity: Views on Parenting and Culture

Introduction
This chapter honours the voices of the South Sudanese-Australian youth who participated in my PhD studies by delving into their perspectives on cultural identity, parenting experiences, and the complexities of being parented in Australia. Through individual and focus group interviews, these young people shared their experiences, shedding light on themes of forced migration, intergenerational conflict, and the tension between parental control and youth autonomy. This chapter presents their stories and reflections, offering a view from the youth's narrative side.

While other chapters focused on the challenges South Sudanese and other African parents face in adapting to life in Australia, this chapter shifts the lens to the youth. It explores how they navigate the cultural expectations of their parents, the pressures of integration, and their struggles to find a balance between their South Sudanese heritage and the demands of their new environment. The chapter also revisits the forced migration experiences of these young people, highlighting how these traumatic events, coupled with the challenges of resettlement, shape their identities and influence their views on parenting and culture.

The youth's voices resonate with a mix of resilience and frustration as they express their concerns about the lack of strong community leadership and acculturation difficulties. Despite these challenges, they show a remarkable determination to succeed, offering advice to their peers on avoiding trouble, respecting their parents, and focusing on their education and future. This chapter serves as a tribute to their strength and adaptability as they carve out their identities in a new land.

The names used for the real stories and quotes that follow from youth participants are pseudonyms.

South Sudanese Youth: Identity, Culture, and Parenting Perspectives

Experiences of Forced Migration

The traumatic experiences resulting from forced migration have had a profound impact on South Sudanese youth, who appear particularly vulnerable compared to adults, who may have developed coping mechanisms or resilience. Kohli and Mather (2003) note that young people are especially vulnerable to the effects of war and natural disasters, and these traumatic experiences often compound the difficulties of adjusting to a new culture upon arrival in a host country. Earnest (2007) underscores that the native culture of refugee children plays a critical role in their psychosocial well-being, often differing significantly from Western perspectives. Adolescents face the challenge of forging a new identity while integrating their culture of origin with their host country (Earnest et al., 2007).

Research indicates that not all adolescent refugees become traumatised by their experiences; some develop resilience, and studies have shown that young refugees are not necessarily more traumatised than their Australian peers when it comes to issues such as child abuse. Many South Sudanese adolescents grew up in war-torn Sudan or in transit countries that were also affected by conflict. They recount witnessing atrocities, such as bombings and violent deaths, which continue to haunt them even as they grow into adulthood. Wol shared that:

"What I saw is different; I was born during the war, and life was difficult in South Sudan because people were always running for safety. Only a few managed to study. The civil war has had a profound impact on our generation, particularly those born during wartime. Some of us have witnessed people being killed and other horrific events. These memories linger with us even though we are now adults."

Koor described the pre- and post-migration challenges, including life in refugee camps, cultural shock, and the difficulties of adjusting to life in a big city:

"After coming here, we encountered different cultures, and the way of life was completely different. Some of us had never lived in a city before coming to Australia. Life in refugee camps was tough, with limited access to food, water, basic needs, and employment. Resettlement was hard to come by. After arriving here, we experienced cultural shock, even in simple activities like going to the

market. It takes time to adapt to the new environment. The system here expects people to adjust quickly, but it's not easy. Many young South Sudanese have witnessed traumatic events, and these memories don't fade quickly."

These experiences, both pre-and post-migration, combined with the demands of adjusting to a new environment, often create parenting challenges within families. As discussed elsewhere in this book, the need to adapt to the host country's culture and laws often requires changes in traditional practices, leading to tensions that can adversely affect the psychosocial well-being of refugees (McMichael et al., 2011; MenjÃvar & Menjívar, 2000). While some adolescents have retained coping strategies from their pre-migration experiences, helping them build resilience, many are still poorly prepared or lack adequate support to navigate these challenges and changes.

Youth Identity Formation

Culture and identity are central to South Sudanese upbringing, forming an essential part of intergenerational connections and cultural transmission (Yenika-Agbaw & Mhando, 2014). Berry et al. (2006) posed critical questions in their study of immigrant youth (Berry, 2006):

> *"How do immigrant youth live within and between two cultures? How well do they manage their intercultural situation? Are there patterns in how adolescents engage with intercultural relations and how well they adapt?"*

The findings sparked further debate and deepened our understanding of how immigrant youth integrate their culture of origin with that of the host country.

In this study, young South Sudanese participants identified themselves as either South Sudanese or South Sudanese-Australian. They generally perceived themselves as integrating their traditional culture with the new Australian culture. All participants were either born in Sudan, South Sudan or in transit countries before arriving in Australia with their families or caregivers. Most were between 18 and 24 years old, and most had been in Australia for over eight years, meaning they arrived between the ages of 9 and 11 or even younger.

These young people were asked to discuss the differences between South Sudanese and Australian traditions and cultures. Many identified key differences, particularly in cultural values such as respect and freedom. Some expressed mixed feelings about the new freedoms they experienced in Australia. Some maintained strong ties to South Sudanese culture through community engagement, while others reported losing touch with their culture and native language. Bakita shared:

"I identify more with South Sudanese culture. I still follow my cultural practices because I don't want to forget them."

As Angeth reflected:

"Honestly, I feel like I'm halfway there. I still follow my cultural values, but I've forgotten my language, which is my main problem. I'm trying to relearn it."

Identity is a cornerstone of South Sudanese culture, shaping an individual's sense of self and connection to their origins. Deng (1995) describes identity as a concept that defines individuals through race, ethnicity, religion, language, culture, and other factors, providing deep psychological and social significance within group dynamics. However, forced migration and the challenges of resettlement in a new environment have disrupted these identities as young South Sudanese strive to balance their new and traditional cultures (Attias-Donfut, 2012; Marlowe et al., 2014).

Intergenerational Conflict: Navigating Between Cultures

As discussed in other Chapters, acculturative stress within families often intensifies when young migrants attend school and experience more rapid cultural changes than their parents. This rapid acculturation, driven by the demands of school and social interactions, often creates conflicts between the original culture upheld at home and the new social environment encountered in schools and other settings (Deng & Pienaar, 2011; Marlowe et al., 2014). This process can lead to a clash of values, causing tensions and struggles between young people and their parents.

Research has shown that many refugee families are not adequately supported or prepared to deal with these challenges (Dunlavy, 2010; Renzaho et al., 2011). An Australian study by Sanders (2002) revealed that changes in lifestyle and cultural environment could negatively influence the lives and behaviours of young refugees. Successful resettlement requires more than finding housing; it involves adapting to unfamiliar systems and customs and engaging in the new country's social, economic, and cultural life.

In this context, South Sudanese youth were asked to share how they navigate between differing cultures, the stresses that arise from this, and their coping strategies. While some young people spoke of adhering to their parents' guidance, others acknowledged the difficulties of growing up between cultures with often conflicting values, leading to tensions and struggles within their families.

South Sudanese Youth: Insights on Identity and Parenting

Some of the young people interviewed believe they must uphold their home traditions and pass them on to their children and subsequent generations. Those who came to Australia as adolescents spoke of not having seen a 'strong culture' in Australia compared to what they had experienced earlier. Most were referring to being together and supporting one another, even just greeting neighbours in the morning. Wol explained the differences he observed in Australia compared to South Sudan.

> *"Our African culture is always about togetherness and support for one another. For instance, when you wake up, the first thing you do in the morning is to check how your relatives, friends or neighbours are doing or even visit them. People eat together and stay together in bad and good times. When practising these parts of our culture here, some people who started to know about such cultural values always give us some positive feedback. For instance, someone told me that if we supported one another like this in Australia, then we would avoid all of these problems due to isolation, which is causing a lot of problems within the wider Australian community."*

The "strong culture" concept in these comments highlights the cultural shock experienced by many young South Sudanese. The absence of key elements of their original culture, such as 'togetherness and support for one another,' in their new environment often leads to feelings of disconnection. These observations also underscore the importance of cultural exchange and the potential benefits of sharing and discussing diverse cultural values within the broader Australian community.

Smith highlighted the challenges that South Sudanese youth face as they transition from adolescence into adulthood in an Australian context:

> *"Turning 18 years is a tough age for many young Sudanese. For example, we have different cultures between South Sudanese and Australians. When they turn 18, most Sudanese boys try to move out of home; they can even fight with their mums, particularly when they ask them to do certain things. According to Sudanese culture, even when you reach 18 or 24 years old, you still live with your parents until you get married and do the right things. But here, the culture has changed, affecting young Sudanese and the community."*

As South Sudanese youth navigate their new environment and culture, their parents simultaneously expect them to adhere to traditional customs and values. Research has consistently shown that acculturation is a significant source of stress for new settlers as they grapple with adjusting to their new country (Berry, 1997). This is particularly challenging for children who, through their education and social interactions, are quickly adapting to Australian culture, while at home, their parents expect them to maintain the values and practices of their original culture (Richman, 1998; Searle et al., 2012). This situation often becomes contentious as parents, holding onto their ancestral cultures, resist any departure from their traditional identity (S. A. Deng & J. M. Marlowe, 2013; Fisher, 2007). The resulting intergenerational conflict mirrors many immigrant adolescents' struggles to balance their original and new cultures.

Power and Control: Youth Perspectives on Respect and Parenting in Australia

Parental Control vs. Youth Independence

South Sudanese youth also shared their perspectives on respect, parenting, and being parented in Australia. As discussed in previous chapters, from the parents' viewpoint, the increased autonomy that young people experience in their new environment often leads to conflicts. These conflicts typically arise around autonomy, freedom, household chores, selecting friends, homework, and sibling care. The tension from these disagreements can create fractures within the family unit, potentially reducing the support adolescents receive from their parents, which may lead to financial difficulties and antisocial behaviour.

The youth provided examples of how parental control often clashes with their newfound freedoms and independence, highlighting the differences in cultural understanding between the South Sudanese and Australian approaches to parenting. For instance, in African culture, young people are not permitted to talk back to their parents; they are expected to listen respectfully and only speak when their parents invite them.

> *"The rules are also different here compared to South Sudan. Here, young people are allowed by law to do whatever they like, while in South Sudan, young people are not… Here, children talk back to their parents and have to listen to them (Bakita)."*

Some youth observed the stark contrast between how they are parented in Australia and South Sudan, where respect for parents is paramount, and children are not allowed to talk back. This was contrasted with their observations of some young Australians, who they felt showed less respect towards their parents.

> *"If I come home late, my parent will ask me, 'Where have you been?' and I have to tell them exactly where I was. But the way I see the other Australians, if their parents ask them, they can disrespect them. South Sudanese young people have to give reasonable answers (Yel)."*

On the topic of parental control, some youth noted that their parents become overly protective and controlling, mainly due to fears of adverse external influences and the potential for legal trouble.

> *"Parents fear that police might catch the young people or maybe that they will go and join a gang (Ker)."*

As discussed earlier, the tension between parental control and youth autonomy often leads to struggles within the families of new settlers. These intergenerational tensions stem from competing understandings of young people's rights and responsibilities and the appropriate levels of autonomy and freedom (Deng, 2016a). However, some younger participants also recognised the importance of parental guidance, suggesting that too much freedom can distract youth from trying to build a better future.

> *"South Sudanese are stricter in their parenting styles. Children have to follow what they say, if not, you get disciplined. But in Australia, there are some kinds of freedom for the kids… Some laws can take parents to court and accuse them of child abuse. It is actually a problem because you are growing up, and you don't know what is right and wrong… Parents are already grown and*

have been through things, so they know what is bad and good for you. Therefore, having too much freedom is bad for some young people (Yel)."

While some youth acknowledge the value of parental control, they also recognise that strictness can create divisions and challenges within the family. Many South Sudanese parents believe being strict is necessary for their children's upbringing. However, this approach often fails to control their children, who are increasingly aware of their rights and freedoms in their new environment. This awareness has posed a significant challenge to traditional parental authority.

Corporal Discipline

The South Sudanese youth who participated in the study grew up in refugee camps and observed a significant difference in disciplinary practices between Australian and South Sudanese parents. Unlike in South Sudan, where corporal punishment is commonly used to correct behaviour, Australian parents are generally seen as less inclined to use physical discipline. Physical disciplining, defined by Straus (1991) as physical attacks on children, includes actions such as spanking, slapping, grabbing, and shoving. While these practices may create immediate conformity, they also increase the likelihood of deviant behaviour, such as delinquency in adolescents (Lansford et al., 2005; Mansouri et al., 2015; Straus, 1991). Physical force is often linked to the need for control and demands for respect. The following comments illustrate the perceived 'good and bad' sides of physical discipline.

> *"The biggest difference is, they (Australian parents) don't beat their kids, but in South Sudan, if you do something wrong, you get beaten until you learn... There are great differences between Australian*

and South Sudanese cultures because the rules here (Australia) are different. Although physical discipline is bad, it teaches you not to do the same thing next time. the way I see it here, they (parents) tell you not to do it, and you still do it because you're not being disciplined... In our culture, they discipline you in a way you will understand so that next time you know the consequences and say, 'I will not do that again (Yoa)."

Angelina recounted the differences between mainstream Australian and South Sudanese parents, noting that South Sudanese parents are more culturally inclined to yell or use physical force when disciplining their children:

"Some Australian parents leave their children without doing much about it (their behaviour), while South Sudanese parents might yell or beat their children up as well as do everything to make sure that their children are listening to them."

The South Sudanese youth were asked to share what happens when they need to follow their parents' instructions and expectations. Most believe that they are treated according to their parents' traditions, which differ significantly from the treatment of their Australian peers, who are often perceived as freer and less controlled.

"Australian young people are much freer than us (young South Sudanese) as our parents expect us to only do things that please them (Angeth)."

As highlighted earlier, many South Sudanese parents were raised in a society where physical force was commonly used to correct children's

Parental Expectations for Youth

This study reveals that South Sudanese parents persist in expecting their children to retain key aspects of their original culture despite the challenges posed by their new environment. These expectations and acculturation stresses contribute to intergenerational gaps and conflicts within families. Milner and Khawaja (2010) suggest that such conflicts within refugee families can increase interpersonal distance among family members. While many South Sudanese parents are deeply concerned about their children's rapid assimilation into Australian culture, the youth often perceive their parents' expectations as overly controlling and an infringement on their rights and independence. This division continues to widen the gap between generations.

> *"My parents expected me to hold onto our traditional culture and language as well as integrate into the Australian culture (Angeth)."*

As discussed in other chapters, research has shown that integrating aspects of the original and new cultures can effectively overcome acculturation challenges, particularly for youth growing up in a culturally conflicted environment. Pouch (2006) observed that these intergenerational gaps have divided South Sudanese families into distinct groups: the older generation, adolescents (12-25 years old), and children born either in transit countries or Australia. In South Sudanese culture, it is traditionally the role of adults to educate younger generations about cultural values, norms, and language (Pouch, 2006). However, the older generation feels that younger people are uninterested in learning about their cultural heritage. At the same time, the youth believe that their community and elders are not providing adequate support to help them cope with the changes imposed by acculturation.

> *"My parents expected me to respect them and other people who are older than me and everybody else (Yel)."*

The study participants emphasised that their parents' expectations of preserving traditional cultural values, such as respect for elders, require active engagement from parents and community elders to bridge the intergenerational gaps. This engagement is necessary to help youth navigate the challenges of integrating into their new environment while maintaining their cultural identity.

> *"My parents expected me not to smoke or drink. It's all about making sure that I grow up in a good way and become a good person (Andrew)."*

However, these expectations often create a dilemma for youth who must choose between adhering to their parents' demands and conforming to peer pressures, such as smoking and drinking. Making the right choices can be challenging in such circumstances.

As discussed in other chapters, South Sudanese young men and women are encouraged to learn and socialise with their older siblings and relatives. Chol, whom I interviewed at his uncle's house, highlighted the importance of spending time with uncles, aunts, and other role models in the community to learn about manhood and womanhood while preserving their culture.

> *"My parents expected me to know my people and how they live and get through things; this is what they want me to hold onto… That is why I came to my uncle's house to learn more about my culture."*

Yoa narrated that his parent's expectation to learn from relatives extends beyond Australia, with encouragement to visit South Sudan as part of cultural preservation.

> *"They (parents) always tell us to follow our South Sudanese cultures, you know, they always tell us to go back home and see how things are done at home, and they always tell us, 'In the future, your life will be based in South Sudan, always keep South Sudanese cultural values, do not lose faith in what our culture is and do not fall off the track."*

As highlighted in previous chapters, parents expect their children to preserve their cultural values and native languages. Some youth agree with their parents on upholding these values as part of their identity. Berry et al. (2006) identified an integration profile in their study of young immigrants. They argued that adolescents who integrate both ethnic and host cultures tend to perform better than those who do not. The study found that immigrant youth who strongly identified with both ethnic and host identities were better able to integrate into their new environment compared to those who either fully assimilated into the new culture or isolated themselves by holding onto their original culture without integrating (Berry, 1997; Berry et al., 2006). Youth who integrated both cultures reported high levels of national and average ethnic language competence, suggesting that using both languages fosters a balance that strengthens adaptation and integration into the new environment.

Youth Views on Resettlement Challenges

Respecting Parental Guidance

As discussed earlier, youth resettlement challenges primarily involve the interpersonal and social conflicts young people face as they transition into a world of greater autonomy. These challenges can be exacerbated by family issues such as parental separation, which often leaves young people in the care of a single parent. Parental separation can significantly impact children's development, as families are crucial to providing stability, support, a sense of belonging, and guidance in navigating their surroundings and future.

The South Sudanese youth participants, despite the challenges, demonstrated remarkable resilience. They were asked to reflect on these issues and advise their peers struggling with resettlement challenges. They acknowledged the difficulties of adjusting to a new environment while meeting their parents' expectations to understand and uphold their traditions. The following comments highlight the conflicting intergenerational perspectives on cultural integration:

> *"My parents taught us to be more careful, not to take everything (we see around us for granted). Parents need to be aware that we are in a different country, and we cannot follow (or hold onto) everything about our traditional culture here (Angeth)."*

These comments reflect the ongoing tension between parents' insistence on preserving traditional practices and the younger generation's emphasis on balancing old and new cultures. As highlighted in other chapters, parents must receive the necessary support in setting appropriate parenting goals that bridge the gap between traditional and contemporary practices. The youth also advised their peers to listen to and respect their parents, acknowledging that parents often bear the blame for their children's behaviour.

> *"We should listen to our parents because if you don't listen to them when they want to talk to us, you cannot succeed. When you do bad things, they return to your parents, and they get blamed for what their children do out there, which affects them... I think that, as a grown-up young man, I should listen to my parents, and if I am doing something wrong, my parents can tell me to stop, and I must stop if I want to be a good person in the future. Also, listen to friends who talk about education and doing the right things, not those who are not following their education (Andrew)."*

These sentiments echo parents' perspectives, who expect their children to avoid misbehaviour, as it tarnishes their reputation within the community. Parental overprotectiveness, often expressed in rigid or orthodox ways, is common in South Sudanese families. This rigidity is compounded by parents' expectations that their children's educational achievements will redeem the family's suffering, a concept widely held among South Sudanese families.

Avoiding Trouble and Street Life

As highlighted by both parents and supported by various studies, young immigrants quickly become familiar with the dominant culture. They may adopt values that conflict with the traditional values upheld by their parents. This can lead to conflicts as youth struggle to adjust to their new environment while being expected by their parents to preserve their culture of origin. Many young people experience intense identity confusion as they navigate these conflicting cultural expectations.

The youth participants advised their peers to "stay off the streets" and focus on their education, emphasising the importance of seeking help.

"Stay off the streets and stay in school (Jok)."

Koor, who had grown up in refugee camps, offered this perspective:

"My advice is that some came a bit grown up while some have grown up here… Most of us who grew up in refugee camps have seen a lot of difficulties in life. I always talk to many young people about using their opportunities in Australia and doing something good for themselves and their community. For example, finishing one's education can lead one to do anything positive in his or her life. A lot of youth here are not making use of these opportunities and have abandoned educational pursuits. I think God gave us these opportunities because here, those who don't want to study or who are unable to study for whatever reason go to work and make money to help themselves and their families. Even older people are still pursuing their studies in this country."

These comments resonate with a survey conducted by Grossman and Sharples (2010) on youth from Sudan and the Pacific Islands concerning safety and policing. The survey highlighted some of the issues youth face in Brimbank, Victoria, and offered practical advice on staying safe. Young respondents recommended going in groups when in public, avoiding violent behaviour, steering clear of bad company, and staying away from places where violence is likely to occur (Grossman & Sharples, 2010).

> *"Do not join bad young people on the streets who are drinking alcohol and using drugs. Seek your own direction rather than following others or those on the streets. This is because there are a lot of bad influences on the streets (Ker)."*

The Grossman and Sharples (2010) survey emphasised the importance of education, self-control, respecting others, carefully choosing friends, and the need for adult supervision and protective measures such as counselling and controls over drugs and alcohol. In line with the parents' comments, the youth also believe that many South Sudanese end up in jail due to antisocial behaviour, which is often exacerbated by intergenerational conflict or identity confusion amid conflicting cultures. Andrew highlighted how easy it is for young people to get into trouble with the law, which can negatively affect their education, employment, and overall opportunities.

> *"You get into trouble, and you will never get a better education, job, or a better life. But if I were in South Sudan, I would still have a better life. The laws here are different, and when you get into trouble with the police, your life is finished, and you may not get a better job; you get rejected. But in South Sudan, people know your family background and may spare you. Yes, most of the time, especially many Sudanese boys and girls are in jail now, and they are not gonna have a better life."*

As highlighted in other chapters and other studies, racism towards South Sudanese individuals (both young and old) has a significant negative impact on them. Both parents and youth often feel unsafe due to their racial visibility and refugee status. This and other studies have also highlighted young people's poor relationships with the police and their lack of trust in the responsiveness and understanding of law enforcement, even when they feel their safety is at risk (Grossman & Sharples, 2010; Losoncz, 2011). Some people claim that youth get into trouble because they lack strong community leadership to voice their concerns and challenges and offer appropriate support.

"If there was strong community leadership, which can present the issues affecting the community to the concerned agencies, they would have the support they needed (Koor)."

However, South Sudanese youth do not attribute all their difficulties to racism, police relations, or the lack of strong community leadership. They recognise that they, too, can contribute to improving their situation, as they expressed earlier in their advice to their peers.

At least Chol also pointed to the distracting nature of technology as a factor contributing to youth issues.

"Growing up here, I didn't have all these distractions like TV and all that. It would have been different… Mum always tells me, 'Don't download this stuff.' … They distract kids; don't be distracted by TV, games, and other stuff."

These comments echo the concerns of many South Sudanese parents about the impact of technology, which they see as a significant distraction from their children's focus on activities that benefit their future. According to Richtel (2010), students often face distractions and timewasters as they become engrossed in using computers and cell phones. Technology's constant streams of stimuli pose a profound challenge to focus and learning.

As discussed extensively in this book, technology distracts young people's (and adults') focus and learning and disconnects them from meaningful interactions with their parents and peers. Research indicates that constant task-switching, a behaviour encouraged by technology, can lead to less sustained attention, particularly in developing brains, which are more susceptible to these distractions (Richtel, 2010).

Supporting Youth for Integration and Future Success

Enhancing Youth Engagement and Education

Many young immigrants struggle to balance their parents' expectations with the demands of their new environment, which can often lead to intra-family conflicts. As discussed in other chapters, many South Sudanese parents come from authoritarian parenting backgrounds where children are expected to obey without question. This parenting style often increases tension between parents and their children, especially as young immigrants strive to assert their understanding of rights and freedoms in their new environment. Thus, the family interprets power, control, and expectations differently. Research has indicated that how newly arrived migrant families manage intergenerational conflict depends on their cultural affiliations and interpretations, mainly how they apply family management models. This perspective aligns with the sentiments of South Sudanese youth, who desire more discussion and proper engagement within their community.

When asked about the most significant support types, South Sudanese youth emphasised the need for assistance to overcome acculturation challenges and build a meaningful future. They expressed a desire to be given options, particularly in deciding what they want to study.

"Support to have a bright future… being given more options in deciding our own education (Chol)."

Some youths suggested the establishment of community homework centres as a specific type of support that would benefit them, particularly those who struggle with their studies.

> *"Help, for example, by setting up a community homework centre for young Sudanese, so that like once a fortnight, struggling students who have trouble doing their assignments can get some help. For example, I might know math; some may not. If the student goes there, they might get help from someone who knows about a particular subject; English is our second language. We need something like that because some young Sudanese do not get help at home when their teachers give them homework, but if there are people out there to help them, then most can go there to seek help (Andrew)."*

Many South Sudanese youth have faced significant educational challenges, as they were often deprived of formal education in their home country or refugee camps. English was not the language of instruction for many, and even when it was, they often lacked access to well-resourced classes with trained teachers. After arriving in Australia, most were placed in classes according to their age but with little or no academic support to bridge the gap in their education.

This created a tension between being in an age-appropriate class and a class that matched their academic level. Consequently, many young South Sudanese have lower English and general education proficiency than their Australian peers, who may have started their education earlier. Moreover, since many of their parents have limited educational backgrounds, they cannot help their children with homework or provide other academic support.

Research has shown that refugee and international students in Australia (and likely elsewhere) face numerous academic, cultural, social, and linguistic challenges (Harris & Marlowe, 2011). Additionally, many schools in Australia are inadequately equipped to provide sufficient English support for students whose first language is not English. South Sudanese youth reiterated the importance of homework centres for educational support, encouragement, and motivation through opportunities to connect with their peers. As this and previous studies have indicated, some young people require ongoing support to stay engaged with their education and focus on their future.

"Parents and community members need to engage with young people by talking to them and helping them in whatever way they can to improve their lives. Advise them to go to school, help them with their studies, and do good stuff (Moses)."

All the youth participants repeatedly emphasised the significance of community centres as a crucial step in providing support. The following comment highlights several issues faced by South Sudanese youth, including enforced idleness or unemployment, lack of engagement in meaningful activities, and the absence of male role models in the family, a challenge particularly noted for single mothers.

"As a new community, we need help. Our community is not very organised like other ethnic communities advocating for themselves. Some ethnic communities are doing very well and have their own community centres, which help their youth since they run programs or activities that engage youth constructively. Many youths are causing problems or getting into trouble because they are doing nothing... When you feel bored, you may end up doing stupid things that you didn't intend to do in the first place. If youths' free time is filled with some activities, it will prevent them from committing

crimes or dropping out of school. The Australian government needs to support the community, particularly young people, so they do not get into trouble (Koor)."

These concerns and solutions echo findings from previous studies, which indicate that when young people are adequately engaged and supported, it helps them succeed educationally. Scales et al. (2006) stated that learning support has great potential in the lives of marginalised youth who do not engage with the community and are often described as vulnerable, disadvantaged, or at-risk. The research highlighted the importance of school and community collaboration, family engagement, literacy development, and support services. The South Sudanese youth in this study reported a lack of collaboration and engagement between their schools and community, which has left some youth without proper support.

Youth Perspectives on Future Parenting

In the final part of the youth interviews, young South Sudanese were asked to reflect on what kind of parents they intended to be. Most expressed a desire to teach their children their native language, preserve cultural values, and give their children more freedom than their own parents had given them, as Angeth stated:

"I want my children to have a bright future, learn my language, be freer, and have a mixture of South Sudanese and Australian cultures."

This question explored how South Sudanese youth's challenges in their new environment might influence their future parenting styles. While they echoed their parents' hopes for a prosperous future for their children, they also expressed a desire to allow their children more autonomy, particularly in choosing their friends, while ensuring they remain focused on their education and future. Although some young people found it difficult to imagine themselves as parents, others emphasised the importance of being good, loving, and caring parents.

"Good care for my children; show them love, spoil them but not too much (Angeth)."

Others envisioned their parenting roles as providing their children with better education, teaching them societal values such as nonviolence, and serving as good role models.

"Well, being a parent is to provide your children with good examples. This is because children copy what their parents do. A strong family is a result of strong parents (Koor)."

While many young people could envision the kind of parents they would like to be, they also revisited the themes of intergenerational conflict and the lack of support and engagement from their ethnic community or service providers. They reiterated the need for community centres where those struggling academically could receive support.

Ultimately, this and previous studies have shown that acculturation is one of the leading sources of stress for immigrant families, particularly for young people, as they navigate the challenges of adjusting to a new environment (Cunningham & Cunningham, 1997; Marlowe et al., 2014; Milner & Khawaja, 2010). As discussed, young settlers often learn their new language and culture at school faster than their parents, leading to tensions at home when parents continue to hold onto their cultures of origin (Richman, 1998). These tensions can escalate as parents insist their children preserve traditional values, creating intergenerational conflict as the children struggle to balance their original culture with the new one (Schweitzer et al., 2006).

Like other immigrant refugees, South Sudanese families spend their first months in Australia learning about the new system and language. However, most parents lag behind in adapting to the dominant culture, while their children begin to question or oppose some of the cultural values their parents hold dear. These cultural shifts and family dynamics negatively impact parenting, leaving many parents struggling to raise their children in a new environment, often with little or no social support.

Conclusion

This chapter has explored the multifaceted experiences of South Sudanese-Australian youth, focusing on their struggles with identity, cultural integration, and the intergenerational conflicts that arise from differing cultural expectations. Through their stories, we have gained insight into their unique challenges as they navigate the complexities of growing up between two cultures.

The youth's reflections highlight the tension between their desire for autonomy and their parent's expectations of them to preserve traditional South Sudanese values. This tension often leads to family conflicts, exacerbated by the challenges of adapting to a new cultural and social environment. However, these young people also demonstrate resilience and a strong sense of responsibility as they strive to balance their cultural heritage with the demands of their new lives in Australia.

The chapter has also emphasised the importance of support systems within the South Sudanese community and broader Australian society in helping these young people navigate their identities and challenges.

The youth's calls for better engagement, educational support, and community leadership underscore the need for targeted interventions that address the specific needs of this population.

Finally, the experiences and perspectives these South Sudanese-Australian youth share remind us of the ongoing journey of integration and identity formation that immigrant communities face. Their voices, captured in this chapter, offer valuable lessons on the importance of understanding, support, and dialogue in fostering successful resettlement and cultural integration. As they adapt and grow, their experiences will shape their futures and the broader narrative of South Sudanese identity in Australia.

Chapter Nine

Promoting Positive Parenting Approaches and Resilience

Introduction

Promoting positive parenting approaches and fostering resilience is crucial for the well-being of South Sudanese and African families in the diaspora. These families navigate a complex journey, preserving their cultural identity while adapting to new and often challenging social environments. Parenting in this context requires a delicate balance of tradition and adaptation, where cultural values are intertwined with contemporary psychological insights. This chapter delves into how migrant families can thrive by maintaining cultural heritage while simultaneously incorporating modern strategies to foster resilience in their children.

At its core, positive parenting emphasises warmth, structure, and open communication, fostering emotional security in children. Coupled with resilience, which serves as a coping mechanism and a source of inner strength, these approaches equip families to face life's challenges confidently and adaptable. Traditional values such as collectivism, respect for elders, and spirituality form the bedrock of resilience for African families. Integrating these values into modern parenting practices allows families to raise children who uphold their cultural identity and develop the emotional and psychological skills necessary to thrive in a rapidly changing world.

Resilience in parenting goes beyond surviving hardships; it empowers children to navigate adversity with a strong sense of identity, purpose, and adaptability. Through the lens of positive parenting, this chapter explores how families can create environments that nurture resilience, foster emotional intelligence, and promote the well-being of future generations. Combining traditional wisdom with contemporary psychological research, parents are provided with a blueprint for raising confident, capable children who can successfully negotiate the complexities of multicultural living.

Resilience as a Foundation for General Wellbeing

Resilience is sometimes described as the capacity to recover from adversity, deal with adversity and maintain a positive outlook, or even optimism, in the face of adversity. However, resilience is also a process or a journey; it is more of a journey than a destination. It is also emergent: how children develop a resilient disposition or become resilient through life, and their level of resilience is shaped by a dynamic interplay of internal and external factors that include their temperament, family dynamics (including intergenerational dynamics), cultural values, and the social support systems they interact within. Importantly, as noted, for the South Sudanese and African families, resilience is definitely not an individual inventory but rather a quality culturally embedded in communal traditions, practices and, above all, a history of surviving great adversities.

Maintaining Culture to Enhance Resilience

Culture, a cornerstone of resilience, provides meaning and prompts adaptive behaviours that help individuals cope with life events. Many strands of African cultural values and practices foster resilience, partly by bringing individuals within the group's purview and promoting participation in communal activities, which in turn grant an infusion of meaning to life. Within various African cultures, resilience is associated with communalism, spirituality and respect for tradition. The community knows the households suffering from eviction, crop failure or death, and communal gatherings provide some cushion during adversity.

Collectivism as a Pillar of Resilience

Collectivism is the continuous repetition of and the focus on: we live, die, and are resurrected together. This is why collective responsibility and mutual support are at the heart of African resilience. It is not a mere principle espoused in fleeting theories or political manifestos here and there, but a value lived in the present. Moreover, the value is so concrete and binding that it permeates all the spheres of social life. Take one of the most evocative African proverbs: 'It takes a village to raise a child.'

This indigenous proverb underpins communalism as a value lived in us, simultaneously a neighbour, a brother and a sister, a beloved, and a saviour to another. It means that in times of difficulty, the community can and will become the extended family that will come to your help, support you and carry you physically, psychologically and sometimes even spiritually. At this point, individuals and families are not left alone to face difficulties. They benefit from communal solidarity, which is central to the community's life. This system of collective support is the glue that holds resilience together.

For example, when a family in South Sudanese communities faces a crisis, such as an illness, the death of a family member or economic hardship, extended family members, neighbours, friends and community leaders/members come together to provide support through various forms such as food, money or emotional support. This act of communal solidarity maintains the view that no family is alone in facing hardship but experiences it together, sharing the burden of adversity as a unit. This heightens the resilience of individuals by providing them with an intricate support network they can rely on in times of need.

Spirituality as a Basic Pillar of Strengths

Spirituality, the final pillar of African resilience, plays a significant role in the lives of many South Sudanese and African families. It is more than a set of religious beliefs and practices; it is a worldview that permeates all aspects of life. For instance, in the morning, families may gather for prayers or to give thanks for the day. In times of crisis, they may turn to religious rituals or seek solace in their animist worldviews. These practices provide a source of meaning, consolation, and direction, particularly in times of crisis. They offer a script for understanding adversity and finding hope through religious rituals, animist worldviews, or connection with the natural world.

In several African cultures, spirituality remains enmeshed with social and community life. Prayer, rituals, and ceremonies are primarily sustained in the community context and reinforce communal bonds and collective responsibility. For example, in crisis situations, community prayers or rituals may be normally undertaken to solicit the divine agency in bringing a solution. These interludes or spiritual practices of lessening anxiety and distress both sustain and enliven the bonds of community and are consolatory.

Moreover, the very notion of spirituality offers hope and optimism, which are essential aspects of resilience. The belief that a greater power is watching over you, that there will be a heaven, and that in life we are all interconnected, as it is in nature, can help you have a wider perspective on your hardships and see your hard times as part of a greater, more meaningful purpose. Thus, the spiritual outlook can be a great source of strength to help you continue and even thrive against adversity.

Admiration for Custom and the Wisdom of Elders

Respect for tradition, customs, and elders is another bulwark of resilience in many African cultures. Elders are widely seen as the repository of cultural wisdom and experience intended to guide and nurture the young. In many African cultures, wise elders are widely revered and deferred to, their minds considered repositories of long-learned wisdom. Their role in inculcating values, norms, and coping strategies that have stood the test of time is particularly valued. Elders often convey the wisdom of their longevity through stories, proverbs, songs, fables, and moral advocacy, providing a morally instructive platform to sort out many of life's difficulties and courtship challenges. Collectively, these lessons contribute to shaping the attitudes and behavioural norms that go to the heart of resilience.

Elders also play a key role in helping to perpetuate a sense of culture so that younger generations are not disconnected from their roots and know where they come from. By preserving and transmitting cultural traditions, rituals and practices, the link between past and future generations remains strong and healthy for cultural survival. A growing body of evidence demonstrates the importance of cultural connection as part of a wellness strategy for all people.

A sense of belonging linked to identity is essential to resilience.

When individuals know where they come from, where they belong, and who they are culturally speaking, they can better weather life's storms, knowing they can leverage the strength of their heritage and the legacy of ancestors who have come before.

Contemporary Psychological Acumens on Resilience
Meanwhile, additional lessons about resilience come from cultural practices and psychological research in recent decades on how to help children and families build resilience. Psychological theories view resilience not as some innate trait but as a set of skills and mindsets that can be cultivated and strengthened over time. Forms of resilience include regulating one's emotions, overcoming obstacles and solving problems, maintaining a positive outlook, and having a robust social support network.

Role of Positive Relationships
Positive relationships, particularly within the family, are powerful tools for building resilience, especially in preparing young people for the transition to adulthood. Children with strong relationships with their parents, siblings, and other primary caregivers develop the social and emotional skills necessary to face and cope with challenges. These relationships provide a secure base for children to explore, take risks, and learn from their mistakes, fostering resilience and a sense of security.

A child who knows she can turn to her parents for help after a tee-ball game will be more inclined to risk stepping up to bat. From the deep sense of security that she provides, she will be able to take on tasks, try activities, stretch and risk failure, and know that she can fall into their arms if need be. More importantly, she will also feel confident that she is prepared to face the challenge without the expectation that she will feel comfortable going it alone. Good relationships between children and parents also serve as a platform for communication. They also give parents information on a child's very private world, opening the way to helping them process that information, seek help when needed, and ultimately develop their own strategies for coping.

The Role of Self-Regulation Skills in Fostering Resilience

Learning and practising self-regulation skills such as managing emotions, setting goals and persisting despite obstacles fosters perceptions of control and agency. Learning to regulate emotions allows children to tolerate and manage their stress, frustration and disappointment –given the inescapable aspects of life.

Nonetheless, parents can do a lot to encourage these skills through 'scaffolding ', a term used in parenting to describe the process of providing support and guidance to children as they learn new skills. For instance, when a child gets upset because he/she cannot find a toy, a parent could help him/her stop crying by explaining deep breathing and doing it together. Then, the parent could ask the child to articulate what was upsetting, help her/him work through possible solutions until an acceptable one is found, and support her/him in initiating the plan. Through interaction like this, with adults supporting and encouraging the process, even relatively young children can practise their conflict-resolving abilities over time. This could translate into children feeling more comfortable expressing their emotions appropriately and standing up for their needs, promoting resilience.

Growing a Mindset to Overcoming Challenges

Having a belief, known as a growth mindset, that abilities and intelligence are not fixed but can be developed through effort and learning also makes a difference in resilience. Children with a growth mindset tend to see challenges as learning opportunities rather than threats to one's abilities or inherent failure. They persist in the face of failure and keep their goals in sight.

Parents can foster growth mindsets in their kids by praising effort rather than innate capability, promoting curiosity and exploration, and re-framing minor setbacks as learning opportunities. For instance, when a child struggles with a difficult task, a parent can say, 'Great job; you are putting in much effort. Let us keep trying.' By promoting resilience, you (the parent) help the child perceive a challenging experience as an opportunity for learning rather than a setback to be avoided.

Parenting Strategies That Foster Resilience

Knowing that they need to develop resilience in their children, forward-thinking parents can take a proactive and intentional approach to the art of parenting, combining the best of traditional cultural practices with modern psychological insight to help their family members thrive and adapt to life's challenges. Below are six specific strategies to do that. Often, clarify your values and strategies since we cannot prescribe a one-size-fits-all approach to parenting.

It helps us clarify the specific values we want to instil in our children so that we can align our parenting practices with clearly defined goals. What is your non-negotiable bottom line in terms of your child's character? First, focus on one specific virtue among identified core social and ethical competencies. Make it relevant to you. Furthermore, clarify your bottom line: the absolute minimum level of development of that virtue that would feel acceptable to you. Avoid getting caught up in unrealistic hopes and fantasies at this stage.

1. Establishing a Supportive and Nurturing Home Environment

A robust home environment where the child can grow up is vital to developing and being resilient when things do not go their way. Unlike a cold or worrisome home, a warm and encouraging home provides more security and stability, allowing for a strong base for the child. Ways a parent can foster a supportive home for their children not only to help develop them but to have a good life could include reducing conflict/yelling, building relationships of trust, having meaningful conversations and family dinners, and discipline being shown in a new manner such as through active listening and logical consequences, giving reassurance and attention, and always being loving.

Developing family bonds

There is no more significant source of resilience than strong ones. These family bonds define who children are by making them feel safe, valued, and loved. These, in turn, let kids feel as if they belong, if only to their family. They are so crucial to their psychological health that parents can do nothing better to foster resilience than to build family bonds with their children. There are plenty of ways to do this; some are obvious. Spending time with one's family is one obvious means of strengthening the bonds between them, and shared activities and rituals such as watching movies, playing sports, or celebrating birthdays together are others.

Such rituals do not have to be overtly family-focused. When kids know they can expect dinner with their family most nights of the week, they know their parents value them and want to be with them. In other cultures, religious holidays and traditional ceremonies play a vital role in strengthening family bonds and reinforcing cultural identity.

Communication must be open: Family communication must be open, honest and non-judgmental so that family members can share their thoughts, feelings and concerns. Parents can facilitate open communication by being available to listen to children and providing them with a non-judgmental and secure space to air their feelings and thoughts. Open communication is one characterised by parents being open about their feelings as well as those of their children and practising transparency. When parents create a safe space for children, they should be non-judgmental, attend to what their children have to say and voice their feelings and difficulties while reassuring them when and where needed. Open communication can also involve talking about family struggles, such as financial worries or health issues faced in a family, yet in a reassuring manner.

Routines and consistency
Routines and consistency can create a sense of predictability and stability. Children benefit from routines that help them to know what they should expect when given the same opportunities. For example, routine mealtimes, bedtimes, homework times, and routines for holidays and other essential family celebrations can help alleviate anxieties. Predictability helps to legitimise and naturalise those experiences we might find difficult, such as illness or death. It is one way to help children feel able to deal with ongoing stressors and uncertainty. There can be great comfort in consistency itself. Something as simple as a regular bedtime story, a bedtime prayer or a brief reflection can help lull a child into sleep.

2. Encouraging Problem-Solving and Critical Thinking
Resilience is finding constructive ways to deal with problems, thinking clearly under pressure and making good decisions. These are the skills

we need to survive in the real world, which is not always how we wish it to be. Parents can guide children to become more resilient by:

Modelling problem-solving behaviours

Children pay attention to how parents and other caregivers approach problems. They will learn by example. Parents can model behaviours such as positively approaching problems, breaking problems into manageable components, and exploring multiple ways to solve problems. For instance, if my child tells me an assignment is confusing or complicated, I can help her by modelling problem-solving. I might ask her to show me what she is working on, ask questions about her thinking, and explore what she is supposed to do. Working through the problem together, I model good, analytical thinking, laying the foundation for a more collaborative, problem-solving relationship and stronger bond with my child. This collaborative approach not only helps the child understand that they are capable of problem-solving but also fosters a sense of teamwork and mutual respect between us.

Independence and responsibility

Responsibilities are an essential way you can actively help your children develop independence and responsibility. These are central characteristics of what we call resilience. For example, you could encourage them to take on more age-appropriate responsibilities, like doing chores, managing their time and making choices. Here's an example of one way you can encourage your children to take on responsibilities and make choices. You could involve your children in household chores such as helping to set the table, make meals or take care of pets. Helping out in the kitchen with essential food preparation, like wiping off the table, setting the table or peeling potatoes, can make children feel that they are contributing in valuable ways to the family.

Learning a growth mindset

Children with resilience often have a growth mindset – that is, they see challenges as opportunities for learning and growing rather than as threats or failures. When parents tell children that hard things, mistakes and setbacks are opportunities to learn how to improve the next time, they encourage a mindset that allows children to persist and overcome obstacles. They see difficulties as a critical part of learning rather than a threat to their sense of self. Learning a growth mindset involves acknowledging children's effort and persistence and developing strategies for turning setbacks into learning experiences. For instance, if their child gets a lower grade than expected on a test, a parent might say: 'I'm really proud of all the work you've put into this. What can you learn from this to help you study differently next time?'

3. Building Emotional Resilience

Emotional resilience includes the ability to regulate and manage emotions, cope with stress, and maintain a healthy outlook. This ability is critical for normal and healthy functioning as we work through the twists, turns, and turbulence of our emotional landscape. How do parents go about fostering emotional resilience in their children? Parents can encourage and support their children's development of these skills in the following ways.

Learning emotional awareness and regulation

Emotional awareness and regulation are important skills for coping with both stress and adversity. Emotional awareness involves understanding feelings, referring to one's ability to identify what emotions they are experiencing. Emotional regulation involves healthily coping with emotions, referring to one's ability to regulate their expression of emotions. For example, parents can help children learn about and identify their emotions and provide healthy ways to cope with difficult feelings, such as deep breathing exercises, mindfulness, or writing in a journal. Parents can encourage children to use deep breathing and mindfulness while upset or help their kids identify their feelings through art (e.g., drawing, writing or music) to allow kids to externalise and manage complicated feelings.

Encouraging positive self-esteem

Positive self-esteem is another attribute of emotional resilience that allows children to develop a healthy and realistic sense of self-worth that improves their emotional perspective. Parents can nurture self-esteem by providing positive and unconditional love and support for their children, giving praise and encouragement, and helping them build a realistic and balanced perception of their own self-concept. This means creating a healthy support environment that allows children to embrace and appreciate their strengths, abilities, capabilities, beliefs, and unique qualities through encouragement and providing balanced opportunities and challenges. Parents help their children develop this healthy self-concept by offering genuine praise while continually reminding them of their own unique tendencies and character traits. This positive approach to building good self-esteem gives children a healthy sense of positive self-perception needed to build resilience.

Social connections are a powerful tool for enhancing children's social-emotional development. These connections, whether with peers, siblings, family, or community members, provide a profound sense of belonging and acceptance crucial for emotional wellbeing. Parents can foster these relationships by facilitating children's social interactions with other children, including setting up playdates, organising group activities or family dinners, or involving them in school events with family members and other parents.

Further, children can benefit from parents being models for positive social behaviours so that their kids might learn empathic concern, kindness, and respect for others. Parents can help children by encouraging greater social engagement in community-based activities, such as sports teams, after-school clubs, volunteering, schools or churches, and other venues. These networks of social support act as a sort of buffer to mitigate against stressful experiences children might endure and instead help them develop the skills needed to get through life's ups and downs.

4. Integrating Cultural Practices and Traditions

Cultural practices and traditions can benefit the parents and children in coping and promoting resilience by providing them with a sense of identity, belonging and continuity rooted in previous generations' values, beliefs and lived experiences. These practices serve as educational tools to teach children different coping styles and as safeguards for their development of healthy adaptation by increasing their flexibility in responses to stress. For instance, parents can utilise cultural practices, which may help children better accept the realities they face and guide them through developmental challenges. Parents can weave cultural practices into parenting by 1) Using it to help children, particularly those from diverse backgrounds, cope and adapt to their migration culture, 2) Using it to teach children different cultural ways of solving problems and coping with different adversities, 3) Using it to foster difference awareness and importance of embracing diversity 4) Using it to maintain their identity.

Celebrating cultural traditions and rites of passage

Cultural traditions and rites of passage express past, present and future cultural life experiences, offering continuity between one's imagined past and imagined future by bridging, acknowledging or integrating different phases of life. Celebrating cultural traditions comforts and soothes. By participating in celebrations tied to family, ethnic, or national history and culture, for instance, holiday celebrations, religious rituals, and traditional practices such as singing, dancing, playing or traditional storytelling, families are reminded of who they are and what they value, reducing feelings of shame and self-blame.

Participating in rites of passage, for instance, celebrating children's birthdays, coming-of-age ceremonies, or graduation families, can reinforce a sense of continuity and cultural belonging despite unfamiliarity with new social and cultural settings. Analysing a specific tradition can help parents understand its rationale for diminishing parental traumatic reactions. Children born in the diaspora can be encouraged to recall traditional holidays, such as Independence Day, or traditional foods, songs, and traditional practices, such as the types of dances their parents would have done in their birth country.

When possible, they can also watch videos of them. Parents can also encourage them to recall religious ceremonies, such as baptisms, communions, or weddings, and discuss the traditions surrounding those practices.

Instilling cultural values and norms is a pivotal aspect of parenting. These values and norms, rooted in the wisdom of successful coexistence, are passed down through stories, proverbs, and instructions. Parents impart valuable insights about leading a fulfilling life by teaching their children these cultural principles. This process fosters a more profound sense of identity and purpose in children, a cornerstone of resilience. For instance, parents can share stories or proverbs that underscore life lessons such as endurance, community, and integrity in adversity.

Cultivate connections within the cultural community
This opens doors to social support and resilience in the long run. These connections, or 'communities', can include other families with similar cultural backgrounds, participation in cultural organisations, and involvement in cultural festivals or celebrations. For instance, a family's participation in a local South Sudanese community organisation, involvement in South Sudanese community festivals, and participation in language classes to connect with other families all contribute to resilience. The sense of belonging, mutual support, and shared understanding that these connections foster form the bedrock of resilience.

5. Promoting Physical Well-being
Adequate physical health is also essential to resilience, providing, for example, the raw energy and stamina required for dealing with difficult situations. Adequate physical health also tends to be a robust predictor of psychological and emotional well-being (e.g., its influence on stress management, mood stability, and cognitive function). Day-to-day, parents can take steps to promote physical health by:

Practising healthy habits
Healthy habits, such as daily exercise, a balanced diet and enough sleep, are the key to a healthy mind and body. Such habits lead to good health, which in turn leads to overall well-being, physical fitness and full of energy, resistance to catching colds and infectious diseases, contribute to mental health by keeping negativity away, enhanced concentration, distance from brain and neurological diseases, boosts mood and promotes mental stability.

As a parent, you can encourage your child to adopt healthy habits. Model good behaviour to your child by doing such things as mixing in periods of exercise in your daily routine, eating fruit every day and getting a good night's sleep. Feed your child nourishing food and teach them proper nutrition so they can learn to do the same into adulthood. Find activities that your child enjoys so that you can encourage them to participate. You maintain a close relationship with your child by joining your child in their activity of choice. Sports or recreational activities like swimming, soccer, and dance are great for physical exercise and social interaction. You can take your child to department stores or farmers' markets and involve them in planning grocery lists and activities.

Provide a safe, healthy environment
The physical environment where children live and the emotional and social support they receive are vital for physical health. Parents play a role in ensuring a safe environment by keeping their home free of hazards, modelling and promoting safe practices such as wearing seat belts and bike helmets, knowing what to do if lost or in danger and teaching their children about personal safety.

For example, parents can practise home safety by anchoring furniture to the walls, using safety gates at stairways, and keeping children away from harmful substances. Parents can also teach children about general safety practices such as looking both ways before crossing the street, wearing a bike helmet, and my favourite rule growing up, stopping and looking left, right, and left again before running onto the schoolyard.

Parents can also provide a safe environment by modelling and promoting safe practices for their children. Parents can provide a safe environment for their children by paying attention to personal safety, not consuming illegal or harmful substances, and accepting help when needed. Parents can also provide a safe environment by welcoming friends and family into their homes, valuing the presence of others, asking for help when needed, and building a support network. Provide emotional and social support: Parents can support their children by providing love, encouragement and positive feedback. These interpersonal aspects of support can enhance resilience in particular.

Health Care and resources
Good health hinges on access to health support and care. Routine medical check-ups, vaccinations, and dental care are critical to preventing disease and maintaining physical health. Engaging the support of health professionals is a great place to start. Parents need to ensure that routine medical examinations are scheduled and completed routinely, vaccination requirements are kept up-to-date, and medical issues and concerns are brought to the attention of the appropriate health care professional(s) for proper evaluation and intervention.

Additionally, it is helpful if parents know about resources and services that might be available to them that support physical health and well-being, such as community health programmes, city and community resources (will vary depending on the community in which you live), recreational facilities like local parks, and even nutrition education programmes that might be offered through schools. Examples of things parents can do include enrolling children in community recreation programs such as sports or physical activities, utilising community recreation facilities, for example, local parks or beaches, and acquiring information through local channels to educate themselves and their children about healthy living and nutrition. Parents also need to remain in the background to allow their children to find their inner strength for coping and continue to foster health-related well-being by helping them manage their health and wellness, making it convenient and accessible.

6. Fostering Spiritual Resilience

Spiritual resilience happens when people discover meaning, purpose, and hope. Spirituality is a critical component of resilience for many South Sudanese and other African families who use it to guide, strengthen and comfort them during difficulties. Along with culture and community life, spirituality offers practical tools for dealing with life's hardships – and helps children to thrive. Parents can boost spiritual resilience by:

Spiritual beliefs and practices

Spiritual beliefs and practices support overall wellbeing and vitality. These beliefs and practices help us to make sense of life's challenges and to reduce suffering. They also provide meaning, purpose and connection to something larger than the self. Parents can help children develop their spiritual life through storytelling about spiritual beliefs and practices, sharing experiences of these beliefs, and encouraging them to explore their own spiritual life.

Parents may, for example, discuss with children the importance of prayer meditation or stillness, engage in these meditative practices with the child, and encourage children to explore their spiritual life through creative work, nature, or service. Parents help children develop their spiritual life while fostering autonomy, self-agency, and an inner lifestyle congruent with the child's own sense of self-nurture values and practices that can sustain the child when the going gets rough.

Fostering purpose and meaning

Purpose and meaning are central to spiritual resilience, a concept that refers to maintaining a sense of purpose and meaning in life, even in the face of adversity. They provide goals that help people engage in the world and provide direction for making sense of life. Purpose and meaning can bolster mental health by helping people cope with difficulties. Parents can help their children develop a sense of purpose and meaning by fostering their involvement in personally meaningful activities that create pathways to a life that gives purpose and meaning.

For instance, they can encourage them to Find a cause they feel passionate about, do volunteer work in the community, and develop talents and skills in creative or intellectual life pursuits. Parents can help their children develop their sense of identity and resilience by helping them cultivate purpose and meaning. For example, parents may involve their child in a local community charity, arrange for them to participate in a community clean-up, or encourage them to become involved in a youth group focusing on social justice or environmental sustainability.

Promoting reflection and mindfulness

Reflection and mindfulness-based practices promote spiritual resilience. These experiences involve looking back, non-judgmentally, at one's experiences, feelings and beliefs and, in the moment of experiencing, being more present and aware. Parents can promote These teachable and precious mental practices in their children. They will help children become more aware and enhance their ability to be spiritually centred and experience peace and stability in times of stress and difficulty. Here are two things that parents can teach their children: Asking your child to write in a journal about their feelings and thoughts when something terrible happens can be an impactful reflective practice. Your child should spend some time meditating or reflecting on their daily life practice.

Experiencing the wisdom of spiritual practice with others

One of the most influential spiritual practices that can be learned and promoted in children is to experience the power of being part of or, at least, recognising the power of spiritual communities and forming relationships with wise and kind people. Spiritual communities and connection to the spiritual knowledge and wisdom of spiritually centred individuals can be a source of comfort, hope and, thus, resilience in the face of tough times and blows to one's wellbeing.

Conclusion

In today's rapidly changing world, promoting positive parenting approaches and fostering resilience is necessary for the well-being and success of South Sudanese and African families in the diaspora. These families face unique challenges, balancing preserving their cultural identity with the pressures to adapt to new societal norms. This chapter has underscored the importance of grounding parenting practices in cultural values, such as collectivism, respect for elders, and spirituality while integrating insights from contemporary psychological research. Together, these elements provide a robust foundation for raising resilient children.

Resilience is not merely the ability to recover from hardship but an ongoing process of growth and adaptation. For African families, resilience is deeply rooted in communal traditions, collective responsibility, and spiritual strength, which serve as pillars in navigating adversity. By embracing these cultural values and combining them with modern emotional and psychological development approaches, parents can create nurturing environments that promote survival and flourishing.

Furthermore, integrating positive parenting strategies such as open communication, emotional regulation, and problem-solving enables children to develop a strong sense of identity and adaptability. This equips them to face the complexities of living in multicultural societies with confidence and purpose. By fostering resilience in their children, parents address immediate challenges and prepare them for future success, helping them become emotionally intelligent, socially aware, and well-rounded individuals.

Promoting positive parenting approaches grounded in tradition and contemporary psychological wisdom ensures that African families can maintain their cultural heritage while thriving in new environments. This powerful combination of cultural and psychological resilience allows families to raise children who are capable of facing life's challenges and empowered to lead fulfilling, meaningful lives in a multicultural world. Through the strategies outlined in this chapter, parents can foster a deep sense of belonging, purpose, and strength in their children, ensuring they are well-equipped to navigate the complexities of the modern era.

CHAPTER TEN

Adapting to Change: South Sudanese Family Strategies in Australia

Introduction

"We need the government and supporting organisations to work with the community to resolve parenting and resettlement challenges. There also needs to be education for parents about child protection and other laws that affect families (Simon)."

This chapter is a tribute to the voices of the South Sudanese community parents, leaders, and members who participated in my PhD studies (Deng, 2016a). It is dedicated to understanding and sharing their perspectives on adapting to the dynamic challenges of resettlement in Australia. The strategies these parents employ to cope with changes within their families and communities are central to the discussion. The chapter delves into the complexities of integrating South Sudanese cultural values with Australian societal norms, highlighting the importance of culturally appropriate parenting support. The South Sudanese community in Australia is a vibrant and diverse group with a rich cultural heritage that they are keen to preserve while adapting to their new environment.

Key themes are explored throughout the chapter, beginning with the necessity of understanding South Sudanese culture and the unique challenges faced during resettlement. Participants emphasised the crucial role of authorities and support services in understanding these cultural nuances to provide practical parenting support. The role of community and spiritual leaders is also discussed, underscoring their importance in offering social and emotional support within the community. This support, often overlooked by mainstream services, is a crucial pillar in the resilience of South Sudanese families, offering reassurance and a sense of belonging.

The chapter further examines the blending of South Sudanese and Australian parenting practices, which requires additional support from relevant service providers. This integration is seen as essential for empowering families and communities to address settlement challenges. The importance of parents taking responsibility for adapting to change, recognising areas for improvement, and embracing the opportunities presented by their new environment is another critical focus. Lastly, the chapter reflects on the role of parents as role models in instilling respect, culture, and language core elements of their identity that they wish to pass on to future generations. The participant names used for the quotes throughout this chapter are pseudonyms.

Navigating South Sudanese Cultures: Effective Parenting Support

Adaptation and social capital: the collective self

Culture is deeply intertwined with the identity of individuals and their communities, shaping how people make meaning of life, respond to challenges, and interact with their environment. It encompasses language, learned behaviours, and values, all of which are crucial in influencing a person's history and socioeconomic context (Copping et al., 2010). In resettlement, culture becomes an essential element, directly impacting how individuals navigate their new environment, understand societal values, and adjust their attitudes (Potocky-Tripodi, 2002).

Many South Sudanese parents in Australia feel that the host authorities do not sufficiently understand their traditions and cultures (Ochocka & Janzen, 2008). They view Australian resettlement policies, similar to those in other countries, as contributing to the persistent separation of family members (McDonald-Wilmsen & Gifford, 2009). Culture significantly influences their attitudes toward and responses to the challenges they face in their new environment. As discussed in previous chapters, community members have highlighted the importance of recognising their culture and leveraging community leadership to address cultural barriers and concerns. In South Sudanese culture, community issues are traditionally resolved by community leaders, chiefs, and elders. However, since resettling in Australia, there is concern among the South Sudanese community that even minor issues are being escalated directly to authorities such as the police, child protection services, and courts.

"I recommend that Australia give us time and value our culture instead of jumping straight to solutions when there are family issues. They need to better understand our culture before involving the police (John)."

Understanding the African and South Sudanese experiences and cultures before devising support strategies is vital for this participant and many others. Identifying the unique needs of these families and communities is crucial to providing appropriate and meaningful services that address their complex challenges. As John explains:

"Before providing support, it's important to identify the specific needs of the South Sudanese community. Parenting issues are often deeply rooted in interactions with law enforcement and welfare agencies that deal with families daily. Understanding and evaluating the community's experiences is imperative to delivering proper support."

Each culture has unique aspects that may surprise or interest others, and understanding these nuances is essential for fostering harmony in a multicultural society. Tribe (1999) emphasised that cultural differences can be significant, particularly between Western and non-Western understandings of family and community. These differences often become more pronounced due to inadequate information provided to new immigrants about their host culture and a lack of cultural awareness within the host community about the newcomers. This lack of understanding can lead to direct and indirect discrimination against new immigrants (Marlowe, 2009; Tribe, 1999). These challenges and the difficulties arising from involuntary migration can create substantial barriers to successful resettlement for some new settlers.

As a result, many participants expressed a desire for government agencies and social support services, particularly those working with families, to coordinate efforts, consult with the South Sudanese community, and work collaboratively to find viable solutions to their parenting challenges. Peter narrated that:

"I felt ignored by the government as a parent. If the government can consult with parents and understand our culture, I am sure we can find solutions to help these children. No South Sudanese parent wants to hurt their children. Government agencies and parents need to work together to address the root causes of problems at home and help keep families together."

Participants also emphasised the need for services to better inform parents about the roles of service providers in areas such as child protection, positive parenting training, and understanding the country's laws. This knowledge is especially important for offering alternatives to traditional physical approaches to child discipline, as Mary explained:

"Parents need support in understanding the parenting styles here so they can balance or modify their practices to fit this country's laws. Parenting training or workshops can help because some parents give up on their children when they feel they aren't being listened to. But parents should never give up on their children; they should keep finding ways to bring them back home."

The lack of access to mainstream services led participants to recommend establishing specific support services that raise awareness and provide education on child discipline and relevant laws. They called on authorities to offer workshops and parenting training on reconciling traditional parenting practices with the expectations of their new environment and on laws and policies related to child protection and family dynamics.

The question of who should educate new settlers about the consequences of using traditional physical disciplining practices remains unanswered. As discussed in this and previous chapters, new settlers often face barriers while mainstream services are available. These barriers range from language and cultural differences to a lack of understanding of the new and often unfamiliar types of services and support available.

The benefit of designing purpose-specific programs to address these intersecting needs and challenges has been demonstrated in other countries. For example, Deng and Pienaar (2011) evaluated a positive parenting program in New Zealand that was conducted with South Sudanese migrants. The program had a significant impact by identifying the needs of families and parents and devising training to suit those needs. It promoted positive parenting in the community by strengthening parents' consistency and application of knowledge, focusing on effective non-physical disciplining to support new immigrant parents and caregivers.

It is crucial to provide parents with tools that substitute traditional techniques (e.g., verbal and behavioural approaches rather than physical discipline) while still valuing the underlying principles of good parenting (e.g., respect, concern for others, healthy choices). This support helps parents cope as they struggle with a sense of powerlessness or uncertainty about correcting their children's behaviour, especially when they feel deprived of the methods they are familiar with in their new environment.

Adaptation and Social Capital: The Collective Identity

As discussed in other chapters and throughout this book, one of the South Sudanese community's most significant forms of social capital is their strong sense of communal culture. This social capital is manifested through gathering and socialising during good and challenging times, offering each other support to navigate the difficulties of resettlement, particularly the feelings of isolation. Research has shown that social support is crucial not only for fostering a sense of care, love, and belonging but also for preventing ill health and positively influencing mental and physical well-being (as evidenced by mortality rates) (Stansfeld et al., 2006).

South Sudanese settlers have developed adaptive coping strategies to overcome the challenges and changes associated with resettlement. Many community members have found common spaces where they can socialise and provide each other with essential support, including sharing and reflecting on their past and present experiences. Deng stated that:

"Some South Sudanese, especially men, have found common places where they can spend time together, socialising and supporting one another. They engage in activities like playing dominoes, pool, and other games, which have been therapeutic for many. This practice is deeply rooted in our culture; we used to gather, share personal challenges, and offer mutual support. Despite many changes, this aspect of our culture has remained strong."

In her study of unaccompanied South Sudanese minors, Goodman (2004) observed that the concept of the communal self was strongly reflected in how participants narrated their stories. South Sudanese individuals often view themselves as integral parts of their community, expressing their experiences through collective pronouns like "we" or "us." This communal approach to addressing challenges, particularly in parenting, is a significant coping strategy. It allows individuals to normalise and mitigate the impact of challenges by externalising them, emphasising that they are not alone in their struggles.

> *"As adults, we always come together to support and counsel each other on the issues we face in our new environment. We meet to talk about these challenges… Those who don't know how to cope often end up isolating themselves or, in extreme cases, committing suicide as they feel hopeless. Those who stay connected within the community benefit from hearing stories that are sometimes worse than their own and realise they are not alone. In these social groups, members provide support and exchange ideas on how to deal with family challenges and changes, as narrated by Mary."*

This comment illustrates how the South Sudanese community is coping with both structural and individual challenges in their new environment. The communal culture fosters a supportive environment where individuals share and discuss their personal issues through socialising and peer counselling. This concept is often absent in more individualistic cultures where counselling is seen as a professional rather than a social activity. Individual counselling is a foreign concept to many South Sudanese.

Previous studies have shown that group counselling, psychosocial support, and psycho-education are more effective for individuals from collectivist cultures, particularly South Sudanese, who perceive individual challenges as collective problems (S. A. Deng & J. M. Marlowe, 2013; Deng & Pienaar, 2011). While individual therapy may work for some, many South Sudanese view parenting challenges as collective issues, so they strongly advocate for positive parenting programs that bring parents together to discuss and find solutions.

South Sudanese believe that collective and community counselling protects the traumas and hardships they have experienced. Relying on each other for support and encouragement helps individuals survive challenging situations by reinforcing that they are not alone in their suffering. Participants also discussed resilience, another vital form of social capital, which they believe has empowered them to overcome parenting and other resettlement challenges.

> *"What helps us maintain our cultures is the determination to remember what brought us here in the first place (Sam)."*

The South Sudanese have endured traumatic experiences due to forced migration, and throughout their refugee journeys, they have developed a remarkable capacity for resilience. This resilience has been built through the necessity of learning survival and adaptation skills to cope with their harrowing experiences (Deng, 2013B; S. A. Deng & J. M. Marlowe, 2013; Marlowe et al., 2014; Marlowe, 2010; Milner & Khawaja, 2010). However, this resilience, a crucial aspect of South Sudanese social capital for coping with settlement changes and challenges, is sometimes overlooked or unrecognised. These protective factors are essential for understanding the resources available to a specific socio-cultural group, which emphasises the importance of considering the interconnections between various protective mechanisms and how they influence each other (Deng, 2016a).

South Sudanese who have successfully survived inhumane conditions often develop a strengthened sense of resilience from their experiences, a response known as "adversity-activated development" (Papadopoulos, 2007). This is an example of the positive effects of trauma, highlighting how individuals, through unique and varied responses, develop psychological resilience that was not present before their adversity (Alayarian, 2007). This discussion explores how South Sudanese individuals utilise their learned resilience to integrate traditional parenting practices into their new settings.

Role of Community Leadership

Kelly (2003) identifies two critical aspects of a community: the warmth and interconnectedness among its members and the subliminal shared values and goals that bind them together. Despite the divisions and rivalries often exacerbated by the political situation in their country of origin, South Sudanese communities continue to provide various support to one another. Like many other immigrant groups, South Sudanese rely heavily on their community for social and emotional support, often drawing on the guidance of community and church leaders, as well as from their peers and broader social circles.

Studies recognise the significant functions of new settlers' associations in overcoming isolation, defending community interests, and generating material support while promoting the community's image. Although "community" can mean different things to different people, for South Sudanese, it often refers to a network of large and small sub-communities from which they draw help and support (Deng, 2016a). These community associations play a crucial role in creating bridges between the new and host society through networking, information-sharing, and enhancing the integration of newcomers into their new environment. (Gamble & Weil, 2010; Rex et al., 1987).

However, reliance on ethnic community members can be both a strength and a limitation. While it fosters a sense of solidarity and belonging, it can also limit individuals' capacity to learn about and adapt to their new environment. As discussed in other chapters, this heavy reliance is often due to language and cultural barriers, particularly a lack of familiarity with the new setting or mainstream culture.

Many South Sudanese parents have highlighted that addressing their parenting and family challenges requires recognising and empowering the roles of spiritual and community leaders. Empowering these leaders to resolve issues at the family and community levels could help mitigate tensions arising from cultural changes, reduce family disintegration, and prevent issues such as divorce, separation, substance abuse, and criminal behaviour among young people.

> *"South Sudanese come from a society where community leaders are highly regarded. Recognising and empowering these leaders to resolve family issues could help reduce problems within the community. Authorities risk causing more breakdowns if they overlook this. Many children end up on the streets, committing crimes and then landing in jail. For example, if a child is caught misbehaving, the police should involve the community leader and allow them to talk to the child first (Sibit)."*

Some participants reported receiving little support from mainstream social services and noted that much of their help has come from within their own community since arriving in Australia.

> *"There isn't much support from outside our community; we usually come together in this place (a park in the city) to share our concerns and support each other (Aluel)."*

Community empowerment at a group-based level, participatory, and developmental processes enable marginalised groups to control their lives and environments. This process helps them acquire valued resources, secure fundamental rights, achieve important life goals, and reduce societal marginalisation. The empowerment occurs over an extended period, primarily in community settings where members live, and requires meeting specific empowering processes and outcomes (Deng, 2016a). These include increasing individual development, improving community well-being, and fostering social change. However, some South Sudanese community members may not understand these empowerment dynamics.

In addition to calling for community empowerment, South Sudanese parents encourage their community members to embrace the changes introduced by their new environment while seeking community and professional support.

> *"It is important to accept the challenges and changes we face and seek help through counselling and community advice, especially from elders and church leaders. This is the only way to cope with these challenges; it's hard to do it alone. You need someone to walk with you, help and guide you through all these challenges... People need to connect and find help (Lado)."*

Blending South Sudanese and Australian Parenting Practices
In the context of resettlement, one of the critical challenges faced by South Sudanese families is balancing their traditional parenting practices with the norms and expectations of their new Australian environment. This part delves into the complex process of integrating these two distinct parenting paradigms. Balancing old and new practices is crucial for effective integration and the family's well-being. While many South Sudanese parents are committed to preserving their cultural heritage, they also recognise the necessity of adapting to their new surroundings. This process, however, requires support,

particularly in understanding their new country's relevant policies and laws.

Some parents in this study expressed the need for targeted parenting training and workshops to help them navigate the differences between South Sudanese and Australian parenting styles. These programs are essential for enhancing understanding and facilitating adaptation, thereby minimising potential clashes between the two cultures.

"As a family and community, we need to adapt and learn our new society's laws, although it will take time. We need to accept the new country's laws by letting go of certain traditional practices that may clash with those laws. If we don't adapt, our children will run away from us and end up on the streets. We must teach them our cultural values and those of Australian society (Peter)."

This perspective underscores the efforts of South Sudanese parents to integrate and adapt to their new environment while highlighting the lack of support and unfamiliarity with the new system as significant barriers to successful integration. Although reconciling the differences between their traditional and new cultures is challenging, most parents must find ways to blend the two to provide their children the best of both worlds.

A positive parenting program conducted in New Zealand between 2006 and 2010 exemplifies how such integration can be achieved. In this program, parents were encouraged to balance their traditional parenting practices with understanding various parenting styles within the New Zealand context (Deng & Pienaar, 2011). The program's success lies in its approach to not replacing traditional practices but integrating new and old methods, thereby enhancing the parental skills necessary to fulfil their roles in an unfamiliar environment.

Participants in this study emphasised the importance of mutual support within their community. They suggested that parents work together to share their experiences and challenges and utilise internal community resources and external support from broader Australian society. Parents must acquire positive parenting and communication skills to successfully discipline their children, particularly knowledge of non-physical disciplinary methods.

"It is hard to reconcile because several changes are imposed on us by the authorities… We are talking to our children to hold onto our cultural values. They say, 'When in Rome, do as the Romans do.' Parents must work together to discipline their children by being consistent. They must also set good examples for their children to follow. For instance, if parents go out, they must inform their children of their whereabouts and expect the same. I always call to tell my family if I am late for work. You cannot expect respect from others if you do not show the same to them (Ngor)."

Children tend to emulate their parents' behaviours, and the comments above align with Joshi's (2015) observation that parents should model the behaviours they wish to see in their children. While not all parents possess the same parenting skills, many believe that sharing ideas and strategies at family and community levels can help bridge this gap.

"The best way to cope with changes and challenges is to address family issues collectively at the family and community levels rather than keeping them private. Today's problem could be mine; tomorrow, it might be my neighbour's. Therefore, parents and the community must work together to overcome family and parenting

challenges. Instead of labelling struggling parents as bad, they need support so that the family can cope with these issues. Moving to a new country comes with many challenges, and it takes years to overcome them. The struggle with challenges often causes fractures within the family (Jak)."

Some parents have begun adopting more lenient approaches, shifting away from the strict traditional parenting styles where children were expected to follow instructions without question. They believe that being more lenient might help prevent the removal of their children by Child Protection due to allegations of abuse or neglect. Instead, they are trying to replace old physical disciplinary practices with closer, more engaging relationships with their children. These changes are not necessarily what South Sudanese parents desire, but they acknowledge the need to adapt their methods in the face of new realities.

"We mix some of our cultural values with Australian ones because if we solely rely on our traditional values, our children will run away from us. Therefore, we must blend the two cultures. We are trying to learn how to talk to our children nicely, not as parents anymore, but as their friends (Ngor)."

Some parents have developed effective strategies to integrate and adapt their parenting styles to the new environment.

"Understanding the parenting issues, I have developed different strategies based on the societal context, recognising the cultural clashes. I identify my children's needs and interests and see if they are important for their mentoring and social connection. If they are,

I allocate resources to keep them connected. Doing so keeps children close to their parents as they are provided with their needs. This is how I have adjusted my traditional styles to meet the demands of the current situation (Madut)."

Identifying children's needs and interests is crucial for building close relationships with them and managing their behaviours effectively. Child discipline, as a form of guidance, provides opportunities for children to develop an internal locus of control, learn to take responsibility for their actions and adopt acceptable values in both the family and society (Deng & Pienaar, 2011). Setting house rules is an effective way to shape children's behaviour. Joshi (2015) suggests involving children in defining these rules, writing them down, and posting them in a visible place while clearly outlining the consequences of breaking them.

However, each parent has their own unique style of parenting, which can be understood through Baumrind's (1991) three parenting styles: authoritative, authoritarian, and permissive (Baumrind, 1991), which are discussed adequately in other chapters. These styles are reflected in the diverse parenting practices of South Sudanese parents. While many are familiar with and have practised authoritarian styles since arriving in Australia, some have been trying to adapt to an authoritative style. In contrast, others have become more permissive due to the inability to apply traditional disciplinary practices.

"I always sit down with my children and teach them important values, like not being violent. If someone wants to fight them at school, I tell them to walk away or inform a teacher. If they see their friends with things they don't have, I teach them not to complain. I usually put our house rules on the wall: love, laugh, kiss always,

say sorry, always share things, and listen to your parents. These are the rules for my children. We are trying to adapt but not lose our traditional parenting practices. I am adapting new parenting styles while holding on to some of my old traditional practices (Ayom)."

Setting house rules and praising and rewarding children for good behaviour is significant in transforming and shaping children's behaviours. These practices include stopping children from engaging in inappropriate behaviour and helping them understand why certain actions are unacceptable within the family and society (Deng & Pienaar, 2011). As discussed in another chapter, this reflects Baumrind's authoritative parenting style.

Transforming children's behaviour requires consistent effort from parents. Research indicates that children thrive when firm boundaries exist, such as saying no to undesirable behaviour (Joshi, 2015). To reconcile modern strategies with traditional parenting practices, some South Sudanese parents encourage each other to build connections with people outside their community. These broader connections provide additional support and help them learn more about the laws and norms of their new country.

"Being connected does not mean only within your community; you also need friends from the wider Australian community because they might have insights on facing challenges in Australian ways. If you only go to fellow South Sudanese, they will advise you based on their knowledge, but that might not work here. You need friends from the wider Australian community to help balance between the cultures (Lado)."

Reconciling old and new parenting practices presents challenges for many South Sudanese parents. However, as most participants noted, they realise that many of their traditional practices are not applicable in their new environment, and they must find ways to integrate them with new ones. To succeed in this integration process, parents need support and empowerment.

Owning Responsibility and Recognizing Shortcomings

The initial years in a new country are often marked by cultural shock and confusion as new settlers grapple with understanding their new environment while trying to reconcile their traditional practices with the demands of their current surroundings. As highlighted in this and previous chapters, South Sudanese immigrants frequently voiced their challenges, sometimes attributing the breakdown of family structures to external authorities they perceived as encouraging disintegration.

Research suggests that many immigrants experience similar stages when transitioning into a new environment. The first few months are often called a "honeymoon period," characterised by excitement and relief at arriving in a new country. During this phase, everything seems possible, and long-held hopes materialise (Adler, 1977; Berry, 1990, 1992a; Deng, 2013B). However, this initial optimism is often followed by a period of disenchantment, during which the disadvantages and limitations of the new country become more apparent, and the novelty wears off. As instant success eludes them and life proves harder than expected, immigrants may experience emotional distress, leading to self-blame and withdrawal.

For many South Sudanese, the realisation of the need to take responsibility for their situation emerges during this second phase. As they begin to view themselves as bicultural or multicultural, they reflect on perceived shortcomings in their parenting practices, often linked to a failure to instil certain values in their children from an early age. This reflection can sometimes lead to a gendered discourse of blame within the community. For example, during a mixed-gender focus group, participants debated the roles and responsibilities of parents in their children's upbringing, with some men attributing perceived parenting failures to the actions (or inactions) of South Sudanese mothers.

"I strongly believe that South Sudanese women are to blame for their children's failures because sometimes children can even fight among themselves while their mothers continue to watch TV or are on the phone talking to their friends. I say this because when kids return from school, their mothers don't look after them at home. They leave the kids to play PlayStation, watch movies, or do whatever they want, which is not good (Madut)."

These views were echoed by a female participant in the same group, who acknowledged that some women might neglect their children while engaging in social activities:

"Some women also have problems as they are always on the phone talking to other friends without paying more attention to looking after their children (Achan)."

However, another female participant challenged the notion that women alone are responsible for parenting shortcomings, pointing out that many men do not fully support their partners, especially in areas where women might lack the necessary education or language skills to assist their children, such as with homework.

"Some women don't know how to read and write, but their husbands or partners are not helping in their children's upbringing. Many South Sudanese men leave the responsibility of looking after their children to the women alone, which is not fair (Yar)."

The discussion also highlighted the diversity in parenting styles among South Sudanese families, with one female participant (Aluel) responding to a male participant who placed the blame solely on women:

"That is not true; it depends on how you raise your children. Here, we have different policies for children's upbringing in every house. For example, in my house, children have specific times for doing certain things. After they return from school, there are allocated times for studying, drawing, eating, showering, and bedtime. We have different parenting styles."

This exchange underscores the participants' recognition that parenting styles vary and children's behaviour often reflects their home environment.

"Parenting means the way of bringing up a child… What the child does reflects where that child is growing up… If the child is good, that means there is something good at home, which also means that children's behaviours reflect their home environment (Garang)."

Despite this recognition, some parents hesitate to share their parenting difficulties due to the stigma associated with being labelled as bad parents. This stigma can lead to social isolation, with some parents avoiding the community out of fear that others might negatively influence their children or because their children are not doing well.

"Some are finding it very hard and start to isolate themselves from the community because they fear that if they associate with other community members, their children may be influenced by those who are not doing well. Others avoid the community because of the stigma that their children are not doing well. In South Sudanese culture, parents are always blamed if their children are not doing well in life (Achan)."

This cultural tradition creates a significant barrier to sharing challenges, yet some participants are beginning to overcome this barrier, allowing community members to provide support. Acknowledging these shortcomings and taking responsibility are seen as crucial steps in overcoming resettlement challenges. Many South Sudanese have progressed from a state of disintegration to one of reintegration and autonomy. Reintegration occurs when new immigrants shift from self-blame to recognising the challenges posed by their culture in the new environment. This phase leads to a sense of autonomy, where they can identify strengths and weaknesses in their new environment. Finally, immigrants achieve a sense of independence, confidently managing conflicts between their old and new cultures (Adler, 1977; Berry, 1990, 1992a; Deng, 2013B).

Embracing Family and Community Changes

The findings of this study indicate that South Sudanese parents have come to recognise the necessity of embracing certain changes within their families and communities as a crucial part of coping with the challenges of parenting and resettlement. Initially, many experienced the "honeymoon period" upon arrival in Australia, where the excitement of new opportunities overshadowed potential challenges.

However, as the reality of resettlement set in, this initial optimism often gave way to disenchantment as the difficulties of adjusting to a new system became apparent. Now, many parents are transitioning toward reintegration, where they are beginning to see their challenges as not solely the fault of the new system but as a product of both old and new influences. This progression is steering them towards autonomy and independence, where they can evaluate their situations from both perspectives (Adler, 1977; Deng, 2013B).

Berry (1992) argued that behavioural shifts occur when individuals move to a new culture, often leading to acculturative stress. These shifts involve a departure from previously learned patterns in favour of those more prevalent in the new society, a process that can be stressful and disruptive to daily functioning (Berry, 1992b). However, these transitions are not uniform for all new settlers, as factors such as language barriers, cultural differences, lack of social support, and socioeconomic conditions all play a role in the resettlement and parenting challenges they face.

Despite the challenges, many South Sudanese parents have also identified certain advantages provided by their new environment. One significant change they have recognised is the reduced support systems they once enjoyed in South Sudan. However, a key benefit of the new environment is the legal protection against excessive force in disciplining children. This practice was once considered normal in their culture but is now prohibited under Australian law. This shift has led to a re-evaluation of parenting values. As Jak narrated:

> *"The big dynamic change here is the fact that parents don't have as much support as they used to enjoy in South Sudan. The benefit here is that those who use excessive force to discipline their kids will be unable to do so because of the law. Many newly arrived immigrants can easily misunderstand parenting in their new environment. ...*

Through these misunderstandings and misconceptions about the laws that protect innocent people, the family tends to guess a lot of things... For example, 'How dare the government prevent me from disciplining my own kids; it is my right as a parent?' Yet, not knowing what the laws are in Australia. So, misunderstandings and misconceptions give wrong impressions about the authorities."

As participants observed, many have realised that their traditional parenting values must be adapted, as practices once considered "normal" are no longer acceptable. For example, physical discipline, such as picking up a stick to correct a child, was common in South Sudan and considered a communal responsibility. However, parents now recognise that each parenting style must evolve to align with their new environment's cultural traditions and laws.

"We have to follow some of our traditions, which are good, but also follow what the policies say and how they work here (Aluel)."

Participants also acknowledged the benefits of their new environment, such as access to education and security. They pointed out that some young South Sudanese have thrived, obtaining education, securing good jobs, and purchasing homes to integrate into Australian society. The success stories of many South Sudanese wished to be highlighted by the media rather than the negative aspects often dominating coverage.

"A couple of advantages: the children who listen to their parents and follow through with their education are now doing very well in life. I have also learned that many young South Sudanese have achieved so well, and some hold good jobs since they have an education and

language ability. Those who failed to be educated are those taken by the government agencies and put in foster care... They stopped going to school and started drinking or using drugs... Some are just loitering on the streets (Achan)."

Further, participants emphasised the importance of integrating their customs with the expectations of their new country. This integration is essential for their children, who are growing up as Australians.

"The benefit is that our children have gone to school and are learning a lot of things, but the challenge is that they are getting confused between the two cultures as they do not know which culture to follow: they are still African, but they do not have much knowledge (of African culture), and when they try to fit into the Western culture, they do not feel they belong there either. 'They are the lost generation'—the only thing is to find how to integrate both cultures. It takes years to integrate, and most South Sudanese have been here for less than two decades (Peter)."

Many young South Sudanese are indeed grappling with their dual identities, leading to significant intergenerational conflict within families. However, many parents believe that their children are now more accustomed to Australian culture and environment than their culture of origin, making it imperative to integrate into the new culture while maintaining key aspects of their original traditions. Another positive outcome of the new environment is that it has brought families closer together, allowing for shared decision-making and more frequent family interactions, circumstances that were not always possible in South Sudan.

"The good thing about these changes is that they create equality or an equal share of decision-making within the family. Sometimes, a family sits and has a meal together. This is good because sitting together as a family and discussing things is very important (Lado)."

Embracing and accepting these changes is a necessity imposed by the demands of their new environment. This does not mean abandoning all-important cultural values but rather integrating them into the resettlement process to enhance the family's adjustment. The dynamic changes in families and parenting practices are a global phenomenon, and adapting to them is crucial for parents and their children. Joshi (2015) argued that "new-old-fashioned parenting" (NOFP) involves finding a balance between modern parenting approaches and traditional methods. The cultures from which immigrants come may undergo significant changes during the migrant's lifetime, making it misleading to assume a timeless past of family traditions. Local cultural beliefs and values often influence immigrants, such as those disseminated through mass media.

Indeed, since gaining independence in July 2011, South Sudan has experienced rapid changes, mainly through increased exposure to the outside world and the Internet. This has led to a return of people from the diaspora, bringing influences from other cultures. South Sudan has also enacted its first legislation on child protection, although it is not yet as strictly enforced as in Australia or other developed countries.

Parents as Role Models

Participants in the study emphasised the critical role that parents play as role models for their children, particularly in teaching them about their cultural heritage and societal responsibilities. Joshi (2015) asserts that a child's parenting experience significantly shapes their ability to manage disappointment and frustration in adulthood. Parents, therefore, are responsible for setting boundaries and fostering effective communication skills, which are vital tools for building and maintaining healthy relationships. This foundational learning begins in the home, where children form their first attachments and learn from those they trust the most.

South Sudanese culture strongly believes that a child's behaviour directly reflects their home environment and, by extension, their parents' success or failure. To be effective role models, parents must teach good behaviour and exemplify it through what Sanders (1999) describes as self-management. This includes being self-sufficient, evaluative, and intentional in setting performance goals and standards. While there is no one-size-fits-all approach to parenting, parents are expected to guide their children toward positive behaviours by setting clear goals and implementing management strategies that align with them.

However, some participants noted that their children occasionally lack role models due to marital disputes. These conflicts often disrupt the family structure and can lead to challenges in providing consistent guidance for children, as Ajak explained:

"Children sometimes do not have role models while growing up. Problems have increased between husbands and wives, which led to this."

The participants also expressed concerns about their community's negative perceptions, often exacerbated by the actions of a few individuals. They stressed the importance of parents taking a proactive and consistent approach to engaging with and disciplining their children rather than fearing intervention by authorities.

"My question is, what kind of people do we want to raise? As a society, we have to comply with the rules… The children go out there and start doing bad things, and then society says, 'Yes, these are South Sudanese who are doing bad things.'… South Sudanese are really confused about what to do. Children's issues are always or partly to be blamed on the parents… Some parents think their hands are tied, but they should remember that children's brains are still developing… Parents must talk to their children about everything… parenting is difficult (Ngor)."

Some parents emphasised the need to change the negative image that has tarnished their community's reputation. They also highlighted the importance of resolving family disputes internally, without involving external authorities in minor issues. As previous studies have shown, the media and politicians often focus on adverse incidents involving South Sudanese while ignoring the positive contributions made by the community. This imbalance in representation has contributed to the stigmatisation of the entire community based on the actions of a few.

"The other thing that the wider Australian society should understand is that not all South Sudanese children are on the streets: some of our children are doing really well, but the media only pick on a few bad incidents to make the entire South Sudanese community look bad. Our community needs to be strong so that such negative connotations and labelling of our community as bad are countered by telling the truth and facts about us. This is a new environment for us; being united and working together to advocate for ourselves and better integration is crucial. In this country, you have to advocate for yourself. According to South Sudanese, there are procedures for resolving family issues (Peter)."

Traditionally, South Sudanese fathers were seen as the breadwinners and protectors of their families. However, these roles have had to change in the Australian context, where many fathers find themselves unemployed, leaving mothers without the familial support they previously received. Some participants believe that the absence of male role models in the family contributes to children's behavioural issues.

"The other thing I suppose is that some are single parents raising children on their own, which is really a challenge because those parents could be single mothers… I don't know whether it is a cultural thing, but most children who are having problems are with solo mothers. Maybe they would have done better if their fathers were there to discipline their sons… The lack of male role models might be playing a big part (Ngor)."

As their children's primary educators, parents are expected to instil positive attitudes, confidence, and essential life skills before their children venture into society. However, this goal requires constructive strategies and concerted effort from parents and the broader community.

"You teach your children to stand on their own feet. You show them their rights and what they can do to be successful in their lives (Bol)."

Teaching children the necessary skills, values, and attitudes for independence involves understanding their behaviours and influences. This understanding is crucial for parents to refine their disciplinary approaches and achieve the desired outcomes. Participants encouraged one another to persist in guiding their children, even when they seem unresponsive, believing that consistent support can lead to positive changes in behaviour.

> *"Parents need to keep trying to convince their children… They need to give them support as this can let the child understand that his or her parents really love him or her, which can even change the behaviours for the better. People should not isolate themselves when they are dealing with difficulties; they need to interact or talk to their friends about these so that they may feel listened to (Mary)."*

As mentioned, parents are held accountable for their children's good or bad behaviour. This cultural belief places enormous pressure on parents to protect their status in the community while raising the next generation. Joshi (2015) emphasised the importance of parents making decisions that are in their children's long-term best interests, even if these decisions sometimes cause temporary frustration or disappointment. Being a role model means being close to your children, listening to them, and involving them in decision-making processes that affect them. Research has shown that when children are involved in setting the rules and understanding the consequences, they are more likely to exhibit positive behaviours (Deng & Pienaar, 2011; Joshi, 2015; Sanders, 1999).

The discussion of parents as role models naturally leads to a broader conversation about respect, culture, language, and identity, which are explored in the next section.

Respect in Culture, Language, and Identity

As explored in other chapters and supported by existing studies, South Sudanese communities perceive respect as deeply embedded in their culture, language, and identity. Respect is not just a value passed from parents to children; it is a foundational element in how individuals interact within their families, with authorities, and in the broader community. It is critical in shaping social inter-ethnic relationships (Buriel, 1993). Research by Losoncz (2013) highlights how respect is crucial in preserving individual reputation, identity, and influence within the South Sudanese community. For South Sudanese, the most significant forms of respect include self-respect, respect for others, and mutual respect, all intertwined with human dignity (Deng, 1972; Losoncz, 2012).

"To be respected, a person has to be proud of who they are, and their culture... Our children sometimes lack these qualities (respect) (Madut)."

Parents in the South Sudanese community expect their children to embody respect, which they see as integral to their cultural and linguistic identity. However, this expectation is challenged when children assimilate new values that may conflict with traditional practices, making it difficult to reinforce these cultural values. Consequently, parents are advocating for open and honest dialogue with their children. This approach is essential not only for maintaining solid parent-child relationships but also for effective family discipline.

"As parents, you don't have to give up on your child because if you are stronger in trying to help your child, you can. (The effect of) your child is the same as going to the toilet - you cannot come out and announce to everyone that you left something terrible and smelly. Your child is a part of you; no matter how bad he/she is, you don't give up on him/her. Parents must be honest and open with their children when discussing these challenges. Being close to your child

is very important... Parents must learn strategies for talking with their children; they need to be friends with them (Peter)."

Many parents are determined to instil and preserve key aspects of their cultural values in their children. Peter shared how he maintained his mother tongue despite growing up in a predominantly Arabic-speaking environment due to his parent's efforts.

"I was brought up speaking different languages (mostly Arabic), but my parent taught me my mother tongue. Since I learned how to speak my language, I was able to fit into my tribe (Nuer); otherwise, if my parent had not insisted on teaching me, then I would have lost or not fitted into my culture. My parent taught me to hold onto my language as it is my identity."

However, some parents acknowledge that they bear responsibility for allowing their children to lose touch with their native culture and language. Mary emphasises that parents must actively teach their children their mother tongues at home, especially after school, to ensure they do not forget them.

"The language barrier between the parents and their children is a real issue. Parents are to blame because they are responsible for teaching their children to preserve their mother tongues. Parents must teach their children while they are growing up. Especially when they return from school, parents and children should speak their language at home, so their children do not forget it."

Participants frequently raised the language barrier between parents and children as a source of intergenerational conflict. They expressed concern that without the ability to speak their native language, children would struggle to maintain their cultural identity, as language and culture are inherently connected. Parents fear their children losing their mother tongues and abandoning their cultural values and traditions. This concern raises an important question: What kind of legacy will parents leave for their children as they grow older? This question is further explored in the following section.

Building a Legacy for the Next Generation

As discussed in other chapters, South Sudanese families take pride in preserving individual and family reputations within their community. Culturally, parents must pass on a meaningful legacy to their children, encompassing strong cultural values, positive attitudes, and ethical behaviours. This legacy is closely tied to a sense of collective responsibility and the continuation of lineage, often symbolised by naming children after their parents, grandparents, and ancestors.

As Deng (2009) noted, maintaining a good name is vital for achieving a permanent identity and influence within South Sudanese society. Respect, deeply woven into South Sudanese culture, is inseparable from one's identity, dignity, and status in the community. It becomes every community member's duty to safeguard others' reputations from being tarnished or defamed (Deng, 2009).

In this study, parents were asked how they wished to be remembered by their children. Most expressed a desire to be remembered as devoted mothers and fathers who worked tirelessly to secure a better future for their children.

"I want my children to remember me as a mother who looked after them very well through guiding, advising them, and doing whatever I could to make them positive people... so that they may do the same

things for their offspring, relatives, and the community. They will remember me, particularly if they can do well (Abuk)."

Others desired to be remembered as role models, caregivers, and protectors who nurtured their children with love and wisdom.

"I would like to be remembered by my children and others as a good role model, nurturing and someone who looked after them. This area needs more research and open discussion since many misunderstandings and misconceptions exist. Sharing information is very important for a proper resettlement of new settlers (Jak)."

Many parents also emphasised that ensuring their children receive a good education is crucial to the legacy they wish to leave.

"I would like to see my children well educated; that is, when they say, 'Thank you, Mum, for not giving up on us and for teaching us to be good and successful or to be who we are today.' I don't want them to remember me as a bad parent but as a good one (Adut)."

As discussed in other chapters, education is highly valued in South Sudanese culture, and the community holds those whose children excel academically in high regard. All the parents in this study shared stories of their struggles during their refugee journeys, motivated by the desire to give their children the opportunity for a world-class education. Many of these parents were denied educational opportunities themselves due to the decades-long civil war in the region now known as the Republic of South Sudan. They now hope their children will make them proud and use their education to support their family members and contribute positively to society.

Although comprehensive research on the educational achievements of South Sudanese migrants in Australia is still lacking, there is evidence that the South Sudanese community is emerging with many graduates compared to other ethnic groups who have been in Australia for much longer. Many South Sudanese parents believe that education will enhance their children's ability to participate fully in their new country.

"I want my children to participate in everything in this country, even in parliament, so that they may say that our mother has made us who we are today (Rose).

As explored in earlier chapters, South Sudanese parents, like other new settlers, often feel powerless when they struggle to control their children's behaviour. Nevertheless, they strongly emphasise leaving a legacy for their children. The comments above outline their aspirations for their children and the kind of legacy they wish to leave. For many, the primary focus is helping their children become successful members of society rather than pursuing personal fulfilment or self-actualisation.

Positive Parenting: Empowering Families and Communities to Navigate Change

As explored in previous chapters, South Sudanese families, particularly parents, are grappling with the challenges of adjusting to new parenting practices and the cultural shifts that come with resettling in Australia. This adjustment has often led to losing confidence in their traditional parenting approaches, as they must abandon the social structures that once upheld their values, beliefs, and strategies (Deng & Pienaar, 2011).

In response, participants in this study offered several recommendations to address these challenges, with a central theme being the empowerment of families and the community as key to overcoming these difficulties. They advocated for open and honest dialogue between their community and service providers to develop appropriate and sustainable support mechanisms, such as education about child protection laws and positive parenting programs. The following summarises these concerns and recommendations.

> *"We want the authorities to listen to parents' concerns and have some dialogue with them. Such dialogue will help find solutions to the challenges facing our community. Parenting training about the laws on children is very important. All we need for our children is for them to have a good future. We are quite strict in not allowing our children to go out as they wish because there are a lot of bad influences out there (Aluel)."*

The call for such discussions and dialogue is crucial, as it could lead to better-tailored support for those struggling with parenting challenges. Achan highlighted these concerns and stressed the importance of collaboration.

> *"We find it very hard to know what to do when our children misbehave because we come from a culture where we discipline them with reasonable force whenever they misbehave, which is not allowed here. Consequently, some of our children have become ill-disciplined and disrespectful and are on the streets. Was the help given to us to bring us here, to fail? The so-called freedom has spoiled many children because children may go out as they wish, and if their parents say anything, they run away. The authorities working with our children need to show us how the alternative disciplining procedures work (Achan)."*

Many participants believed that programs bringing parents together to discuss their parenting challenges could provide valuable opportunities for interaction and mutual support (Deng & Pienaar, 2011). These programs should be designed to meet the specific needs of families by teaching alternative disciplinary approaches. Adapting to a new environment with different parenting practices can be daunting and depressing for new settlers.

However, previous studies and parenting programs have shown that when new settlers are properly consulted, when their needs, cultural values, and beliefs are understood, and support programs are developed with their involvement, the outcomes are more effective (Deng & Pienaar, 2011; SKIP, 2011; Westoby, 2008). As stated earlier and illustrated by the above comments, many participants suggested equipping parents to tackle their parenting challenges. Empowering the community to resolve some of these issues at their level is significant because it aligns with traditional practices.

"We came from a culture where we used to resolve our issues at family and community levels… we used to have chiefs or sultans. Our community members know who can help in resolving problems. Such people can be identified here and organised to help… A basic agreement can be drawn up in conjunction with Australian laws and some of our cultural values to be used by the appointed mediators (South Sudanese) in the community. This can help minimise the issues, especially for young people who are always having trouble with the always have (Deng)."

Another participant echoed these sentiments, emphasising the importance of involving community elders to mentor struggling younger parents.

> *"Open and honest discussion within the family and community about parenting challenges is critical. Older people also need to provide support or mentoring to younger people. Parenting training is strongly recommended. Parents need to share experiences and ideas on their parenting challenges. Parents do not have to fear that if they ask for help, they will be labelled as bad parents. Elders and wise people need to be engaged in helping parents and young people. There are a lot of misunderstandings and misconceptions about the new settlers in the wider Australian community, in which some consider African/South Sudanese to be hostile to their children. Nobody can hurt his or her child intentionally, but they think that we abuse our kids. There is a need to share cultures within the wider Australian community. A program that provides cross-cultural experience is paramount. Service providers and most people within the wider Australian community know very little about the good parts of our cultures. Sometimes, they get their information about our culture through negative media about poverty, violence, or war (Jak)."*

Despite these challenges, some South Sudanese parents lack knowledge about where to take their children for leisure and extra-curricular activities, leading to conflicts between parents and their children.

> *"We strongly need parenting support such as positive parenting training, workshops, and even going out camping with our children. Sometimes our children say they are bored at home and need to go out (Bol)."*

There was a strong emphasis on parents needing to solve their parenting challenges by setting up communal spaces where they can socialise and share experiences. However, participants also noted that they have become more individualised and scattered across different suburbs, making it harder to support one another.

> "Parents need to create a parents' club, which may not need many resources: a place where parents can go to share their experiences of their parenting styles as well as how they are overcoming the parenting challenges. The problem is we are becoming very individualised, and we don't even care so much about others but only about our own children. People are not sharing ideas as they used to in South Sudan (Ngor)."

Despite the challenges, the resilience of many participants shines through. They believe that solutions to their parenting challenges can be found within their families and communities. They stress the importance of taking action before placing all the blame on authorities. Their suggestion of working together in discussions and brainstorming sessions to identify possible solutions for their resettlement issues and challenges is a testament to their unwavering determination. This strength in the face of adversity is truly inspiring.

> "There are things we can do as families, parents, or community to resolve some issues affecting us before we blame the authorities. We have to accept that we are in a new environment. Therefore, let us change our culture to cope with the current challenges. There is a need for discussions about these challenges and to find ways of resolving them (Yar)."

Some participants identified the importance of having community centres where parents can share their experiences and support one another. There was also an emphasis on empowering the community and creating a better understanding of South Sudanese culture by employing its most educated members in relevant support sectors.

> *"The way parents can be helped is to employ some of our community members to work in different sectors, particularly with social workers, counsellors, police, and other relevant sectors. Having our community members in these sectors will help address some of the problems facing parents, families, and the community in general since they will better understand our cultures and have greater inside knowledge about the current issues and challenges (Rose)."*

Participants consistently stated their belief in the power of community support. They emphasized that if their community is empowered, community leaders and members can help resolve some family issues, such as domestic violence, through acting as mediators. They identified the need for community support, particularly from elders, and advocated for positive parenting training as an essential solution to their challenges. This collective action and support from the community, demonstrating the power of unity, are crucial in addressing the complex issues faced by South Sudanese families in Australia.

Conclusion

This chapter has highlighted the resilience and adaptability of South Sudanese families as they navigate the challenges of resettlement in Australia. Their strategies, rooted in a deep respect for their cultural heritage while adapting to new societal norms, are essential for a successful transition. The participants' voices have underscored the importance of understanding, support, and collaboration between the South Sudanese community, government agencies, and support services.

Central to this discussion is the participants' call for culturally appropriate support. They emphasise the need for support that respects and integrates South Sudanese cultural values with Australian laws and expectations. Participants strongly desire educational programs and workshops that bridge the gap between traditional and contemporary parenting practices, empowering parents to navigate the complexities of raising children in a new environment.

The chapter has also emphasised the significance of community leadership, the blending of cultural practices, and the role of parents as role models in shaping the next generation. The participants recognise their challenges and are committed to embracing the changes within their families and communities. South Sudanese parents are adapting to their new environment and laying a strong foundation for their children's future.

As the chapter concludes, it calls for continued dialogue and collaboration to ensure South Sudanese families receive the support they need to thrive in Australia. The legacy they leave for their children, built on a balance of traditional values and new opportunities, will testify to their strength and resilience in the face of change. This emphasis on continued support is essential for the audience to understand the ongoing needs of South Sudanese families and to feel the urgency of their continued involvement.

CHAPTER ELEVEN

Navigating Challenges and Embracing Educational Opportunities

Introduction

Education is a cornerstone in the lives of South Sudanese and African diaspora families, serving as more than a tool for economic advancement. It becomes vital for preserving cultural identity, ensuring intergenerational continuity, and fostering community cohesion in new and unfamiliar environments. For these families, education transcends academic achievement; it symbolises hope for a prosperous future and connects their rich cultural heritage to the demands of their new society.

This chapter examines the deep significance education holds for South Sudanese and other African diaspora families, particularly in the context of migration. It explores the challenges these communities face in navigating the educational systems of their host countries, such as language barriers, cultural differences, socioeconomic hurdles, and discrimination. These obstacles are compounded by the complexities of adapting to a new environment while striving to preserve cultural values. Understanding these dynamics provides a clearer picture of the educational journeys undertaken by diaspora children, whose success is often rooted in the collective efforts of their families and communities.

Moreover, this chapter highlights strategies for fostering academic success within these communities, emphasising the critical role that parental involvement, community support, and culturally responsive schools play in shaping positive outcomes for students. The chapter underscores the transformative potential of education as a pathway to academic and personal success while preserving cultural identity. These strategies include creating community centres for sharing experiences and support, employing community members in relevant support sectors, and advocating for culturally appropriate educational programs and workshops.

As we delve into the intersection of education, cultural preservation, and diaspora life, we aim to shed light on education's integral role in shaping the future of South Sudanese and African youth in the diaspora. It is a vehicle for individual achievement and a means of retaining cultural pride and continuity across generations.

The Vital Role of Education in Diaspora Communities

People often assume that new parents, especially among the South Sudanese community and other African diasporas, see education primarily as a means to get ahead economically. However, for most parents, education represents something more significant: a source of social, cultural, and generational continuity. It is a reliable modality that ensures generational continuity, and parents often describe how help from older generations, especially grandparents, allowed them to get through school.

Asking about a family's experience with education quickly becomes a shared moment of learning about how these families persevered through scarcity, conflict and marginalisation. Parents became teachers in refugee camps, children moved in and out of farm schools or schools that turned into refugee camps, and others left everything behind in pursuit of the promise of better education.

The family I have been interacting with in the diaspora for about two decades and a half had experienced all these things, and the experience of surviving shaped how they approached and valued education. For our own children, education was the answer to a brighter future, said one of the parents during my research interview. Most of the refugee parents I got to know identified the shame of illiteracy as one of the most complex parts of their existence when they were living in camps and then in their newly adopted countries.

People who had never been to school felt self-conscious around their peers during daily tasks, especially when filling out forms for rations or other aid. As parents, they worked relentlessly to ensure their children were never made to feel like they did not fit in or were somehow less. Learning was seen as the antidote to feelings of inferiority and inadequacy. It offered a rare sense of self-reliance and anti-dependency in a world where it became clear that they no longer held sway.

Education is treated as a near-sacred endeavour. Parents and (grand)parents might sell land or use other resources to get their children to school or even to become scholars. The wellbeing of the wider family or community is often considered bound up in educational success and failure. Such pride in educational accomplishments highlights that the rewards of success might be inappropriately appropriated by only the student, denying the wider group the benefits of hard work.

For diaspora families, education also assumes an added element of importance. It becomes a (often critical) vehicle of transition into a different and challenging sociocultural and economic milieu in an adoptive nation. Children who do well academically are likely to be better able to conform to the demands of the host country's social, cultural and economic texture, for instance, being sensitive to and acquiring the language and cultural skills and socialisation in social networks that are critical to success in a competitive environment.

Education thus also provides children with a sense of retention and anchoring in their strangely familiar diasporic world. Education in this context assumes added significance. It becomes a wellspring of achievement and a maternal act of self-preservation, ensuring that the offspring in a diasporic milieu continue to help perpetuate the culture of their kinsmen and kinswomen back home – their very roots.

Moreover, it is an intergenerational imperative as parents invest in transferring their dreams for a better life in the host country via their children's education. For parents who have left their home countries, one indirect result of that decision to migrate has been the chance for their children to gain access to education that may be otherwise unattainable. This intergenerational aspect of schooling promotes stability within families that might feel otherwise torn apart.

Having something that keeps the family together, regardless of one's age, level of educational attainment, or familiarity with the host country's cultural context, provides some sense of continuity between the families' past in the home country and their present in the host country all of which is of more excellent value than the daily struggles of living as a migrant. In this manner, having children in school can also become a means of family cohesion, a shared goal for families to come together.

Education is also crucial because it is believed that doors that were once closed would be opened, and opportunities would be available if you had more education. For many South Sudanese and other diaspora African families, education presents the opportunity to have finances to get themselves out of poverty, be secure economically, and open up more chances at better jobs and higher careers. This belief is also perpetuated by parents who would have experienced limited educational opportunities in their own countries because of conflict, discrimination or economic hardship. This way, parents desire to provide their children with the necessary academic tools to push against these barriers and gain greater opportunities.

However, the pressure to succeed in university does not come without difficulties. The educational system becomes opaque for families as they struggle with an unfamiliar landscape laden with new norms, expectations, and values. They also struggle to overcome the barriers that different cultures and languages may create. Nonetheless, such commitment to education is unwavering as the high stakes of 'making it' in the diaspora continue to drive families toward pursuing the diasporic dream.

Educational Challenges for South Sudanese and African Diaspora Families

Parents and relatives from South Sudan and the diaspora generally see education as 'the golden ladder', but different challenges often hinder student success. These challenges usually involve multiple layers of culture, language, and social and economic factors, intersecting in complicated and frequently unpredictable ways.

Overcoming Language Barriers

The central barrier is access to English (or the language of the host country); many South Sudanese and other African families speak a language other than English as their first language in the home. As a result, children are expected to learn, communicate, and excel in school in a language that may be foreign to them.

Children can be disadvantaged at school if they are unfamiliar with the language of instruction. This can prevent them from understanding lessons, completing homework or asking questions in the classroom. All these factors can contribute to low self-confidence, frustration, and shame. Furthermore, classroom assessment can negatively reflect the lack of command of the language of instruction. Young children who do not handle the language of instruction well are more likely to be disadvantaged in standardised tests and examinations that rely heavily on language skills. So, this can undoubtedly affect their overall performance in class and their prospects for promotion.

Language issues impact a child's academic achievements, social interactions, and relationships with peers and teachers. Non-native speakers of the language of instruction may be reluctant to explore the school culture and become involved socially. This makes such pupils more isolated and prone to feeling excluded. This fragmented and isolated experience may be particularly pronounced for children recently coming to the host country. Newly arrived children are often unfamiliar with the cultural norms and expectations of their new school and culture.

Language hurdles may include parents' inability to communicate effectively with teachers and school personnel. This includes their lack of ability to advocate for their children and support students' learning behaviours and academic growth. For instance, when parents do not speak fluent English, they might miss communicating with school officials about school policies and procedures, be unable to participate in parent-teacher conferences, access resources and support services, or have a disconnect between the home and school.

However, language development challenges need to be proactively addressed at home - either by parents taking their kids to language support programs that could immensely benefit children, practise language at home and interact with native speakers, and look to the school for tutoring, language classes or bilingual support or by parents trying to improve their own language skills for better communication with the school and for better supporting their child's studies.

Navigating Cultural Differences

Cultural differences between home and school can be an issue for children from South Sudanese and other African families as well. Expectations of what children should do, how they should behave, the goals of education and its processes, norms of deference or authority, and who takes responsibility for learning might all be quite different in the host country's education systems from those of the child's culture of origin. In many African cultures, education is seen as a collective endeavour for which the family and community are responsible. In contrast, many of the world's education systems place high value on individual effort and achievement, as well as on independence and self-reliance.

Not surprisingly, such cultural differences underpin multiple sources of misunderstanding and friction among children, parents and teachers. For instance, while parents might be sceptical about their children's abilities, attributes and achievements, the school is expected to provide an accurate report. In most African cultures, likewise, children are trained to be deferential to authority and to value respect and obedience more than self-expression. This might create considerable tension in a school setting that promotes independent thinking, questioning, and critical engagement. The conflict arises because children might struggle to reconcile what they have been taught to value at home with what they might encounter at school. In short, children could experience cultural dissonance between inherent core values and those acquired at school.

Other cultural differences can show how education is valued in the family. Many South Sudanese and other African parents will be strict and insistent on rote learning and discipline as essential to academic success. Those approaches are not valued in Western educational systems, which emphasise critical thinking, creativity, and problem-solving more. This mismatch in educational philosophy can place significant stress on a child who has to manage between two sets of expectations.

Furthermore, a family must have a way to keep open lines of communication with teachers and school principals to facilitate the discussion of and agree on these cultural differences. Communication in both directions from parents to the school about 'home' and from the school back to the parents about 'school' enables the formation of a proper understanding of the expectations of each set of institutions. Another helpful response is for parents to convey to their children that there is no need for shame about their different cultural values and even that their cultural identity can serve as a source of pride and strength when they encounter challenges moving forward in school.

Third, schools can respond to cultural differences by educating teachers about culturally responsive teaching. Culturally responsive teaching entails making the classroom culture engrossing and open to diverse perspectives and designing teaching and learning strategies attuned to the student's diverse cultural backgrounds. For example, the teacher can include stories, literature, and historical examples in the classroom that engage pupils from African cultures or create spaces for learners to share their cultural perspectives and experiences. By making and bringing in this kind of classroom stimulants and designs, the school can bridge the environment and context within the home and the classroom, enhancing and supporting all students' educational success.

Addressing Socioeconomic Challenges

Despite the specific socioeconomic challenges facing South Sudanese and African families in the black diaspora, these families toil with great fortitude in their commitment to their children's academic success. Families facing financial hardships, including low income, unemployment, and unpredictable resource access, can limit educational opportunities. Despite this, families prioritise educational materials, technology, and extracurricular activities in their efforts to achieve academic success. Children from low-income families, despite the additional stressors experienced, such as food insecurity, housing instability or having to become caregivers at home, continue to achieve and persevere in their schooling (Deng, 2016a; Maher et al., 2018).

The family's limited financial resources in the diaspora means that children do not have the necessary resources to excel. This could be due to not having access to textbooks or supplies or a computer or the internet that is often needed to be able to complete assignments and participate in class. The family might be unable to afford extracurricular activities, such as sports, music lessons or tutoring, that might be vital to their children's development.

Socioeconomic realities can also provoke animo, as children may face stresses that put conditions for learning and their wellbeing at risk. As we have seen with food insecurity, children who live in poverty are more likely to worry over their inability to provide adequately for themselves and their loved ones than their non-poor peers, and they might have a more challenging time paying attention and learning in school. Some children in poverty live with housing instability, worrying over moves from one furnished, temporary rental to the next and perhaps lacking a stable refuge where they can find stability, relaxation and healthy sleep, all key to their ability to learn. Some children in poverty lose time and energy to managing household responsibilities that include watching younger siblings or even working a part-time job to help pay the bills.

Parents can rest by creating a home environment that strongly focuses on education, provides students with the necessary resources, and encourages them to succeed and embrace their studies. It is also important for parents to reach out to the community for additional resources or help when needed, such as financial assistance, food programs, or after-school programs. Schools and the community can play an important role in accessing the materials students need for school, such as school supplies, tutoring, or scholarships. School could be a significant factor that contributes to students' success. Parents play an active role in their children's academic success.

Confronting Discrimination and Bias

Other out-group factors, such as discrimination and bias that occur both within the school and in society, might also impact children's academic achievement, especially from South Sudanese and African students. For example, children might face racial or ethnic discrimination from classmates or teachers, which in turn may or might not be significantly associated with autonomy, self-perceived competence, self-esteem, affectivity, personal responsibility, social responsibility, and academic achievement. Discrimination might manifest itself in someone not being served in a restaurant, being beaten, receiving a false accusation or being stereotyped.

Discrimination and other forms of bias can be particularly harmful to children. Children who experience disadvantages or discrimination can perceive themselves as outside the 'mainstream' or might feel unwanted or disliked, leading to decreased motivation or engagement at school. Stress, anxiety, or depression can also lead to lower academic productivity. In the worst cases, children who experience discrimination can adopt negative stereotypes about themselves, leading them to become less confident in their own academic abilities.

Likewise, bias can impact children from South Sudanese and other African families by limiting their education and training options. For example, children can be denied admission to gifted- or advanced-studies programmes, sports or other extra-curricular activities, and either formal or informal leadership opportunities that would otherwise facilitate their academic and developmental growth and provide them with a sense of inclusion and belonging.

Parents have a role to play; they can stand up for their kids and their rights. With their guidance and help, parents can partner with a child's school and build an environment where the young person can speak out against discrimination, turn to adults they trust if targeted or bullied, and appreciate their cultural heritage with pride. It is essential that schools and educators also take responsibility for addressing discrimination and enhancing diversity and inclusion in the school environment. However, parents can make a difference in creating a culture of support and inclusion for school kids.

Classroom teachers are critical in combatting discrimination and bias since they can create an atmosphere that encourages the exchange of ideas and the sharing of diverse cultural aspects, encourages students to challenge stereotypes and prejudice, and promotes respect and inclusivity among their students. Due to their efforts in creating learning environments that are safe and inviting for all, classroom teachers will help students of various backgrounds realise their academic potential and enjoy the educational experience. Classroom teachers are an important asset in the fight against discrimination and bias. Their role is not only confined to teaching but extends to that of a student mentor and a role model.

Effective Strategies for Promoting Academic Success

Despite these hurdles, several approaches exist to fostering children's success in South Sudanese and other African families in the diaspora. These approaches encompass a blend of home, community, and school involvement.

The Power of Parental Involvement

Parental involvement is one of the most critical components in children's academic success. Studies show that children of parents who are involved in their education generally have better academic performance, a more positive attitude towards school, and higher self-efficacy. This emphasises the vital role that parents can play in their children's educational success.

A fundamental strategy in the parents' control is creating an emotionally supportive home environment for their kids' educational pursuits. That might mean setting aside a specific, quiet workspace at a kitchen table at a specific time every night after dinner when they can do their homework. Alternatively, it might mean providing stationery supplies and creating access to textbooks and other instructional materials or resources. It might also mean providing encouragement and praise for their education so their kids understand they are supported in their learning efforts. For instance, parents can also model learning-positive attitudes and behaviours for their children by committing to their educational pursuits, such as aspiring to learn another language.

In addition to providing a supportive home environment for their children, parents can help foster academic success by contacting the school. Schools often hold events such as parent-teacher conferences where parents have the opportunity to talk to teachers about their children's learning and progress. It can also be helpful for parents to keep track of their children's learning at school so that they can help with their homework at home. If parents feel like their children are not doing well in school, they need to speak to their child's teacher or the principal to address any problems and make a plan to improve their child's performance.

Still, another behaviour is supporting their interests and passions. Children with interests and passions invest more time studying the topics or activities they are most drawn toward. Parents play a role in supporting their children's interests and passions by providing opportunities for them to engage with their interests, signing them up for extracurricular activities, providing books or other resources they might need for their projects, or showing genuine interest in their favourite topics.

Parents can also promote their children's social and emotional capacities, which go hand in hand with academic success. This may involve teaching children social skills, such as how to make friends, resolve conflicts, or cope with stress, and providing emotional support and guidance. Children with strong social and emotional skills are more likely to succeed in school, partly because they can better cope with challenges in the classroom setting and develop positive relationships with peers and teachers.

Harnessing Community Support

Another critical factor in promoting children's school success is community support. Like parents, members of the broader community can offer diaspora South Sudanese and African families support, encouragement and resources for their children's education. Community organisations, cultural groups, and congregations have provided much-needed programmes and services to support children and their families, as well as spaces for children to interact with other diasporic African children and role models and to foster intergenerational conversations about their heritage.

Also, parents can work with the extended community, for instance, coming together with other families who share the same experiences and challenges to build supportive relationships. This includes joining parent groups and cultural organisations or networking with other parents online to provide information and advice, share experiences and support one another. In this way, parents can also support the notion of cultural community and belonging among children by helping build a more comprehensive social network that can, in turn, support their children's learning and help them integrate within an academic environment. In addition to providing material support for the study, community organisations can also help with cultural pride by offering children regular access to cultural celebrations, such as cultural festivals, religious events, or community celebrations for families. In turn, a strong sense of cultural identity can help children to integrate with their new families and peers and the wider community in their new country of residence positively and successfully.

These same organisations could help South Sudanese and African families in schools and advocate for their needs within the education system by working with schools to ensure culturally responsive teaching and demanding that school curricula incorporate culturally relevant perspectives. They could also train teachers and other school staff on how to interact with parents. Both community organisations and schools might succeed by working together to create a school environment where everyone feels like an essential part of the community.

Building Partnerships with Schools

Supportive relationships with schools are essential for children's pursuit of academic success. Schools and their personnel are individually and collectively key players as children develop in educational attainment that indiscriminately caters to the needs of all children. For South Sudanese and diaspora African families, relationships with schools involve their effective and supportive collaboration with the school system and its staff.

Parents can work with schools through participation in their child's education (attending parent-teacher conferences or other school-related activities), and by working with the school on their child's needs (e.g., language barriers, cultural differences, discrimination), and in helping to ensure that the child's culture is respected and valued by that school (e.g., sharing information about the cultural background, attending cultural events, and influencing the curriculum to reflect diverse perspectives).

Schools can also work with families to create a climate by providing opportunities for parents to be involved in children's education. Examples of this might include having parent-teacher conferences, regular communications on children's progress, or hosting workshops or resources for parents. School systems can better partner with families by creating family-friendly environments to support children's academic success.

Fostering a Growth Mindset

Another key strategy in helping children develop a love of learning is encouraging a growth mindset, which is the idea that one's intelligence and abilities can change and grow through effort, practice, and learning. Kids with a growth mindset are more likely to see challenges as something to embrace, work through, learn from and see failure as an opportunity to learn rather than a reflection of their abilities.

Nevertheless, parents can nurture a growth mindset in straightforward, simple-to-implement ways. For instance, they can praise specific strategies and pay special attention to their child's efforts. Rather than saying, 'Wow, you are so smart; you got an A,' parents can say something like ', I am really proud of how hard you worked on your project. I knew you could do it when you put your mind to it.' Similarly, parents can encourage their children by acknowledging their challenges and anxieties when tackling new things.

Research has shown that children whose parents shared learning and growth experiences were less likely to give up on complex tasks and were more willing to stretch their abilities in new situations. The claim that effort, practice and learning make people more capable foreshadowed the scientific notion of a plastic brain. Parents can also model a growth mindset by sharing stories about times they made mistakes and how they learned from those experiences. They can provide their children with challenging and varied experiences that are beyond their comfort zone, and they can encourage them to engage in new activities, even if they seem like they might be difficult.

Secondly, schools might convey a growth mindset by having a culture that promotes taking risks, exploration, and problem-solving. For instance, they might give students hands-on learning experiences or opportunities to work together on projects. No matter what, schools can help all students cultivate a growth mindset by having a culture that values effort.

Nurturing Cultural Pride and Identity

Instilling cultural pride and identity is equally important to support your child's academic success. A tight connection to your cultural heritage and tradition for South Sudanese and African young people in the diaspora is often a source of stability and support in students' lives. It gives your child a sense of belonging and self-worth, which could also be a locus of self-regulation when facing academic challenges. You can ensure that your child has a tight connection to their culture by celebrating your traditional cultural celebrations and holidays, sharing their cultural history, and encouraging your child's cultural pride. You may want to participate in cultural events (e.g., festivals, religious celebrations) or family gatherings and share stories, music and art from their culture. A robust cultural identity will help your child to develop a positive view of themselves and foster a sense of pride and belonging in the school culture.

Schools can promote cultural pride and identity by developing a curriculum that reflects students' histories and perspectives and teaching in ways consistent with students' cultural needs. For instance, schools can include stories, literature, and historical examples from South Sudanese and African cultures in the curriculum and provide opportunities for students to share their own cultural experiences and perspectives or stories. When a school creates a culturally responsive learning environment, it can support the achievement of all students.

The Critical Role of Schools and Educators in Academic Success

Schools and educators have crucial roles in supporting South Sudanese and African students in the diaspora to thrive in their learning. This involves creating safe and supportive learning environments that enable students to build connections with one another and with the local community. To create these environments, teachers must commit to equity, diversity, and inclusion.

Embracing Culturally Responsive Teaching

Culturally responsive teaching acknowledges and values all students' cultural backgrounds and experiences. It aims to foster a curriculum that embraces diverse perspectives and adopts a teaching style that resonates with the learning needs of students from different cultural backgrounds. Culturally responsive teaching can increase the chance of a more inclusive and supportive learning environment for children from South Sudanese and African families by ensuring their cultural background is respected and valued in the school.

Teachers can use culturally responsive teaching to respond to their students' needs by 1) embedding cultural perspectives into the curriculum, ensuring that new content lasts longer and is revisited, 2) Using culturally responsive teaching materials, ensuring that teaching resources reflect cultural representations of students 3) Create room for students to talk about their feelings and thoughts on the curriculum, 4) Bring in books, stories or podcasts featuring teachers, friends, and family with 'different' characteristics, 5) stories or podcasts from South Sudanese or African cultures 6) Create a project where students learn about or bring in items from their home, or someplace they are from 7) Ancestry project where students interview someone and share their story. Considering these culturally responsive teaching principles is significant, as students will more likely be willing to learn, feel a sense of belonging, and be proud of their roots, which enhances integrating into a new environment and embracing different cultures.

Beyond a culturally responsive curriculum, educators can develop culturally responsive teaching strategies such as using teaching approaches that match their students' cultural values and learning styles, for example, cooperative learning, storytelling, experiential learning, creating classroom spaces for students to experience and appreciate other cultural heritage, for instance, offering opportunities for cultural events, inviting guest speakers, infusing multicultural themes and practices into the lessons.

Empowering English Language Learners

Another critical aspect of promoting academic success for children of South Sudanese and African families is supporting English language learners (ELLs). Language can often be a barrier to academic achievement, so schools must provide the necessary support and tools to ensure ELLs can be successful, too. Schools can provide more language support programmes like English as a Second Language (ESL) classes, tutoring, or bilingual education classes for students. These help the ELLs develop and improve their language skills to succeed academically, gain confidence, and build self-esteem. Furthermore, educators can incorporate some teaching strategies that are responsive to ELLs. These strategies could include using visual aids, allotting more time for assignments, or providing extra help in class.

While support with language is one type of support schools can provide ELLs, schools can also create a welcoming and inclusive environment for the ELLs through providing translation services for parents, providing culturally relevant resources, or providing an opportunity to meet with other peers who have a similar language and culture background. Creating a supportive environment and opportunity for ELLs to succeed will improve academic achievement for ELLs.

Combating Discrimination and Bias

School is essential for this so that children are not afraid of going there to learn and become educated. There also have been issues of racism against South Sudanese and African families within the school environment as a result of discrimination and bias. Teachers and school leaders are responsible for ensuring diversity and promoting equity and inclusion among students within school communities.

Teachers play a crucial role in tackling discrimination and bias. They can make the classroom inviting, challenge stereotypes and prejudices, and encourage students' respectful and inclusive behaviour towards each other. Schools can tackle discrimination and bias through anti-discrimination policies, teacher and staff training, and initiatives that promote diversity and inclusion. This is vital to making schools welcoming spaces for all students.

However, cultural competence for students and staff is not simply a strategy. It is a necessity. While this helps students feel more comfortable with the diversity surrounding them, being sensitised to the culture of others promotes improved relations among ethnic groups, which certainly will foster a more supportive and congenial learning environment for all students. Such an environment may be accomplished through training in cultural awareness and sensitivity, inter-class multicultural exchanges, the development of multicultural clubs, or the infusion of multicultural ideas into the curriculum.

Conclusion

Education remains a powerful tool for South Sudanese and African diaspora families, bridging their cultural heritage and the realities of their host countries. Throughout this chapter, we have explored how education is more than just a pursuit of academic success; it is a vehicle for cultural continuity, social mobility, and personal empowerment. In navigating migration challenges, these families have shown remarkable resilience, overcoming barriers such as language difficulties, cultural dissonance, socioeconomic hardship, and discrimination.

Education, amidst its challenges, stands as a beacon of hope and opportunity. It equips children with the skills to adapt to a new sociocultural landscape while instilling a strong sense of identity and pride in their roots. For parents, investing in their children's education is not just an investment in their future, but also a means of preserving cultural values and reinforcing a sense of intergenerational continuity and communal cohesion.

Schools, families, and communities are critical in this process. Schools must create culturally responsive and inclusive environments, empowering students to thrive academically while embracing their unique backgrounds. Through active involvement and support, families play a pivotal role in shaping their children's educational experiences, instilling a sense of confidence and capability in parents as they reinforce the importance of education as a tool for success. Communities, in turn, offer essential support systems, bridging gaps between the school and home environments.

As we look to the future, it is essential to recognise the transformative power of education in shaping the lives of individuals and entire communities. By fostering an educational environment that embraces diversity, promotes inclusivity, and supports academic achievement, we enable South Sudanese and African youth to navigate the complexities of life in the diaspora while maintaining their connection to their cultural heritage.

Finally, education provides a pathway to greater opportunities, personal growth, and collective success. By embracing the challenges and seizing the opportunities it presents, South Sudanese and African families in the diaspora can ensure that their children succeed academically and carry forward their communities' values, traditions, and aspirations into the future.

CHAPTER TWELVE

Parenting in the Digital Age: Balancing Technological Benefits and Risks for Child Development

Introduction

The digital age has transformed nearly every aspect of daily life, and parenting is no exception. From communication to education and entertainment, technology now plays a pivotal role in shaping how children grow, learn, and interact with the world around them. This transformation adds additional complexity for South Sudanese and African families living in the diaspora. These parents must navigate the challenges of maintaining cultural traditions and values while helping their children adapt to and thrive in a digital environment. This dual responsibility introduces opportunities and risks as technology is increasingly interwoven with family life and child development.

This chapter delves into the intricate relationship between technology and modern parenting, focusing on its effects on child development and family dynamics. It explores the benefits of technology, such as enhanced educational resources and stronger connections to cultural heritage, alongside the potential pitfalls, including screen addiction, exposure to harmful content, and erosion of meaningful family time. By examining how technology influences parenting in the context of migration and acculturation, this chapter seeks to provide practical strategies for parents to help their children navigate the digital landscape responsibly while preserving their cultural identity.

The central question that guides this discussion is: How can parents strike a healthy balance between embracing technology's educational and developmental benefits and protecting their children from its potential risks? In the diaspora, where technology serves as both a bridge to cultural roots and a gateway to new opportunities, finding this balance is crucial. The goal is to equip parents with the tools they need to raise children who are not only digitally literate but also grounded in their cultural identity and well-prepared to navigate the complexities of both the digital world and their cultural environment.

The Role of Technology in Shaping Modern Family Dynamics

The advent of 21st-century technology and, more precisely, its growing centrality to everyday life shapes many aspects of family life. It influences how parents communicate with children, how children learn and entertain themselves, and how families spend leisure time. Indeed, whether it is staying updated with relatives overseas or accomplishing simple daily tasks like communicating with relatives, core moments in the daily life of South Sudanese and, more broadly, African families in the diaspora revolve around technology. This reality raises significant challenges related to the structural use of technology, including managing screen time, fostering a sense of safety and security in one's online environment, and ensuring that children use technology for productive and enriching reasons rather than those that distract from, or negatively impact, their holistic development.

Technology's Role in Strengthening Cultural Connections

One of technology's most significant contributions to diaspora families is its ability to bridge geographic distances, making cultural ties remain as vibrant and resilient as possible regardless of duration, context or location. For most South Sudanese families and other Africans who are physically separated from their homeland and feel estranged from their extended families, technology provides an essential lifeline that keeps families and cultures together. This role of technology in preserving cultural connections is not just a convenience but a reassurance that families can remain strong and connected, no matter the distance.

For example, WhatsApp, Zoom, Facebook and other platforms that enable users to set up virtual calls are vital to families who want to communicate and interact with relatives in their home country. These platforms allow relatives and friends to speak, share photos and videos, celebrate cultural milestones in real time, and make family members feel part of a close-knit community. Video calls allow users to see and hear each other in impossible ways, even with the standard letter or even the phone call. Such a feeling of belonging is a powerful tool that could bring families together to restore global unity, fostering a sense of connection and support among family members.

In addition, technology offers access to a wide array of cultural content related to her heritage, including traditional music, films, literature, and news from the parent's country of origin, which are widely captured and available online. Engaging with this kind of content includes having children's videos or phone conference sessions with parents or grandparents back home. Watching documentaries about the history of the child's home country, listening to traditional African music and joining a social-media forum or group that discusses topics relevant to that country can all help children learn about their cultural heritage, understand how life is lived in their homeland, or learn about their place of origin, and thus reinvigorate their connection to cultural identity.

Educational Opportunities and Challenges Presented by Technology

Technology is also changing the learning landscape for children, offering them an almost unlimited selection of learning resources, tools, and materials. For South Sudanese and African families who move to new countries with different educational expectations, technology can be a valuable source of support to help their children through learning challenges associated with language, cultural differences, and education.

Children can learn English, History, or any subject of their choice adaptively and speedily through interactive eBooks and educational apps on a tablet or a smartphone. Numerous video tutorials on Khan Academy or Coursera allow children to learn at their own pace and interact with the material in a different way that will capture their attention (Bhatt & Hackney, 2014). Children can adjust to a new educational system with new language skills with greater ease, or children struggling to keep up with peers in certain subjects can access online courses and additional resources that will help them catch up. For example, a newcomer to an English-speaking country might start learning English through language-learning apps, such as Duolingo, which deliver personalised lessons in an engaging and fun way (Shortt et al., 2023).

Technology can also help children explore their cultural education, particularly relevant in the diaspora. Kids can watch videos about their homeland, opt to take free language courses online, watch documentaries featuring their culture and heritage, tour world exhibits and museums virtually and more. Parents can present these digital and digitised resources to their children and help them cultivate a worldview that encourages them to view the world through the lens.

Studies have shown that individuals who actively engage in their cultural learning with the support of their parents have more profound insights and an enriched understanding of their cultural identity. Parents can guide their children in finding these resources, empower them to own their cultural learning and open new doors of exploration and self-discovery.

However, even as we appreciate the possibilities technology brings to learning, it is crucial to recognise that the risk factors associated with technology may outweigh the benefits. While technology can bring countless learning opportunities to the classroom, from student-led inquiry to connecting with peers across the globe, the use of technology also brings a high risk of those using it being distracted by games, misinformation or exposure to inappropriate content. With all the benefits that come from technology, there is undoubtedly a cost associated with it, especially when students have the opportunity to overuse devices recreationally and at a young age without any limit.

Excessive screen time leads to physical inactivity in children who might otherwise prefer more active outlets such as outdoor sports, creative arts, or social activities. It can also result in social isolation or difficulty making friends. Excessive screen time use also restricts students' ability to practise and develop essential life skills and competencies such as thinking critically, solving problems, and modulating and regulating emotions. The overload of online information makes it difficult for children to evaluate sources and distinguish between reliable information and inaccurate, biased sources.

Nevertheless, parents can help their children set their agendas so that the use of digital resources is balanced, and purposeful balance parents can advocate for that can make them less anxious and more in control. This might take some work, of course: it would likely include putting firm boundaries on screen time, practising mindful limits and breaks from devices and digital content, and encouraging children to engage in the full spectrum of activities that support physical and cognitive development. With a well-balanced agenda, parents can feel confident, and kids can maximise the benefits of technology in their education.

The Impact of Technology on Family Communication

Technology has undoubtedly made it easier for families to communicate, offering new ways of staying in touch, sharing experiences, and maintaining relationships. There is evidence that technology could bring families closer together and may provide ways for South Sudanese and African families to come to terms with acculturation issues, identity, and a foreign environment to communicate and bridge the generation gap.

Digital means of communication, including messaging apps, social networks, and video calling platforms, are increasingly used by family members to keep in close touch when living geographically apart. Of course, we can think of many scenarios, but one that immediately comes to mind is a family with some of its members living in other parts of the world due not only to immigration but also to work, college, or school.

With the help of applications such as WhatsApp or Viber that enable messages to be sent for free instantly, one parent may check in regularly with their child at midday, ascertaining whether they are all right and then learning more about their day. Family members could also have face-to-face conversations via video calls made using popular applications such as Skype or Zoom for more substantial exchanges, offering the opportunity to see expressions and share moments in real-time, even though family members might be thousands of miles away.

They can post pictures and videos and keep in touch with their extended families through the photos and videos they share, creating a sense of closeness and engagement. These platforms can also be used to celebrate cultural events such as holidays, birthdays or achievements. For diaspora families, social media can be a tool that helps connect them to their cultural community, where they can interact and discuss issues and engage with news and events from their country of origin.

However, an even greater danger is that those augmented forms of digital togetherness may become a substitute for actual face-to-face family interactions. For parent-child families that have become increasingly digital, especially those that are more passive in their use of new media technology, the risk exists that they might begin valuing their relationships through the artificial medium of the screen over the actual medium of family life itself: the family dinner table and conversation, family gatherings and togetherness, and the soft rhythm of shared family beginnings and endings.

The fears that new technology flattens the experience of the world and that digital renderings offer substitutes and simulations for the richer, fuller, more robust reality of living it out in the real world are real. Furthermore, for those families who might be substituting more monitored, directed, and filtered relationships with others via new and social media instead of real, human-to-human interaction face-to-face, these fears may well turn into realities.

Parents can create tech-free zones in the home, such as the living room or dining room, where no technology is allowed. They can also designate tech-free times when specific family members must live without devices. For example, a family might make the dining room tech-free and have everyone put their devices away during meals to focus on conversation or bonding, or parents might rule that the bedroom space or particular hours of the day are off-limits to devices. When tech-free zones or times are created at home, children are less likely to view technology as a threat to the family.

Balancing Screen Time and Family Time

One of the biggest problems of parenting in the era of digital technology is how to balance screen time and family time, as technology has many benefits, such as aiding learning and enjoyment and as a means of social contact. However, there are many adverse consequences of excessive use of computers, phones and tablets, and this can harm the child's physical and mental health, leading to their deprivation in essential aspects of their social connections in the family, which can seriously impair the quality of their lives.

Spending too much time with screens can have serious health risks for children, including obesity, poor sleep and eye strain. Too much screen time can also mean too little physical activity, contributing to social isolation and difficulties with communication, problem-solving and emotional regulation skills necessary to navigate life away from the screen still further. The risks are even more significant in the digital age when most children start spending time on screens early and when it can be too easy to spend an unhealthy proportion of their lives online.

One way to achieve this balance would be for parents to put rules in place regarding how many hours each day their child can access screens and explore various other activities that will fulfil the child's developmental needs. For example, a child's exposure to screens could be limited to no more than one hour a day, and to achieve the remaining time, activate a different set of physical, social, and life skills by focusing or participating in play outdoors, playing a game such as hanging basketball rings or a board game that does not include a screen, or for older kids walking or riding bicycles and for older kids playing recreational sports.

Parents can complement boundaries and limits on screen-time use by modelling and co-experiencing healthy technology and sharing their experiences with their children. They can practise what they preach and strive to become role models for what it means to set boundaries and priorities while co-experiencing with their kids a 'real' world of stimulating interactions that do not get 'stolen' by or disconnected from real-time interactions and play. For example, they can use social media as little as possible, rarely check emails at home during family time, or disregard or postpone them as necessary. They may arrange family activities such as cooking, gardening or playing board games together. In this manner, parents can model healthy behaviour to optimise the benefits, limit the health-related risks of technology use for their children, and limit the intrusion of screens in the domain of family life and family interactions.

Recognising and Managing Risks in the Digital World

On the one hand, there are many advantages to today's technology. Still, on the other hand, serious harm to children could arise as they remain online in schools for longer hours and are vulnerable to online hazards. Hazards can be available unless many vigilant methods are employed to contain online settings for children and mould their parents and teachers as morally solid role models. For South Sudanese and many African families, these hazards could range from cyberbullying, pornography and foul language, with overexposure to technology or, worse, online predators representing life's most significant risks.

Addressing Cyberbullying and Online Harassment

Children and teenagers are increasingly communicating on social media and through messaging apps. While these sites allow young people to create and share content, they can also be used as weapons. Sending hurtful messages, spreading rumours or making threats of physical and emotional abuse can break a child's spirit, tearing down a long-held vision of a supportive, caring world.

Migrant children, or children in a broader situation of cultural shift, may also have a peculiar vulnerability to cyberbullying: their appearance, language or cultural practices may make them targets of ridicule, contributing to feelings of shame, perhaps foreignness, and fear that children and youth in their peer group will identify them as different or inferior. The humiliation and public nature of the harassment can be visible to the child's peers, and the difficulty of 'walking away' from a computer or phone screen are hallmarks of this new form of abuse.

Parents can use digital tools to protect their children from online bad behaviour. For example, they can teach their kids about cyberbullying and answer their questions. They can explain the risks associated with digital technology to their children and demonstrate how to protect their online privacy and safety from abusive behaviour. They can teach their children how to configure their social media accounts to prevent others from abusing them online, including privacy settings and blocking or reporting abusive users. They can also explain how to spot and react to digital abuse.

Parents can also help their kids speak up if they experience or witness this kind of abuse. This can be a particularly challenging conversation for parents and children because the child might think that they and their friends and relatives are to blame for the abuse. They might believe that, somehow, they deserve how they are treated.

So, parents can reassure their children that people are not perfect; they make mistakes.

Parents can also offer education and support to their children in order to help them avoid the pitfalls of online abuse or bullying. At the same time, it is essential for parents to proactively monitor their kids' online activities and opportunities for abuse. This could mean reviewing their Facebook posts regularly, perusing apps and sites they use, and implementing parental controls that block particular material.

Dealing with Inappropriate Content and Potential Harm

For every educational, entertaining and uplifting article on the web, there is one that can be inappropriate, hurtful or ugly, including violent or pornographic content, hate speech, conspiracy theories and even fake news. All this has the potential to hinder a child's development and health. Seeing that sort of material may have damaging consequences, for instance, causing children anxiety and confusion or desensitising them to violence or other socially unacceptable behaviours. Exposure to online disinformation might also crowd their understanding of the world or make distinguishing between factual claims and fiction harder.

Parents can use parental controls, filters and monitoring tools to prevent their children from viewing explicit and obscene content to prevent them from accessing certain websites and apps, as these can help safeguard children and provide a family-friendly environment. Parental controls and filters forbid children from using sites or apps classified as not for their age. At the same time, monitoring websites can prevent children from accessing pages where obscene or harmful material is available.

Alongside utilising the technological tools available to protect their children, parents can converse with their children about the different types of content they might come across online and the steps they could take if they do find a scene online that makes them uncomfortable: they could question what they were observing; they could explore if the information is correct or not; they could contact their parent if they have any queries or reservations. Consequently, conversations can provoke openness, where children know they can assertively engage with dad and mum over the challenges they may encounter online.

It creates a permissible environment where children feel reassured that their responsibility will not be reduced because they have witnessed sexually explicit content online. Instead, they can pose any queries to their parents, who will cater to their questions constructively. It generates a purposeful atmosphere where children have acquired the best tools to cope with the realities of cyberspace, correctly identifying how they can have fun with their peers online while practising wisdom and thoroughness in their online explorations.

Protecting Against Online Predators and Their Threats
Children are vulnerable to online predators, who use the comfortable air of anonymity of the internet to coax, manipulate and exploit particularly susceptible kids. An excellent example of this type of threat is the efforts of so-called paedophiles to lure young people into sexual activity through dating and gaming sites, social media platforms, or online messaging apps.

Perhaps our greatest fear is of the online predator. Not only do a high percentage of children report scary stuff online, but half of them also know someone who has been confronted online by a predator. One distressing problem is the predator's vote of confidence. A man might, for example, take the role of a peer or an adult, attempting to win over a child with toxic flattery, playing on a child's need to please adults, or convincing her to like him with gifts or talking about shared interests. Then he will escalate. As a child becomes attached to her online friend, this frightening stranger will lure her into intimacy, showering her affection, sharing secrets and forming a deep bond with her, leading her to believe she is safe. In real life, a predator would typically attempt to influence a child's habits so that she is home alone for more and more hours. He would gain possession of her trust, then pressure her for more details about herself or send photographs of herself, eventually blackmailing her into more dangerous territory.

Parents need to teach their children not to share their names, addresses, phone numbers or school information to avoid falling victim to an online predator and to recognise the warning signs of predatory behaviour, such as someone who asks them to send a photo, makes inappropriate comments, or requests an in-person meeting.

If your child does get into a situation online with somebody who makes them nervous or puts them in danger, they should feel able to speak to their parents about it. By developing a level of trust with your child and making sure that the lines of communication remain open between you both, the chances of them feeling embarrassed about asking for help if they need it are reduced.

In addition, parents can monitor their children's online activities and use parental controls to filter access to certain content or notions and block users who may engage in unscrupulous or potentially damaging behaviour. Through information and engagement, parents can mitigate some of the risks of children encountering predatory online paedophiles and ensure safer and more positive experiences overall.

Fostering Digital Literacy and Responsible Online Behaviours
Children should be developing digital literacy and responsibility in today's digital world. Digital literacy is using computers and technology

effectively, safely, and ethically. Digital responsibility means making appropriate choices with your digital life, respecting others, and using the internet responsibly.

Teaching Digital Literacy

What is crucial for raising tech-savvy and responsible citizens in the digital age is to involve children in learning how to use these tools. Parents can assist their children in developing digital literacy by teaching them how to use search engines, apps, and software programs, as well as how to judge the credibility and reliability of the web-based information they find. For instance, parents can show their children how to check whether the information is credible and trustworthy: if the information can be evaluated by checking information from different sources, checking the background of the author and the organisation/website from which the information is obtained, or looking for other signs of factual errors, bias or outright misinformation. They can teach them that their personal information is valuable to people or organisations that wish to exploit or manipulate them and share best practices for protecting information, such as developing strong passwords, not sharing sensitive information online, and being wary of the apps and sites they use.

Parents can also help their children navigate technology's educational pursuits, such as art, music, writing, coding or research, by offering support to hone her skills and helping to develop her expertise. Better yet, it is when parents take a positive and forward-looking approach to the technological landscape that is emerging in front of them. They can also share experiences related to the technological milieu and devise and help children pursue their technological goals. This holds the promise of bringing about a paradigm shift in how children engage with technology and how they are more inclined to grow creatively and confidently in order to thrive in the technological world we eventually find ourselves in.

Promoting Responsible Digital Behaviours

For most parents, the greater goal is: Will it prepare my child to become a responsible digital citizen? Digital literacy not only enables but also disables students. It does not have to be so dichotomous, however. When schools treat digital literacy in isolation from any ethical or social contexts, they merely hope that students will become decent human beings despite interacting predominantly through devices lacking human features.

It is unrealistic to assume that students will grasp digital responsibility without clearly understanding their words and actions online and their impact on others. When adults share stories of antisocial behaviours linked to online activities, they usually do not claim there is no connection to digital literacy (the ability to read, write and interact online). Questions about the reach, potential, or intent do not emerge.

For example, if children spread rumours online, write mean comments during a live stream, or cyberbully, parents and teachers often equate this antisocial behaviour with a malicious intention to harm individuals. While reprehensible, this can also be seen as a failure to consider the implications of a word, comment or statement on the emotional well-being of others. Gamers engaging in insult wars do not merely utilise new technologies to express their malevolent intentions; they also show a deficit in recognising online words and actions as genuinely reflecting their intent. The same goes for the inability to treat other people's property with respect or their privacy with discretion.

Parents who want to instil digital responsibility can model it themselves. They can use technology responsibly, have a good online presence by taking responsibility for their comments, respect their children's expectations of privacy, and show their children how to use technology responsibly, balanced and ethically. Our children then become powerful advocates of digital responsibility and, perhaps, create a much more respectable online community in the future.

Integrating Technology into Everyday Family Life

While technology carries with it risks and dangers, it can also be a powerful retooling of family life when it is consciously incorporated into family activity through carefully selected apps that promote learning and interaction, for instance, through time-shifting television to create family viewing opportunities; and through digital media that foster moments of increased interaction, fun bonding and creative expression all by keeping technology on mission and target with the family's values and goals.

Using Technology to Strengthen Family Bonds

Technology can also improve family bonds. Consider, for example, how you and your family members could connect, share experiences, and maintain memories via new media and technology, such as video calling applications to contact relatives who live far away, sharing photos and videos through social media, or collaborating with your family members on creative projects.

Technology can also help them plan family activities, view a film or television programme together, play computer games, or explore educational websites and apps that help promote fun, learning and connection and allow parents to model their own positive technology use. Suppose parents create opportunities to incorporate technology into family life without excluding it. In that case, they can provide children with a context that feels normal, non-druggy and nurturing while supporting positive interpersonal connections and their loved one's sense of belonging.

Blending Technology with Learning and Play

Technology can also foster learning and play, enabling children to learn more about topics of personal interest, enhance their skills, and engage in creative expression. For example, parents can encourage their children to use educational apps and websites to play games and learn more about subjects that pique their curiosity, such as science, history, and art.

Moreover, parents can help their kids hone their interests and creativity by giving them a computer and internet access that personalises their music or drawing program or by assembling a home recording studio. This would give their digital achievements an audience and develop positive experiences with online creation. It would foster further creative activity and offer a creative, engaging, positive outlet for their excess energy and imagination.

Balancing Technology Use with Offline Activities

Technology will always have its place in the digital age as a learning tool to enhance children's play. However, it should be balanced with offline activities that support children's physical, social, and emotional well-being. These activities could include playing outdoors, engaging in sports like soccer or basketball, creating arts and crafts, reading, or playing family games without screens. For example, a parent can set up a daily routine where their child has a prescribed amount of 'screen time' as well as non-screen time activities that involve reading a book, going outside to play a specific sport, or working on a puzzle together. In this way, your child can learn to self-moderate their technology use. Meanwhile, the parent can use daily routine and prompts to ensure their child gets their daily dose of physical activity, social time with their peers, and healthcare professionals.

Recommended Screen Time for Children: Current Australian Research Evidence

Australian research on children's screen time has explored guidelines and evidence-based recommendations for how much time children should or should not spend on devices daily. The guidelines vary by age group, and the recommendations are rooted in physical, cognitive, and social health considerations.

1. Infants and Toddlers (0-2 years): The Australian Government's 24-Hour Movement Guidelines for the Early Years recommend that children younger than 2 avoid screen time, except for video chatting with family members or friends. The research emphasises that exposure to screens in this age group may impede healthy cognitive and social development.

2. Preschoolers (3-5 years): The same guidelines suggest that children aged 2-5 years should be limited to less than one hour of screen time per day. Studies show that excessive screen use in this age group is not just a matter of concern, but is associated with delayed language development, reduced attention spans, and poorer social interactions (Hinkley et al., 2018). This information should make us all more attentive to the potential negative effects of screen time on our children.

3. School-aged Children (5-12 years): The Australian Physical Activity and Sedentary Behaviour Guidelines recommend no more than two hours of recreational screen time per day for older children. Research indicates that screen time beyond this threshold can contribute to adverse health outcomes, such as increased sedentary behaviour, a higher risk of obesity, and disruptions to sleep patterns (Straker et al.). However, research also acknowledges the educational benefits of technology, especially for school-aged children, when used in moderation and combined with physical activity.

4. Adolescents (13-17 years): The guidelines also recommend limiting non-educational screen time to two hours per day for teenagers. Studies indicate that prolonged screen use in this age group is linked to increased risks of mental health issues, including anxiety, depression, and poor sleep quality (Mathers et al., 2009). However, the research also suggests that a balanced approach, where adolescents engage in regular physical activity, social interaction, and sleep while using devices for educational and recreational purposes, can help mitigate these risks. This guidance should reassure you that there is a way to navigate the digital world for your teenager.

Generally, these Australian guidelines and research that suggested daily screen time limits: no screen time for children under 2 years, less than 1 hour for ages 2-5, and no more than 2 hours of recreational screen time for children aged 5-17 are significantly imperative for parents to guide them in mitigating risks while balancing the benefits of technology.

The Importance of Setting Boundaries and Limits

As a parent, you hold the power to set clear boundaries and limits, such as overall screen time or other online activities. This control allows you to shape your child's relationship with technology to align with your family's values and priorities. By doing so, you empower yourself to guide your child's technology use confidently and responsibly.

As discussed throughout this book, this might include being home, for instance, or creating a tech-free zone, such as the dining room or bedroom, where devices are not allowed during specific times or activities. Alternatively, it could be concerning setting aside periods where technology was not allowed, such as mealtimes, family activities or before bedtime, to emphasise mutually respectful face-to-face interaction and ensure that technology does not re-order aspects of family life, like sleep routines. Setting limits can also help parents establish a healthy balance between technology and other areas of life. For example, they can give their children some control as they agree on their shared rules.

Conclusion

Parenting in the digital era presents unique opportunities and challenges, especially for South Sudanese and African families living in the diaspora. While technology has the potential to enhance learning, communication, and cultural preservation, it also introduces significant risks that must be carefully managed. As this chapter has explored, finding the right balance between leveraging the benefits of technology and mitigating its adverse effects is a key challenge for modern parents.

The digital world offers new ways for diaspora families to stay connected with their cultural roots, enabling children to engage with their heritage and maintain a sense of identity even while adapting to their new environment. At the same time, technology provides access to educational tools and resources that can support children's academic success and personal growth. However, the risks from excessive screen time, exposure to harmful content, and the potential erosion of face-to-face family interactions are ever-present.

To navigate these complexities, parents must take a proactive approach. By setting clear boundaries, fostering digital literacy, and creating balanced routines that incorporate both online and offline activities, they can ensure that technology enriches rather than diminishes child development. Equally important is their role in guiding their children toward responsible and safe online behaviour, helping them build the skills needed to thrive in both the digital and real worlds.

For South Sudanese and African families, the digital age is not just a challenge but an opportunity to bridge cultural divides and build resilience in the face of change. By integrating technology thoughtfully into family life and maintaining a strong focus on cultural values, parents can raise a generation of children who are not only tech-savvy but also deeply connected to their heritage. Ultimately, the goal is to reassure parents that they can foster a harmonious relationship between children and technology, ensuring that it serves as a tool for growth, learning, and connection rather than a source of disconnection or risk.

CHAPTER THIRTEEN

Balancing Tradition and Innovation: Parenting in the Digital Age for African Diaspora Families

Introduction

The rapid pace of technological advancement over the past few decades has transformed nearly every aspect of human life, including parenting. Today's technology is deeply embedded in daily routines, influencing how we communicate, learn, work, socialise, and entertain ourselves. For South Sudanese and other African migrant families in the diaspora, understanding the impact of technology on parenting is crucial. It offers both a unique opportunity and a complex challenge, bridging between preserving cultural heritage and embracing the new realities of their host societies.

When used thoughtfully, technology can revolutionise education, offering flexible and innovative ways to learn and connect that are especially valuable to migrant families. However, it also brings considerable risks, such as exposure to harmful content, as discussed in the previous chapter, cyberbullying, and the potential erosion of traditional values. These challenges can seem at odds with the family-centred ethos prevalent in South Sudanese and broader African cultures.

This chapter explores the complex dynamics of technology's role in parenting, focusing on strategies that South Sudanese and African families can adopt to harness the benefits of technology while mitigating its risks. It continues to explore similar challenges to those explored in the previous chapter. It may sound repetitive, but it provides an in-depth understanding of these and how to overcome them.

Through a deeper understanding of how technology is reshaping the parenting landscape, families can make informed decisions supporting their children's growth in a world dominated by digital devices and online interactions. A clear understanding of how technology is transforming parenting in our world will assist families in making informed choices and decisions about how they want their children to grow up in a world of iPad-armed, tweeting, Wi-Fi-dependent digital natives.

Technology's Impact on Contemporary Parenting Dynamics
Technology has become a central part of day-to-day life in the new South Sudanese and African families. Smartphones, tablets, computers, and the internet have become the primary ways parents and children interact, learn and communicate with the broader world. Technology has literally become part of the fabric of families' daily lives. Parents use it to transmit images of family rituals to their loved ones, while children access more educational opportunities than ever. Most African families in the diaspora have always used the phone call or postal service to communicate with relatives back home. However, technology has revolutionised this by allowing families to quickly talk

to each other, see each other, and learn more about each other's lives. The newspaper no longer controls the narrative.

Probably the most significant aspect of technology's impact on parenting in the contemporary world is the ability to keep in contact with family and friends over long distances. For many families that have migrated to a new country, maintaining links with the homeland and extended family is essential to preserving and instilling their cultural identity and providing continuity of existence and a feeling of belonging together.

The advent of communication technologies like video calls, social media and messenger apps have enabled families to stay in contact with loved ones, regardless of the physical distance involved. For example, a family living in Australia could connect with relatives living in South Sudan via a video call, allowing the children to also interact and share a piece of their everyday life with their grandparents, learn more about their cultural background, and participate in family events and celebrations. This maintains familial links and reinforces their sense of identity and belonging, essential aspects of a child's emotional and psychological development.

At the same time, parents who can communicate regularly with relatives and friends back home can achieve a measure of control over the process of their transition to their new setting by asking for advice and support from their extended family. For instance, a mother might call her relatives at home for guidance on using traditional medical remedies to treat ordinary children's health problems that she grew up with.

Alternatively, she might call her parents to find out how they have addressed certain challenges her children are now facing as they grapple with growing up in a new culture. With each other's help, a parent can reach out to a broader circle of past life experiences, making it easier for her children to maintain their cultural identity while adapting to their new environment.

The internet has made connecting with our families back home easier and serves as a gateway to learning about a wide range of topics in our native language. Today, we have at our disposal resources that can enhance our children's education and deepen our understanding of our host country's culture. Parents and children alike can tap into a wealth of information to explore new languages, customs, and opportunities, bridging cultural gaps in the process.

We have an advantage in drawing on the expanding world of information to acquire this knowledge and these tools. For instance, a less literate child who struggles with mathematics can watch online tutorials or play educational games to support this learning and this development. A parent who wants to form deeper bonds with another culture and language can access parenting blogs and forums, seeking advice from families in a similar position.

Moreover, technology enables parents to play a more active role in their child's learning and development trajectory by providing them with online learning grounds, educational apps and games. Learning to utilise diverse technology-enhanced resources at home becomes crucial for families navigating complex schooling systems in the diaspora. Along with our hardware engine, parents can use technology as a software tool to support their children's learning inside the learning rooms and at home through online learning platforms, educational apps and games.

Parents of diverse ethnic minority populations residing in the diaspora have much more to worry about when it comes to their children's learning and education. Some parents might be utterly clueless about how the public school system works. Similar to technological and informational assistance, familial assistance can also help diaspora children navigate the social landscape of public schools. Parents can utilise technology to track their children's academic standing, communicate with teachers and access educational resources online. For example, parents can log into online grade portals to track their children's academics, participate in virtual parent-teacher conferences and utilise online school resources aligned with their children's curriculum.

Furthermore, technology has broadened how families can gain or provide access to resources and support. Online communities, social media groups and support circles have granted parents access to resources and information and offer pools of peers from whom parents can seek or provide support. For many South Sudanese and African families in the diaspora, these online communities can serve as an avenue of connection or belonging, on the one hand, with practical advice and assistance throughout the process of navigating the realities of life in a new country on the other.

Parents can join parenting, culture, or immigration-themed groups to discuss their experiences, give advice, or both. Such groups could provide a forum for families who have moved to feel less isolated and more empowered as they face the challenges of assimilating into life in a new country.

Technology now structures the relationship between the family and the community at large: one example is the increasing availability of what might be called virtual trans-local diasporic support networks online groups that connect families with an affinity based on culture and/or experience but living across multiple locations. These networks allow parents to share ideas, resources and support. A South Sudanese parent living in London may join an online group for African parents in the African diaspora and diaspora communities. Such groups might discuss parenting experiences, cultural adaptation processes and raising children in transnational contexts. These virtual communities provide concrete support to families while reinforcing a cultural and diasporic identity and a sense of solidarity.

Navigating the Challenges and Risks of Technology in Parenting

Today, technology offers practically countless benefits to parents and children. However, technology meant to make life more efficient and meaningful can also bring significant challenges and grave risks for many parents and children. The most common concern for parents is that children are easily exposed to harmful content while online. The internet is an uncontrollably huge space. Video, music, books, and all kinds of information are offered everywhere and are all accessible to children, which could result in children watching violent videos, viewing obscene pictures or dealing with online predators. These are not just annoying emotions, but many are aroused trauma and hinder the normal development of children. In other words, it can be an extremely stressful experience.

Therefore, parents need to oversee their children's digital lives and create some limits to keep them safe from the worst content. Parents should use parental control software or watch their children's actions on the net and create some boundaries to keep off the worst content. They should install filters to block access from some websites, which their children are wise to avoid and monitor apps to track the children's actions on the net and how they use social media or online games. In addition, parents can converse honestly with their offspring, providing information about the dangers the internet holds for them and teaching them to surf the digital world with caution. Parents can help their children escape the dangers of the digital world by educating them about online safety and creating clear expectations.

One significant risk is cyberbullying. Social networks, messaging apps and online games offer new opportunities for bullying by children's peers or by strangers. Cyberbullying can have a severe impact on children's mental health, leading to anxiety, depression and, in worst cases, suicide. Cyberbullying is different to regular bullying. It can be a genuinely inescapable experience, as it can happen anytime and anywhere the child can access the internet.

For the parents, steps must be taken to prevent a child from being bullied online. First, they must instruct their children about good behaviour regarding respectable online behaviour, including being an active informer if they witness someone being bullied online or becoming a cyberbullying victim. They must be aware of the signs that indicate bullying of their children online; this includes recent changes in their behaviour, withdrawal from their social activities, and shying away from using digital devices. Suppose parents think that their child is a victim of online bullying. In that case, immediate actions must be taken, such as reporting that incident to an appropriate platform, communicating with the school, and providing emotional support to overcome it. By promoting positive communication and listening to their children, parents can help them foster good behaviour online and build immunity against online bullying.

Another concern aside from the difficulty of harmful content as well as harmful cyberbullying is that technology tends to promote the decline of the family microcosm by eroding traditional values. This is because family members themselves have been heavily influenced by information technology. They have formed a habit of using smartphones, tablets, computers, and related digital devices all the time. Many children and adolescents spend all their free time playing games on their gadgets. Simultaneously, they chat with their peers or strangers online after school. As a result, they can no longer spend precious time with their parents, sharing feelings or having quality face-to-face communication.

Eventually, close relatives become distant due to a lack of socialising together. For families where technology has become an overriding concern, parents need to enforce clear rules and routines that increase face-to-face interactions and time spent together. To begin, parents might create specific times of the day that are 'tech-free', such as mealtimes or evenings, in which all family members put away their devices and engage in some activity as a group. While some examples may include board games or walks, the most crucial aspect of these tech-free times is that parents and children engage in meaningful interactions. When busy families make the space for such interactions, they reduce the constant connective pull of technology, bringing them more fully into the present moment and strengthening their family bonds.

A third risk is the potential for addiction and overuse of technology. Digital content, such as social media, video games and online streaming, can be highly addictive, leading to excessive screen time and a corresponding decline in physical activity, social interaction and academic performance. Children who spend too much time in front of a screen risk becoming lonely and inactive, disenfranchised from other pursuits, such as school, clubs, pursuing passions and spending time with friends and family.

There are several ways to tackle this problem of technology addiction, including setting time limits on digital devices and modelling healthy habits that children can adopt. For instance, setting time limits, such as children only being allowed to use these devices for two hours daily, can help them develop a balanced lifestyle. In addition, children should also be encouraged to participate in physical exercise and engage in social interaction and creativity to ensure a healthy lifestyle.

In addition, the best people to model healthy reuse are their parents because they are their guides, and they will learn by doing good behaviour. Parents need to control the use of digital devices and also model healthy habits for their children. By doing so, their children will develop balanced use of technology and good habits that will help them.

Another area of worry for parents is the long-term effects of technology on children's mental development. Evidence is emerging to support the idea that screen time can adversely impact children's cognitive development, attention to tasks and interactive skills. An example is the link between children's time on digital devices, lack of focus/concentration, problem-solving strategies, and face-to-face communications. This can negatively impact children in the long term at school and in their social lives, as they may lag behind their peers in their ability to keep up.

Parents can mitigate many of these risks by encouraging their children to engage in activities that support technology-free cognitive development. These activities also help children manage their attention spans, control their impulses, and improve their social skills. Whether it is a few minutes reading a book for fun, playing an educational game with a parent, or a few minutes drawing a picture or building with blocks, such activities should be supported as the child and parent do everything together. Not only might they support your child's cognitive development, but they might also provide a needed healthy balance to their screen time.

Secondly, despite the positive effects technology can have on cognitive development in children, it also may adversely affect their physical health by encouraging a sedentary lifestyle. Behavioural studies have shown that additional time spent on digital devices has been linked to unhealthy habits like obesity, poor posture and eye strains among children. For instance, children who spend more time in front of a screen are less likely to participate in physical activities such as sports or outdoor games, which are essential for their health, growth and development.

Parents can promote physical health by encouraging their children to participate regularly in physical activities and limiting screen time. For example, parents can sign their children up to play on neighbourhood sports teams, take them on regular nature walks, or encourage children to play outdoors whenever possible in safe environments. Parents can also emulate these behaviours by remaining physically active and participating in some physical activity as a family. For example, a family can go for a bike ride together, play soccer in a neighbourhood park, or attempt to learn how to dance together.

Another angle for parents to ponder over here is children's psychological and emotional health. Facebook, Twitter, Instagram, personal websites, online gaming, YouTubing, and other forms of content for consumption have created an environment where children can build high expectations for peer impressions and conform to their idealised image of 'normal'. As a result, children who regularly follow social media accounts tend to develop unrealistic expectations for themselves and others, which often leads to depression, anxiety, low self-esteem, and negative influences. For example, children and adolescents regularly exposed to images of beauty, wealth, and success on Instagram and Facebook are likely to compare themselves with peers they see on social media. They may feel unconfident about how they look, dress or behave. Often, these comparisons significantly influence their worldviews.

Beyond fostering self-worth, parents can empower children to interact with technology in healthier ways. In fact, research has shown that explaining social pressures connected with behaviour on platforms such as Instagram, Snapchat, or Twitter, setting attainable goals for behaviour, and referencing one's own past experiences can help children feel like they are in control of their actions and avoid feeling disempowered and overwhelmed (Alhabash & Ma, 2017).

Parents can also help children cope with feelings of shame and anxiety associated with social media comparison, which is linked with anxiety and depression, by emphasising their felt strengths and accomplishments. Finally, parents who cultivate a positive emotional baseline for their children across all life domains will likely enhance their ability to trust in their own competence when they have to make crucial decisions, which in today's world is frequently about their interactions with the online ecosystem.

Harmonizing Technology with Traditional Values

For South Sudanese and other African diaspora families, one of the biggest challenges is understanding how to leverage technology for good without sacrificing cultural values. On the one hand, technology is used to both support and undermine culture, depending on how we use it. Conversely, our relationship with technology is only as positive or negative as we intend it to be. As parents, we must show intentionality and thoughtfulness about how we engage with technology so that it empowers rather than undermines our cultural identity and family values.

Parents can also ensure this balance by using tech as a tool for cultural preservation and education. There are an overwhelming number of Internet sources of information available concerning heritage, including libraries, museums, educational websites, and many more resources parents can use to educate their children about their culture, religious values, heritage, tradition, history, morals, community and overall world view, and reinforce the value of perpetuating cultural identity. Parents could provide their children access to traditional fables and stories, music, and art from their home country online so that their children feel connected to the source of their heritage.

Crucially, parents can use technology to strengthen linkages to their cultural community. Social media, messaging apps, and online groups can help families forge connections with other members of the cultural community, both locally and worldwide. Bridge-building activities are often associated with positive feelings of belonging, connection, shared mutuality, shared understanding and support, all of which could promote cultural resilience and help families perceive themselves as both belonging to and bridging across multiple worlds. For example, a parent might create a group online or join another group already composed of other parents who share their cultural background. They become virtual cultural 'friends', confidantes or comrades who can assist with challenges, provide solidarity and hope, and nurture a relational sense of belonging.

Meanwhile, parents must be aware of how technology may erode many of these same values and practices. From online social media, TV, and other online entertainment, children can be exposed to values and behaviour contrary to their parents' values, such as consumerism, materialism and individualism, which are often viewed as contributions of digital media. This can gradually move their children away from key cultural values central to many group-centred African cultures around the communal, family ethos. For example, they prefer their children to be part of a larger social group defined by their parents rather than be defined as an independent economic unit, as in industrialised economies.

To meet this challenge, parents can help children become mindful consumers of digital media by fostering their critical reflection on the messages and values conveyed by digital media, either with or without their parents and by developing savvy skills for source triangulation, risk assessment, and other critical skills. They can cultivate interventionist skills by modelling effective media use, setting limits on TV and other media, and rejecting offensive portrayals; they can role-model media literacy and critical thinking in the family.

For instance, they can set rules about the type of television shows or movies children can watch and discuss the messages and values conveyed by the digital media their children access. They can encourage their children to be critical consumers of information they read or see online, rejecting racist or sexist portrayals. They can work to support their children in maintaining their cultural authenticity or identity: parents can foster cultural pride, media literacy and mindfulness by helping children to 'critically assess the portrayal of their cultural values and identity in and through digital media'.

Aside from helping children make better choices about media consumption, parents may also increase the opportunity for kids to use technology for activities consistent with parental cultural values. For instance, they may use digital media to support family communication, collaboration and creativity. Parents can amplify children's exposure to digital tools used for activities that involve family co-production and cultural production because those kinds of activities support a child's identity as part of a family—for example, helping a child make holiday cards for mailing to relatives or produce a digital narrative of a family event or as part of a cultural group. In other words, ask children to record stories from a family member as part of a family history project. Technology then appears to children as a tool and extension of their cultural identity and family relationships rather than as a distraction or source of discord.

Furthermore, technology can help to maintain intergenerational ties, especially for parents who may feel isolated. Grandparents who live abroad could read stories, share family culture or traditions, or offer advice to their grandchildren through shared media platforms, such as video calls or messages. This strengthens family bonds across generations. Parents can encourage their children to use technology to explore elements of their culture and ethnicity, such as courses, documentaries and virtual tours of cultural heritage sites. This active learning approach using technology can help children deepen their understanding of their culture.

However, an additional byproduct is that parents can use technology to encourage their children to preserve their native language and increase their language proficiency. Technology has many language preservation and development resources, such as language apps, online dictionaries, and video calls. Engaging with technology for language preservation via these tools means that there are various practices that a parent can guide their children to undertake.

For instance, with language apps, children can practise vocabulary and grammar and watch videos in their native language. They can also engage with peers from other cultural groups through online language swapping and establish relationships with relatives in their home country through technology. Language preservation can be a crucial component in identity maintenance, essential for those who live in countries that have historically not shown excellent tolerance towards cultural diversity.

Fostering Healthy Technology Habits within the Family

Staying healthy with technology in the family requires parents to clarify expectations, establish routines and provide role-modelling behaviour. Parents are integral in setting the tone for how children engage with technology. They have to be intentional in how they approach the task. One of the first steps to promoting healthy technology use is clarifying the expectations and boundaries around screen time. This might involve setting family rules regarding when and how much time children spend on digital devices.

For instance, parents can define specific times of the day in which screens are allowed, such as after homework is completed or during the weekends. Additionally, they can set rules regarding the type of content permitted, such as being clear about not allowing violent or adult content and encouraging educational or creative apps. Parents can help children develop a mindful and healthy relationship with technology by clarifying the expectations.

Beyond setting expectations, parents need to create routines centred around family time. Tech-free zones (e.g., no electronic devices at mealtimes or in the evenings), where the whole family can come together to talk through their day, play board games, or go for a family walk, are an excellent way to re-centre family relationships at regular intervals. Screen time need not mean relationship time off.

Positive behaviours must be modelled within the family, and parents must be positive role models for using technology. Children are great observers and learn a lot from what they see as critical adults, including their parents. This means a parent needs to engage in positive behaviours with their technology use actively, for example, not using it all the time, being present with their children and fostering communication when sharing a device with their phone at the dinner table. Modelling positive behaviours will maintain the sense of values and habits that parents want their children to adopt throughout their lives.

A vital part of this is fostering a balance in how children spend their time, encouraging plenty of physical activity, social interaction and other creative activities. They can encourage physical activities at home or elsewhere, involving sports and other personally appealing forms of exercise, such as outdoor activities and play. Social activities can focus on interacting with friends in person or over the phone and participating in clubs, teams, or other forms of social gatherings such as travel, as well as groups often organised by organisations such as churches and synagogues.

Encouraging children's creativity, such as withdrawing, writing stories and poems, composing music, or singing, can be increasingly helpful in developing a range of interests and skills outside of the digital world. By promoting a balanced lifestyle, parents can prevent children from becoming sedentary and instead participate in activities conducive to healthy habits, even if they limit persistent screen use.

In turn, parents can leverage technology to empower their child's development. Just as kids may gain various physical or social benefits from their iPads, but their parents can use them to promote their learning. In fact, parents can also capitalise on other forms of technology, such as a computer, educational apps or web games, online museum tours or other virtual expeditions, team chatrooms or other online communities based around shared interests or pastimes. Such activities can bolster children's learning, expand their worldview, and develop their curiosity and adventurous spirit.

Another is to centre children in conversations about the place of technology in their lives. Parents can invite their children into conversations about the pros and cons of technology, the limits and risks of technology, and how it can support their health and wellbeing. By naming the impact of technology on their children, parents can encourage children to increase awareness of their own technology use and to make more conscious decisions about it. For instance, parents can ask: 'How do you feel when you spend time using your devices? How does it affect your mood and energy? How much is a healthy balance for you?' and more.

Parents can begin by modelling their desired behaviour: taking breaks from technology by participating in other enriching activities. For example, parents can encourage their children to spend time outside taking a walk, engage in an innovation effort, or participate in another family activity that's not on a screen. Breaks from technology will allow children to recharge batteries, become less stressed, and pay greater attention to the world around them. Of course, it is also vital that parents remember that they are first and foremost models for their children. Parents must be mindful of their screen habits, prioritise face-to-face interactions with children, and keep tech-free zones at home. Parents reinforce the values and habits we hope our offspring can emulate by being exemplary.

The Evolving Intersection of Technology and Parenting

Technology's role in parenting will be a much more significant part of parents' worlds in the decades ahead. Newer technologies such as artificial intelligence, virtual reality and wearable devices could continue transforming how families live, learn and connect in significant and perhaps unwanted ways. 'Also, a range of challenges and issues will come up due to these technologies along with a whole new set of ethical questions.' 'There will be educational advances and ways to support child development and family connections.

One of the significant challenges for parents on the horizon is staying informed and involved with new technologies as they are introduced. Because technology is increasingly a part of everyday life, parents must stay informed about new technologies, consider their risks and benefits, and find ways to navigate them within their family's interconnected lives. This could mean educating themselves about new technologies, looking around for resources and support, and setting limits and ground rules.

A third important dimension will be ethics. As technologies such as artificial intelligence and biometric data-gathering proliferate, parents must grapple with tough questions regarding privacy, data security, and the potential effects on their children's development and wellbeing. For example, a new parent might consider the consequences of using an AI-powered tutoring app, which promises a personalised learning experience yet complicates privacy matters and potential bias. A biometric wearable device that tracks children's health and activity could offer new insights into the childhood routine, but it raises vital questions about surveillance and autonomy.

Faced with these problems, parents need to think more critically and reflectively about technology. For instance, they need to be able to assess the pros and cons of new technologies, explore alternative views and contexts, and discuss ethical choices and problems associated with using technology with their children. Children can only become critical thinkers if their parents show them how.

On sight of the fundamental values that underpin their parenting by fixating on the next piece of tech to try. Just because tech provides new tools, opportunities, and resources does not mean that it replaces the core values of parenting, which remain the same, such as the need to provide love, care, nurture and help children grow into responsible, kind and respectful individuals. Good parenting remains about a strong relationship between parent and child, which includes open communication, emotion and connection, as well as trust and mutual respect. Sound foundations based on traditional values enable parents to integrate tech into family life without it taking over and compromising the ethos of their family values.

The future holds challenges for all of us to see how technology will bolster, or not, the broader value system of society at large. Furthermore, suppose technology reshapes children's work, education and socialising as it seems destined to do. What will become of the family and its cultural heritage in the context of the broader backdrop of the transformation of society and its value system? The challenge for parents posed by the digital age will be to act proactively as technology has become yet another opportunity for the family to bring its cultural values to the fore.

Since its appropriate use would help their children master the challenges of the network while maintaining and retaining a strong allegiance to the profound and fundamental values of family and its cultural heritage. Societies must resolve the 'question of survival' and the 'question of the concrete values' that will allow future families to thrive. Parents, too, are required to wield their cyber pickaxe for this, building a walkway through the fog of the digital world. This task can be made more accessible by parents who maintain a robust sense of identity rooted in a deep sense of belonging to successfully navigate this digital era's challenges.

Conclusion

Technology's rapid evolution presents opportunities and challenges for South Sudanese and African families in the diaspora. On the one hand, technology has become an invaluable tool, enabling families to maintain connections across continents, access educational resources, and preserve cultural heritage in ways previously unimaginable. It empowers parents to navigate the complexities of raising children in a new cultural landscape while staying rooted in their traditions.

However, this digital era also introduces significant risks, such as exposure to harmful content, cyberbullying, and the erosion of traditional family values. The challenges are not insurmountable but require intentional, thoughtful planning. Parents must establish clear guidelines for technology use, promote healthy digital habits, and ensure that technology serves as a bridge, rather than a barrier, to family cohesion and cultural preservation.

As technology continues to advance, it will inevitably reshape the parenting experience. However, the core values of love, care, and nurturing remain constant. Parents can successfully balance tradition with innovation by staying informed, critically engaging with new technologies, and fostering strong family relationships. In doing so, they ensure that technology enhances rather than detracts from their children's development and their family's cultural legacy.

Finally, it is not the technology that defines modern parenting but how families integrate it into their lives. By making deliberate choices, parents can harness the power of technology to support their children's growth while preserving the essence of their cultural identity. This balanced approach will enable families to thrive in a digital world while remaining anchored in the values that matter most.

CHAPTER FOURTEEN

Human Development and Wellbeing Amid Migration

Introduction

Human development and well-being are critical pillars of a meaningful life, especially for individuals and families navigating the profound changes that come with migration. For South Sudanese and African migrants in the diaspora, migration is not just a physical relocation but a transformative journey that impacts every facet of life culturally, psychologically, socially, and economically. The migration experience presents a complex blend of challenges and opportunities that reshape health, social ties, emotional resilience, and economic stability, all while requiring migrants to negotiate new identities in their host countries.

This chapter examines the intricate relationship between migration and human development, focusing on the experiences of South Sudanese and African migrants. It explores how migration affects physical health, mental well-being, social connections, and economic prospects while highlighting the resilience and cultural continuity that can help mitigate these challenges. By providing insights into the various stages of human development and how migration influences each one, this chapter offers a comprehensive understanding of how migrant families can foster well-being, navigate barriers, and build fulfilling lives in their new environments.

The chapter also delves into how migrants can maintain a sense of identity and cultural pride amid the dislocation of migration. Understanding the role of culture and resilience is essential for ensuring that migrants not only survive but thrive as they adapt to their new circumstances. By addressing these dynamics holistically, this chapter aims to equip parents, community leaders, educators, and policymakers with the tools and knowledge necessary to support migrant families in their human development journey, enhancing their well-being and creating pathways for success in their host societies.

Stages of Human Development: An Overview

Before we discuss the implications of migration on human development and wellbeing, let us first look at the stages of human development and the role of human development in parenting. Human development is a complex and lifelong journey that starts from conception and goes through various stages, from infancy to adulthood. There are essential physical, cognitive, social and emotional stages that are integral components of human development, shaping the reason every child needs to grow and develop well throughout their lives to stay mentally and physically healthy and be able to be active and productive members of their communities (Ambasz et al., 2023; Bronfenbrenner, 2000; Song, 2012). Understanding the different stages of human development allows parents to become supportive agents of children's development and provide them with information to assist with the journey of some of the most beautiful and vulnerable stages that will lead the child into adulthood (Table 1 below).

Table 2: Eight Stages of Human Development

#	Each stage of Human Development	Observable changes	Parental role in child life as they grow
1	Prenatal Stage (Conception to Birth):	Foetal development and maternal health	Ensure proper prenatal care, balanced nutrition, and a healthy environment to support optimal foetal growth.
2	Infancy (0-2 Years)	Rapid physical growth, brain development, and the formation of emotional bonds	Provide a nurturing and safe environment, responsive caregiving, and stimulation through play and interaction to foster secure attachment and cognitive development.
3	Toddlerhood (2-3 Years)	Development of motor skills, language, and autonomy.	Encourage exploration, support language development through conversation, and offer guidance to help toddlers navigate their growing independence.

4	Preschool Age (3-5 Years)	Refinement of motor skills, cognitive abilities, and social interactions.	Engage in activities that promote learning and creativity, establish routines, and foster social skills through play and peer interaction.
5	Early School Age (5-8 Years)	Formal education, literacy, and development of self-esteem.	Support academic learning, encourage positive social interactions, and provide a stable home environment that promotes self-confidence.
6	Middle Childhood (9-12 Years)	Development of logical thinking, peer relationships, and moral understanding.	Reinforce problem-solving skills, support healthy friendships, and guide moral reasoning through discussions and role modelling.
7	Adolescence (13-18 Years)	Identity formation, abstract thinking, and emotional regulation.	Offer emotional support, respect growing autonomy, and guide decision-making and coping strategies.
8	Young Adulthood (18+ Years)	Independence, career development, and forming adult relationships.	Encourage independence, support career choices, and model healthy relationships.

Table 3: Effective Parental Strategies

In these stages, parents and caregivers provide a supportive environment in which their children's development can take place by using the following skills, described, discussed and expanded on in various chapters (Table 3 below):

#	Parental strategies	What parents need to do
1	Responsive Parenting	Be attuned to the child's needs at each stage, offering warmth, affection, and consistent support.
2	Encouragement of Exploration	Allow children to explore their environment safely, fostering curiosity and learning.
3	Structured Routines	Establish clear routines and boundaries for security and predictability.
4	Active Engagement	Engage in meaningful conversations, play, and activities that stimulate cognitive and social development.
5	Positive Reinforcement	Use praise and encouragement to build self-esteem and reinforce desirable behaviours.

Because parenting takes many forms, it is not so much a doctrine as a practice, and it needs to be flexible. Parents need to adapt to who their children are and to grow along with them. This speaks to the importance of flexibility in parenting and the practices that help children thrive and succeed. Understanding these human development stages and what our children need from infancy to adulthood is crucially important, especially equipping the new parents and caregivers with tools to understand the stages of human development and guide them through the complex questions that arise when guiding our children through life's opportunities and challenges.

Migration's Influence on Human Development

Migration is a transformative course that affects every area of human growth. Individuals choose to migrate for a reason. In many cases, it is a mix of push and pull factors. Push factors such as conflict, persecution, and poverty leave little to no choice but to relocate. In contrast, pull factors such as security, better opportunities, and improved living standards are significant attractions. Although fraught with difficulties, the experience of migration often demonstrates the resilience of families and individuals who manage to cope with risks and access opportunities, which in turn fuels hope for better wellbeing.

Challenges to Physical Health

The often most pressing issue related to physical health concerns of individuals and families, either during or following the migration journey. While on the move, internal migrants and newcomers can be exposed to various health risks, such as infectious diseases, malnutrition and physical injuries. Upon arrival at their destination, migrants may face new health risks, such as dietary changes, changes in lifestyle and availability of care services.

In particular, the dietary transition can become a significant hindrance to South Sudanese and, indeed, African families. Traditional African diets are rich in fresh or whole foods such as vegetables, fruits, grains, and lean meats. This often changes upon migration to countries in the Western World, where dietary construction is mainly comprised of convenience and processed foods that come with extra calories, sugars, and unhealthy fats. Consequently, it is no surprise to see a rising prevalence of obesity, diabetes, heart disease and other chronic health disorders in these families.

For example, a family that was used to dining at home-cooked meals using foods from local markets will find alternatives to fast food and buy snacks conducive to their lifestyle if these meals provide easier or cheaper options or are the only available choices where they come from. Eventually, if followed persistently, the change can have serious health consequences.

Other risk factors for physical health differences come from dietary and lifestyle changes due to migration. For instance, rural- or semi-rural-dwelling South Sudanese or African migrant families who move to urban environments of Western countries have decreased physical activity. In rural settings, daily activities often start early and involve manual labour, walking longer distances, working collectively and communally, and asking people for anything. In Western urban settings, such individuals might spend more time sitting at desks and commuting via public transportation and less engaging in traditionally active or rigorous exercise behaviours, such as running or community farming. With more physical activity, healthy weights are easier to manage with less physical activity, weight gain, reduced cardiovascular fitness, and elevated chronic disease risk.

In addition, the anxiety and uncertainty of migration may affect physical health directly because chronic stress is a well-documented risk for hypertension, gastrointestinal disturbances, and immune dysfunction. The acute stressors of migration, such as the challenge of learning a new language and culture, finding work, and securing housing, may generate biochemical and physiological changes that compound the burden on the body. For example, a recently arrived and underemployed migrant whose stress level appears chronically high and who is experiencing headaches, sleeplessness and digestive upsets might find the situation becomes chronic if it is not addressed with medical or psychosocial resources.

Accessing to Healthcare Services

Another is access to health care. For many South Sudanese and other African families, the first challenge involves having access to the pivotal resources that support good physical health and wellness. In their new home, South Sudanese and other migrants face language, cultural, economic and other barriers to care.

Language barriers can hinder migrants' communication with healthcare personnel, their comprehension of medical advice and navigation of the healthcare system. For instance, an English-as-a-second-language mother might struggle to relay her child's symptoms to a doctor. As a result, a paediatric appointment might end with neither parent nor doctor coming to a proper and effective diagnosis or treatment.

Culturally, attitudes toward healthcare vary, leading to misunderstandings. For example, in some African cultures, traditional medicine, community elders, or healers might be the first sources of health-related advice. Where healthcare workers neither understand nor respect these practices, their disdain can create mistrust and familial reluctance to engage in medical care.

Economic limitations can be crucial to access to health care: South Sudanese and other African migrants may be in minimum-wage jobs or work without health insurance. Given these considerations, policies that guarantee access to Medicare for all migrants seem imperative; persons without health insurance may delay or avoid treatment altogether and worsen existing health conditions.

To combat these challenges, systems must develop culturally sensitive and linguistically appropriate services that offer interpretation during office visits, train healthcare professionals in cultural competency, and develop outreach programmes to educate migrant communities on available healthcare. As people in need feel understood and respected based on their cultural values and beliefs, this leads to an appreciation of medicine that translates into utilisation, ultimately improving the lives of newcomers.

Mental and Emotional Health

Migration is a part of human development, perhaps the most crucial, neglected, or forgotten, especially for refugees and other migrants. Migration itself is a hugely stressful time, and for many South Sudanese and other African people, it is compounded by the stresses of conflict, persecution, or severe economic hardship … People often talk of adverse coping mechanisms. In fact, most migrant have similar sad stories to tell.

The alienation of migrants arises from attempting to adjust to a new culture, language, and social environment, as well as the loss of social support networks and acculturation challenges (Deng, 2016a; S. A. Deng & J. Marlowe, 2013). In contrast, existential alienation arises from the fact that life is ultimately meaningless and that any attempt to find meaning will fail. Existential alienation goes beyond the social and can be understood as a deep-seated loneliness that no superficial remedy can rectify. An inward-oriented perspective on alienation can help to explain why so many people who are migrating experience forms of social isolation, loneliness and alienation.

The arrival of a migrant is united, in many cases, with the loss of social and familial networks. On top of this, migrants also face acculturation challenges: the newly arrived migrant will inevitably experience a lack of social contact with anyone within her host country who speaks her native language or shares her own cultural background. This is mainly the case in cities with widespread immigration, where language and cultural barriers in one neighbourhood will be bordered by another neighbourhood with little knowledge of the migrant's native language. This can lead to homesickness. Experiences of racism, discrimination or xenophobia in host countries will add layers to these feelings of separation and can profoundly undermine an individual's self-worth.

The very reasons why a migrant or refugee has left their home country often account for their mental health issues. For instance, those who flee conflict or persecution may do so having experienced extensive traumatic experiences of violence, loss of loved ones and dangerous situations, which, if untreated, can lead to mental health symptoms such as flashbacks, nightmares, heightened alertness, anxiety and emotional detachment that can affect their day-to-day safety, security and potential for a new start.

The stigma attached to mental health problems can further impede their access to help. Some South Sudanese and African migrants might believe that acknowledging a mental health problem is a sign of weakness and is shameful, and this can lead them to hide symptoms or avoid any interaction with mental health services altogether.

Other factors can, therefore, intensify the problem: a feeling that mental health services might not be available in the host country and/or a set of worries over how others might treat them, which could even result in legal consequences for some. For example, the migrant with depression who is fearful of how his community and his friends are going to respond or the fear of deportation upon disclosure of one's mental health status can further hinder access to help.

Mental and emotional wellbeing should be prioritised and made accessible by ensuring that culturally sensitive mental health services are offered to migrants, allowing them to navigate challenges specific to their migration journeys and helping cultivate therapeutic relationships by considering their cultural backgrounds. By offering counselling and therapy services based on migration drivers and proximal challenges and providing orientation and support groups to help those who have endured trauma or loss, psychological interventions can be adapted so migrants with varying levels of English-language proficiency and cultural contexts can understand them. Moreover, attention should be paid to fostering mental health within migrant communities so that individuals know what mental illness looks like and where they can seek help.

Social Wellbeing and Community Ties

As discussed in the previous chapters, social well-being can be considered part of human capital: quality relations and social well-being are contexts in which people maintain relationships with family, community or the wider society. As much as they want to, the social wellbeing of the South Sudanese and other African diaspora families remains a challenge. Migration often comes with the disruption of social networks and the support systems that enable these forms of human capital.

Loss of social ties for collective meaning and belonging in the home country is one of the most critical threats to social well-being in the diaspora. For migrants, leaving close family members, friends, or community ties is often the most challenging part of the migration. The lack of social protectors may lead to loneliness, isolation and a sense of alienation, which in turn can undermine one's own well-being. A family from an extended family in the home country might feel lonely and unconnected in a more individualistic society abroad, where they have less social or cultural ties.

Acculturation migrants' participation in and adoption of the culture and value system of the new country is a relative newcomer to the literature, and it can also represent an essential stress on social wellbeing. The term 'acculturation' is usually taken to mean migrants' participation in the cultural and value system of the host country. Most definitions explicitly demarcate the difference of acculturation in terms of power. Acculturation is an act of new beings being incorporated into or subjected to a different culture. All integration processes involve tension. However, acculturation is often conceptualised as balancing the competing demands of emphasis on the migrants' cultural identity and adaptation to the cultural context of their new home.

Research has demonstrated that acculturation and adaptation occur at all levels of society, including those of the family, where tensions emerge between parents and children as one, or the other tries to push through their understanding of how to navigate the host society (Berry, 1997; Deng, 2016a, 2016b). Parents often identify tensions between the wish to transmit familiar values and the need to support their children's participation, even integration with the context of the new country. For example, acceptable dress for women, language use with parents and outsiders, social respect (e.g., drinking habits), method choice and aspirations for their children's education, and so forth are all subjects where parents report tensions between generations.

Moreover, the absence of social prestige and the presence of prejudice and/or discrimination (which can rise to the level of racism) in a host country can compound social wellbeing challenges. New migrants might have been respected members of their home country but now find themselves the subject of prejudice, marginalisation or outright hostility in the new community. In these circumstances, a sense of estrangement and powerlessness arise, making it challenging to forge new social connections and feel like one has a 'fitting place' in the host society.

For example, a former community leader, now working some low-wage job in a host country, might experience emotional ambivalence and feelings of 'status frustration' that erode the ability to engage with people meaningfully and form new social networks. For social well-being and meaningful community connection, families must re-invest in finding company in cultural/religious organisations, social or recreational groups or special community events to meet others who share their stories.

Community organisations can play a vital role by fostering social wellbeing, socialising migrants into the community, offering a safe space to meet people, organising social activities, and accessing services and opportunities as they integrate into the new country. Social services provided by community organisations can be as diverse as language classes, cultural events, workshops and social gatherings, and support groups for specific needs. They all have the potential to help individuals and families build social networks, preserve and maintain their identity and culture, and access essential services, information and opportunities. For example, a community centre that offers language classes and social activities to migrants might facilitate social interaction among new migrants.

However, building social connections with the wider host society (e.g., involvement in civic activities, volunteering, or joining the local community and/or cultural groups or organisations that reflect their interests and values) can also help. This will facilitate belonging and inclusion in any community, whether a small subgroup or the wider society. For instance, a migrant who volunteers at a community centre or a school or engages in neighbourhood initiatives such as community gardening may appreciate that this kind of involvement helps her build relationships with people from a wider range of social backgrounds and that her efforts enhance the quality of life in the community.

Economic Wellbeing and Financial Security

Economic well-being and financial security are important to meaningful human development and well-being. The post-conflict situation in South Sudan and economic discrimination in foreign countries have made it very difficult and more challenging for South Sudanese and African Diaspora families to achieve and maintain financial well-being.

Lack of decent employment is one of the key obstacles to economic well-being in the diaspora. Migration usually represents a quasi-clean slate for migrants forced to set up home in the new country, often resulting in commencing from a standing start. Language barriers, non-recognition of foreign qualifications and discrimination in the labour market can all contribute to developing a 'normal' experience of the labour market characterised by low wages, insecure 'precarious' employment or overqualification. The engineer or teacher who is drastically underemployed, taking low-paid work in a bar or cleaning public toilets, will develop a sense of frustration, loss of self-esteem and a growing sense of economic deprivation in a status-driven world.

Economic hardships, for example, that many South Sudanese and other families experience could penalise wellbeing because if you are feeling a lot of stress and anxiety about not having enough money, that could lead to worse outcomes in health and health risks. Financial constraints can limit access to modern services vital for human development, such as healthcare, schooling and housing. For example, if a family is spending all of its money on rent or food, they may not be able to afford to go to the hospital when sick or buy notebooks, pens or books for school children.

One possible route to addressing this need is economic and financial empowerment avenues, such as education and training to increase employability, financial literacy and management services, or entrepreneurial opportunities. For instance, a migrant going back to school or earning a certification in a high-need industry may put themselves in a position to increase their wage and benefit from more stable jobs. Likewise, a family returning from abroad may attend financial literacy workshops and offerings to acquire skills to manage their income, savings, and debt expenditures to reach a happy medium on the financial prowess spectrum.

While solutions at the individual level may be helpful, systemic changes are also needed to overcome the economic hurdles South Sudanese and other African diaspora families confront. These are the types of policy changes that could help to promote economic inclusion, for instance, anti-discrimination-policy initiatives that could be implemented in the workplace in addressing settlement challenges, recognising foreign credentials as a complement to alternative approaches, programs to admit immigrants and refugees to education and training. For instance, a government programme that offers a credential-recognition service or skills upgrading funding can assist migrants in acquiring the needed certifications and better realise their economic potential.

Economic wellness is also strongly related to financial literacy and management. Financial management can be especially onerous for many families if they are unfamiliar with their new country's financial systems, practices, and resources. Financial literacy, understanding how to manage personal finances, and the ability to implement that understanding effectively are necessary to ensure and sustain economic wellness.

To increase financial literacy and competence at home, families should search for programmes and classes to help them be informed about financial issues. Families can get help as needed from their banks, financial advisers, or online tools. For example, a family that attends a financial literacy seminar may learn how to create a budget, set financial goals, and build an emergency fund, which may help them gain financial confidence and security.

Culture and Resilience in Human Development

Culture and resilience are vital components of human development and well-being for a person or family facing challenges during their migration process. Culture provides a sense of identification, continuity, and belonging, while resilience helps people and families adapt to and recover from adversity.

Maintaining a sense of tradition is not just a luxury but a necessity for South Sudanese and other diaspora African families. Traditions, practices, and values can serve as a beacon of solidity and continuity amid migration's economic, social, and cultural shifts and dilemmas. When individual families continue cultural traditions and practices, for example, celebrating cultural holidays, participating in spiritual or religious rituals and practices, and passing the culture to their children, they establish a sense of cultural pride and educational backbone.

For instance, rituals or celebrations that maintain a connection with tradition, such as holidays, baptisms, weddings, funerals, or religious services, could protect the family's sense of connection with the culture they regard as their own. These traditional practices might inform the value children take away, foster their sense of identity, and embed them in a larger community of meaning.

Resilience, the ability to move, make and recover from adversity, is not just one element in the recipe of human flourishing; it is itself a superpower that can be learnt and practised. Expressed in this way, resilience has the potential to become a tool, practised and developed to harness the challenges inherent in parenting in the diaspora. We can expand and refine our reservoir of skills, such as building social support networks, positive coping, and finding purpose and meaning in our lives to become resilience champions that enable us and those who love us to parent in an otherwise disorienting world.

Cultural traditions and practices can be a powerful resource for building resilience to migration for many South Sudanese and African families, for instance, through storytelling, music and dance as forms of emotional processing and expression, connecting with others and cultural identity maintenance, and through religious and spiritual practices and resources across a range of faiths as sources of meaning, hope and strength.

Culture provides resources for building resilience and wellbeing through migration for individuals and families. These might include sharing stories of strength with others in the community, participating in traditional dance and music performances, and communal religious expression.

Community associations like cultural associations, worship associations and social clubs can foster culture and resilience through support, resources and opportunities to continue cultural connection. Cultural events, social gatherings and support groups may be valuable for South Sudanese and African families to continue cultural expression, mitigate online harassment and bullying, and continue to build family resilience while living in the diaspora. Social support groups may also offer the opportunity to promote a cultural identity for many South Sudanese and African families who came to Australia and other Western nations through displacement and migration.

However, these community organisations' service providers and policymakers need to be culturally competent and also can serve other families engaged in these communities. If a community association were to host a cultural event for South Sudanese and African migrants, this could be an excellent activity for families living in cultural isolation. Similarly, social engagement groups within the community could also foster resilience among families seeking social engagement groups.

However, they may feel unwelcomed due to racial disparities, stereotypes and discrimination within these groups or if these groups were holding racist policies. Second, community organisations can be a great resource to address the challenges faced by South Sudanese and African families in a more cultural and language-relevant manner than service providers and policymakers within mainstream systems. Many community organisations could also help lobby policymakers, educators and service providers for cultural competence and alignment with the needs of South Sudanese and African families in the diaspora.

Community organisations can also advocate for the needs and rights of South Sudanese and African families in the diaspora. They can engage with policymakers, educators and service providers to promote cultural competence, challenge discrimination and create a more inclusive environment for all families. Cultivating connectedness to cultural pride, building resilience and advancing social capital can be a powerful tool for families to develop a "We feel at home" sense of belonging and purpose in their new locales. For those families, this can mean surviving, thriving despite adversities, and engaging in the hopeful and inclusive vision of forward-thinking for all.

Conclusion

The intersection of human development, well-being, and migration presents a complex and multifaceted journey, particularly for South Sudanese and African diaspora families. Migration is not simply a physical relocation but a profound shift that reshapes every aspect of life, including health, emotional resilience, social ties, and economic stability. For these families, migration comes with unique challenges that influence the developmental trajectory of parents and children as they strive to adapt to new cultural contexts while preserving their identities and traditions.

As explored in this chapter, migration impacts each stage of human development, from childhood to adulthood, creating opportunities for growth while posing significant challenges related to physical and mental health, access to social and healthcare services, and economic well-being. Navigating these changes can strain family dynamics, test resilience, and threaten social cohesion. However, the cultural heritage, values, and communal ties that many South Sudanese and African families bring serve as powerful tools for navigating these challenges.

Culturally grounded approaches to parenting, preserving community connections, and fostering resilience are essential strategies for ensuring that migrant families survive and thrive in their host environments. Community support structures, culturally competent services, and policies that recognise the distinct needs of migrant families are crucial in this regard. By offering pathways for inclusion, social support, and economic empowerment, host societies can create environments that promote the holistic well-being of migrant families.

Most importantly, the success of migrant families in their new environments is a testament to their resilience and adaptability and a reflection of the inclusiveness of the host society. As migration continues to shape the global landscape, the ability of South Sudanese and African families to flourish in their host countries depends on a shared commitment to building strong, supportive communities that value diversity and inclusivity. This chapter highlights the importance of understanding the dynamic relationship between migration and human development. It offers insights into how families can navigate these challenges to achieve long-term well-being and success.

CHAPTER FIFTEEN

Charting the Future: Conclusion and Next Steps

Introduction

As we reach the culmination of Parenting in the Digital Age: A South Sudanese and African Guide, reflecting on the unified vision that has shaped this journey is important. The final chapter serves as both a conclusion and a guide for the future, offering practical strategies, insights, and pathways for navigating the complexities of parenting within the African diaspora, particularly for South Sudanese families. As we revisit the central themes of cultural preservation, resilience, and adaptation, we are reminded of the balancing act families face in preserving their cultural identity while integrating into new societal landscapes.

This chapter is a reflection and a call to action, offering concrete recommendations for parents, community leaders, policymakers, and institutions. It emphasizes the continued need for cultural preservation, community support, and systemic changes that ensure the wellbeing and success of African diaspora families. The challenges of acculturation, the influence of technology, and the pressures of migration require not just individual effort, but a collective one, resilience, and strategic adaptation. Therefore, this chapter aims to inspire hope and resilience for the future, empowering families to continue navigating these complexities with strength, grace, and a sense of unity and support from their community.

In revisiting the key themes explored throughout this guide, we reaffirm the power of cultural identity, the importance of mental and emotional wellbeing, and the need for educational and economic empowerment. These principles provide the foundation upon which South Sudanese and other African diaspora families can build thriving, resilient communities. As we chart the course forward, this chapter will offer a blueprint for action, ensuring that the lessons learned not only inform but also transform the lives of those in the diaspora for generations to come.

Reflecting on Core Themes: Expanding Insights for the Future
We have seen how the many chapters of this guide have woven together various themes integral to the experience of families from South Sudan and Africans abroad. These themes include the complexities and challenges of migration as well as the opportunities offered by migration. With this in mind, we hope that the stories of the women and families in this guide can paint a vivid picture of a totality that marks the best modern parenting.

Preserving Cultural Identity: Foundations and Future Directions
One of the most prominent recurring themes in this guide is the central role of cultural identity and the need to protect it in the context of migration and integration or assimilation. For many South

Sudanese and African families, cultural identity is not a mere label but rather the very foundation of identity. It is the fabric of a rich heritage of traditions, values, beliefs, languages, and practices handed down from generation to generation. Cultural identity also offers a sense of belonging, continuity and stability. It is particularly crucial in the context of migration and uprooting from a known environment into one that is not always seen as welcoming.

Maintaining cultural identity in the diaspora requires significant, intentional effort and investment. It is a balancing act, as families pivot between cultural remembrance and expression on one hand and cultural adaptation to the new context and citizenship on the other. One of the challenges in this process is the dissonance experienced, especially by children, who may find themselves with competing expectations of their parents, on the one hand, and those of their peers and society more broadly. For instance, a child growing up in a Western country may find it increasingly difficult to meet his parents' expectations of dressing traditionally, speaking the heritage language, and doing so faithfully with the attitudes and expressive behaviours of the novel situation.

Beyond struggles within the family, external pressures into the broader community can undermine cultural continuity. Cultural homogenisation that comes with globalisation can flatten some traditions and heritage values, especially when these are not supported from within the community. An increased influx of Western-influenced media, social media, consumer culture and values can create a gap between parents and their children and threaten the intergenerational propagation of their heritage. The question for parents is how to shape their children's identity by keeping their pride in their cultural heritage and ensuring its continuity while allowing them to adapt and succeed in a multicultural modern world.

Here is the point at which this guide has advocated for a hands-on approach to cultural education and maintenance on families' part. It is one thing to pass on information about your heritage and culture to your children, a common practice for many parents. However, it is another way to create opportunities for children to experience and hopefully practise it. Participation in cultural events such as ethnic festivals, religious celebrations, traditional rites and rituals, for example, has been a tried-and-true way to achieve this aim, as have integrating features of their culture, be it language, music, dance or cuisine, into family life.

Building Resilience: Adapting to New Realities

Resilience is another core concept we have discussed in depth in this guide. The life of migration is inevitably tricky. Resilience is the quality that allows individuals and families to adjust to and cope with adversity. For South Sudanese and African families, in particular, ideas about resilience are rooted in traditions, community, and shared histories of survival.

However, rather than merely living through, these families draw on what could be called 'adaptive' or 'culturally appropriate' resilience, a response to stress that allows for survival and includes new learning and growth as part of the process. Families resettled after flight from conflict, for example, resettled immigrants of Syrian descent in the US. They do this by simultaneously adapting to new environments, learning from daily stressors, and affirming their solidarity, faith, and endurance culture. The community becomes a source of support and sometimes survival.

By learning from their country of origin, they can navigate the emotional toll of migration and integration more effectively. Their sense of identity and family is included. However, it continues to be their guide to a safer, more stable society and often contributes to their new homeland's material or emotional well-being. These culturally-rooted ways of navigating the obstacles of exile were passed on from parents to children. The latter adapt and coalesce these resources and values and choose to pass them on yet again, ultimately to their children. An intergenerational advantage emerges built upon the foundation of community support that fosters identity and stability.

In fact, adaptation is a critical component of resilience both in migration and more broadly. Families must adapt to new cultural mores, social systems, and economic realities while often trying to maintain their cultural practices and values. This can mean demarcating their spheres of adaptation in raising their children and their relationships with the broader culture. For instance, parents may have to adapt how they parent to fit the expectations of the values embedded in the host country's schooling system, but at the same time, reject popular cultural trends and values.

Through this guide, we have shared ways to strengthen resilience and adaptation through community support, cultural continuity, and healthy coping behaviours. Building and sustaining strong social connections can create a support network that provides families emotional, practical, and cultural support. Families can assist each other in navigating migration challenges by affiliating with community members while fostering a sense of community, continuity, and belonging in the face of change.

Navigating Integration: Balancing Acculturation and Identity

While integration and acculturation feature centrally in the migration experience for South Sudanese and other African families relocating to the diaspora, it refers to a complex and multilayered process involving integration into host country socio-cultural systems that often necessitates accommodating national laws and social norms while retaining cultural distinctiveness. This process usually involves striking a delicate balance between the duality of assimilation and ethnic fragmentation.

Not all acculturation follows the same pattern; it depends upon the person, the family, and the community. Some families opt for total assimilation, learning the language and ways of the host culture (and, often, abandoning their traditional language and cultural heritage). Others prefer to remain close to their original cultural background in ways that might prevent them from fully participating in the broader society. Most, however, find themselves somewhere in between. They want to integrate without sacrificing all sense of what is distinctively and inspiringly their own.

This guide has analysed the distinctive obstacles and benefits characterising the acculturation and integration experience. One of the major threats is cultural incongruity, particularly between the parents and their children. Children who have assimilated and internalised the host country's culture from an early age, through school, media and peers, will develop attitudes and habits that differ significantly from those of their parents, especially if those parents are attached to more traditional beliefs. In fact, children's departure from the traditional norms of their parents can give rise to remarkable conflict and misunderstanding within the family unit, as parents struggle to come to terms with their children's identity and reconcile their expectations with the reality of their children's new world.

Other challenges are discrimination and racism, which can lead to difficulties in integrating and leave people feeling alienated and isolated. For instance, a family experiencing workplace, housing, and education discrimination will likely find it more difficult to integrate fully into the host society and feel like they belong or have a meaningful connection to the broader society. This Guide has promoted a focus on these challenges through community support, advocacy and education, fostering cultural competence and diversity in the wider society.

On the other hand, integration and acculturation present opportunities for learning, growing, and establishing a mutual understanding of the host culture. An enriched family life can be adapted and integrated into the new community it is moving to. The family members themselves can acquire new skills and competencies in the process of intercultural exchange. Family members can learn a new language, explore a new culture, and create new relationships and communities that they can identify with. The outcome of integration and acculturation can, and should, be a success for the new individuals and the community they enter. With this guide for integration and acculturation, we have aimed to outline strategies and tools for a practice based on open communication, cultural exchange, and mutual respect for the other.

Empowering through Education: Pathways to Economic Wellbeing

Education and economic stability are the keys to a better future for South Sudanese children and families abroad. High-quality education and economic opportunities can help children reach their full potential, and families can build a prosperous and secure life for themselves and their children.

Education is a recurring topic in this guide, as it is widely viewed as an essential route to social mobility, individual and community development, and empowerment. Many in the South Sudanese and African diaspora often see education as a key to the survival and flourishing of the next generation. The 'education moment' is not seen as an end but as a practice deeply valued by those concerned about their children's wellbeing and future prosperity. This Guide has highlighted parents' active engagement in education, culturally responsive teaching, and the role of schools in promoting the educational gains of the most marginalised children.

Education is an essential factor in driving economic well-being. It can enable you and your family to hold onto financial stability, security and prosperity, especially in times of hardship or temporary setbacks. However, economic well-being can be hard to achieve, especially when, as a migrant family, you face obstacles to employment, including language barriers, non-recognition of your foreign qualifications and professional experience, economic, social and cultural discrimination, or a combination of these barriers. This guide has examined these barriers in-depth and offers concrete paths to overcoming them through education and training, financial literacy, and entrepreneurship.

Another key message within this guide is that financial literacy and management are critical skills for achieving and maintaining economic wellbeing. Financial literacy refers to understanding and managing personal finances, such as budgeting, saving, investing, and managing debt. Often, diaspora families must learn how to manage their finances in a completely different country with potentially different processes, practices or resources than at home. For instance, we discuss the importance of understanding the system in a new country and how to handle banking and diaspora remittances.

Fostering Mental and Emotional Wellbeing
Individuals' and their families' emotional and psychological wellbeing is a central dimension of human development. Emigration is an emotionally charged process that can create a range of mental health

issues, such as stress, anxiety, depression and trauma and, for many South Sudanese and African families, these are issues compounded by the experiences of conflict, persecution and displacement that often precede migration.

Good mental and emotional health are functions of the more prominent themes of resilience, cultural continuity and social wellbeing. Families that retain cultural connections and develop strong social networks and practical coping skills are more likely to experience good mental and emotional health. The strategies outlined in this brief focus on practices that foster mental and emotional health, such as access to culturally sensitive mental health services, open dialogue on mental health, and a protective ecosystem that allows for

Stigma about mental health issues is often a significant barrier to mental and emotional wellbeing in the diaspora. Some South Sudanese and African beliefs can frame mental health problems as weakness, shame or blame, and even as a curse due to what the person, or their parents, might have done wrong. This can lead to covering up symptoms or avoiding treatment. Stigma from family, community and friends, ignorance or lack of familiarity with services in the host country and fear of discrimination or prosecution may also discourage people from seeking help. This guide has highlighted the value of destigmatising mental health issues, raising awareness of mental health among migrant communities, and providing culturally sensitive mental health services.

A third challenge is discrimination and racism and the ways that they can impact severely different aspects of mental and emotional health. The experience of discrimination and feeling marginalised, isolated and alienated as a result can cause considerable psychological distress and, ultimately, result in serious repercussions. Strategies in this guide for countering or minimising the impact of discrimination and promoting social inclusion include advocacy, education and community support.

The Vital Role of Cultural Preservation

As we have seen in this guide, South Sudanese and African families' resilience, well-being or success in diasporas hinge on preserving cultural heritage. The preservation of cultural heritage is not about being anchored in the past but about nourishing what we stand for, what we believe in the values, practices and traditions that make us who we are, and transferring that cultural human capital to the next generations to help them thrive and play an active role in the community.

In times of mass migration, preserving culture takes on an added urgency. To migrate usually means that a family has lost its connection to the culture they left behind. They inevitably bring only a fraction of what it takes to sustain culture in a new land, community and society. When families are dispersed across generations across the globe, new, often strained ways of keeping tradition alive can usually emerge. Sometimes, this is easier, other times remarkably difficult, especially in the presence of globalisation, which often seeks to homogenise cultures and diminish timeworn ways of living from the consciousness.

Cultural preservation can also be a proactive, dynamic process rather than merely a defensive tactic. It can mean maintaining traditional practices in new environments and drawing inspiration from other cultures, a method of hybridisation that can enrich culture and even strengthen identity. For example, a family celebrating traditional holidays and rituals in a new land might incorporate practices from the host country.

Nevertheless, cultural preservation is not only about identity. It is about pride, self-confidence, and self-respect. Connecting with and learning to value the culture of our ancestors can empower diasporan children, giving them an infusion of pride that can help them successfully face the challenges of integration and discrimination and provide them with the voice, confidence, and opportunities to contribute positively to their cultural community and broader society. As we have seen, cultural education at home and in the community is vital to fostering cultural pride and identity.

Moreover, cultural preservation has wide-ranging societal benefits beyond familial and personal benefits. The maintenance and celebration of cultural diversity play a vital role in the vibrancy and richness of a host society. Cultural preservation does not serve solely as an anchor that ties the present to the past; it is an anchor that roots the present and the future to the past. Societies that embrace and value the cultural diversity of today's migrants stand to gain a great deal from their unique knowledge, experiences and narratives as they contribute to and enrich their new society.

Final Reflections: Looking Back and Moving Forward

As we reflect on the complex and often unpredictable journey of South Sudanese and African families in the diaspora over the past few decades, I hope that, despite the uncertainties of the future, these communities will continue to renew, evolve, and transform both themselves and the societies in which they live. The migration path is never straightforward and fraught with twists, turns, detours, and obstacles. Yet, within these struggles lie the seeds of hope, renewal, and opportunity.

The resilience of South Sudanese and African families is demonstrated by their ability to navigate new environments and their capacity to reframe their experiences across cultures. They engage in the global community, continuously reshaping their lives and adapting their rich cultural heritage from Africa to Western societies and beyond. They remain deeply rooted in the traditions of their ancestors while simultaneously embracing their roles as 'global citizens', fluidly moving between worlds, acquiring knowledge, and seeking livelihoods wherever opportunities arise.

Despite the inevitable challenges of adapting to new social, economic, and cultural realities, these families work tirelessly to preserve their identities. They strive to secure homes and create environments that reflect the warmth and familiarity of their native countries, from the food they prepare to how they cultivate community bonds. Their unwavering commitment to family, education, economic survival, faith, and the pursuit of a better future, whether in Africa or elsewhere, remains a powerful constant throughout their diaspora experience.

However, the well-being of migrant families does not rest solely on their shoulders. The responsibility to support their integration and success is shared, extending to broader community organisations, educators, policymakers, and allies. Through our collective efforts, we can provide an environment that welcomes and nurtures diversity, fostering a more just and inclusive society for all.

As we look to the future, it is essential to recognise the strengths of South Sudanese and African families in the diaspora. By acknowledging their challenges, celebrating their achievements, and learning from their contributions, we can develop more inclusive systems that enable them to thrive. This necessitates a steadfast commitment to building frameworks that embrace cultural diversity, support family structures, and empower individuals to succeed in their personal and communal aspirations.

This guide has sought to lay the groundwork by offering practical strategies informed by research, lived experiences, and community insights. These foundations provide a platform for meaningful action for families, communities, policymakers, and researchers. Whether you are part of a migrant family seeking resources or a stakeholder invested in shaping a more equitable future, the next step is to build upon these insights and take decisive action toward a more inclusive and supportive world for all.

Actionable Strategies for the Future
In closing and with reference to the major themes discussed throughout this guide, here are three pragmatic recommendations that can aid families, communities, and policymakers in supporting the resilience and flourishing of South Sudanese and other African diaspora families:

First, South Sudanese and other African diaspora families should be encouraged to connect to their social and natural environments. These connections are critical for their wellbeing, help maintain their sense of self-worth, and place their children on a path of success. Parents should do all they can to incorporate traditional rituals and values into their family dynamics and, when possible, to pass on the language of their country of origin through parent-child interactions.

Second, promoting parents and their children's reconnection with their country of origin is significant. Regular return visits and/or prolonged stays in the country of origin will allow them to make continuity with their heritage and get a sense of place and belonging. Many platforms facilitate return migration from ethnic-based organisations and diaspora groups on social media to larger humanitarian and nongovernmental agencies. It is highly recommended that these resources be utilised in addition to actively supporting South Sudanese and other African national development programmes to benefit South Sudan, the wider region, and the diaspora.

Lastly, the case of South Sudanese families in the diaspora should be used as a microcosm to assess the ability of mainstream policymakers in Western countries to implement more culturally understanding best practices in their work with these and other African diaspora families. In addition to these, I would like to highlight the following strategies I believe might expand our knowledge in tackling our day-to-day challenges:

1. Strengthening Cultural Education and Preservation
Parents should reinforce cultural education and preservation at home and in the community. This means teaching children about their cultural heritage, history, values and traditions and providing them opportunities to participate in cultural events and observances. Community organisations can provide essential resources, programmes and opportunities for cultural education, including language classes, workshops, and cultural festivals. Policymakers can support cultural preservation by promoting policies that honour cultural pluralism and multicultural diversity, including policies that fund cultural organisations or community-based organisations that support cultural exchange or foster appreciation of cultural differences.

2. Strengthening mental and emotional wellbeing
Promoting mental and emotional health can be the combined work of families, educators, and service providers. This includes providing access to culturally sensitive mental health services, encouraging free and frank discussion about mental health, and creating mental health-supportive and nonjudgmental environments where people feel safe to seek help.

Mental and emotional health promotion can also be facilitated within families through the creation of a home environment that is positive and respectful, especially for those who are facing challenges, encouraging children and youth to talk about their feelings openly and to develop coping strategies and social supports to combat stress and negative emotions in their daily lives. Community organisations can provide guidance, counselling and support groups based on the needs of migrant families. Policymakers can play a role in promoting and funding mental health services through programmes to increase the community's awareness and reduce the stigma associated with mental health problems.

3. Advancing educational success

Fostering children's eventual academic success is of critical importance to families; hence their involvement in the educational development of their offspring, be it liaising with schools, advocating for their children's educational rights and needs, supporting growth mindset that values growth (i.e., effort and learning), or helping to maintain a positive home learning environment conducive to learning (e.g., setting up a specific time for homework, providing educational resources, and encouraging a love of learning). Schools and educators can increase academic performance through culturally responsive curricular and teaching practices, as well as support for English language learners within the school context (e.g., testing and demographic tracking services), not just navigating the nuances of a second language but ensuring that language differences are not misunderstood for lack of academic competence. Policymakers can help increase education through education policies that aid students, regardless of their backgrounds or circumstances, in having access to 'good quality' education.

4. Boosting economic security

Family wellbeing relies on economic stability, and families can prioritise economic empowerment. This might include pursuing further education and training to increase employability, accessing financial literacy resources, and exploring entrepreneurship opportunities. Families can also provide economic security by empowering members to effectively manage their finances by following and enacting budgets and saving money and investment (both of which can help plan for the future). Community organisations can contribute to economic empowerment by providing job placement services, financial literacy programs, microfinance schemes and other types of empowerment opportunities. For example, policymakers can create policies that will foster and facilitate education and training for learners and workers, inform and accept the value of foreign qualifications, and facilitate economic inclusion and opportunity for all.

5. Fostering social connections and community building - is vital to social well-being.

Families can do this through opportunities to get to know more people in the community, such as other cultural organisations, religious institutions or social groups that can allow the exchange of ideas and create social connections and feelings of belonging. Community organisations can foster human connections and community building by providing space for social and cultural exchange and community involvement. Policymakers can support social well-being by promoting social inclusion and diversity through funding community organisations and initiatives fostering intercultural dialogue and exchange.

6. Advocating for policy change

Politicians can advance policy change to make the world more family-equitable, but to do so means encouraging legislative, structural and programme change. Political leaders should push for policies promoting cultural competence, economic inclusion, and access to healthcare and education for migrants, refugees, and their families. This means supporting efforts at the international political level and engaging at the local, regional and national levels. Families and communities can push for policy change by being aware of the challenges facing migrant communities, engaging directly with policymakers and other political leaders, and voting for and creating policies that foster equity for all people and families. We know there is power in coming together to create a world that values and supports all people regardless of their origins, abilities, races, gender identities or sexual orientations.

7. Harnessing Technology for Positive Impact

Technology can disrupt culture and cultural identity, yet it can also help foster and build connections, education and empowerment. Families should use technology to support their cultural identity and connection with their local and global community through social media to connect with others who share similar cultural backgrounds, by using online educational platforms, and by participating and engaging in various cultural events and activities held virtually. Community organisations can utilise technology to enhance cultural preservation and social inclusion by developing online civil society platforms that support cultural exchange and education, by providing virtual support services for migrants and communities, and by using technology to reach and engage migrants. Policymakers can help young people and migrants positively utilise technology by promoting access and digital literacy policies for all individuals and communities, regardless of their background and social reality.

Cultivating Hope and Resilience

We want to end this primer on a hopeful note. Despite everything, as families approach these hopes, they are much more than simple failures or successes to be quantified. Forced migration and the following process of healing and reconnection are some of the heaviest burdens a family can face. Still, they are also some of the most significant moments of learning, growth, and transformation. South Sudanese and African families have proven their resilience for thousands of years. They sure as hell will be doing it for another thousand.

Made possible by the resilient components of cultural rebirth in emigration, adaptation to new environments, and determination towards dreams, South Sudanese and African diaspora families can thrive in tradition and innovation. We are not alone on this road or path. We are in the community and, in concert, the solidarity and mutuality of an ever-further consolidating worldwide that is twinning toward the regenerative future of full and capable life for all.

Overall, this guide has provided a roadmap for immigrants and refugees in modern parenting, with tools, information and suggestions to help South Sudanese, African and other migrant families in the diaspora experiencing migration to a foreign environment, with the centrality of culture, resilience and social inclusion. We must build on these strengths, celebrate our successes, and continue to create greater justice, inclusion and prosperity worldwide.

Finally, as we bring this journey to a close, it is essential to acknowledge the strength, resilience, and adaptability that have been central to the experiences of South Sudanese and African diaspora families. This guide has offered a roadmap for navigating parenting challenges in the digital age while preserving cultural identity, fostering resilience, and promoting integration within new environments. However, the journey does not end here; it continues through the everyday decisions, actions, and strategies employed by families, communities, and policymakers to ensure a prosperous future for the next generation.

The challenges we have explored are real and complex but also present opportunities for growth, connection, and transformation. By embracing our rich cultural heritage while adapting to the evolving world, we create a foundation for future generations to thrive. The strength of our families lies not only in our ability to withstand adversity but also in our commitment to fostering hope, building strong communities, and advocating for a more inclusive, supportive, and equitable society.

As we look ahead, let us do so with confidence in our shared values and collective strength. The future is bright, and by continuing to prioritise cultural preservation, education, economic empowerment, and emotional wellbeing, we can ensure that the next generation flourishes in an increasingly interconnected world. Together, we will continue to light the path forward, grounded in our traditions, enriched by our experiences, and united in our vision for a better tomorrow.

REFERENCES

Adler, S. (1977). Maslow's need hierarchy and the adjustment of immigrants. International migration review, 444-451.

Alayarian, A. (2007). Trauma, resilience and creativity: Examining our therapeutic approach in working with refugees. European Journal of Psychotherapy and Counselling, 9(3), 313-324.

Alhabash, S., & Ma, M. (2017). A tale of four platforms: Motivations and uses of Facebook, Twitter, Instagram, and Snapchat among college students? Social media+ society, 3(1), 2056305117691544.

Ambasz, D., Gupta, A., & Patrinos, H. A. (2023). A Review of Human Development and Environmental Outcomes. World Bank.

Attias-Donfut, C. (2012). Citizenship, belonging and intergenerational relations in African migration. Palgrave Macmillan.

Baumrind, D. (1991). The influence of parenting style on adolescent competence and substance use. The journal of early adolescence, 11(1), 56-95.

Berry, J. W. (1990). Understanding Individuals Moving Between Cultures. Applied cross-cultural psychology, 14, 232.

Berry, J. W. (1992a). Acculturation and adaptation in a new society. International Migration, 30(1/2).

Berry, J. W. (1992b). Acculturation and adaptation in a new society. International migration, 30, 69-69.

Berry, J. W. (1997). Immigration, acculturation, and adaptation. Applied psychology, 46(1), 5-34.

Berry, J. W. (2006). Acculturation: A conceptual overview. Acculturation and parent-child relationships, 13-32.

Berry, J. W. (2017). Theories and models of acculturation. The Oxford handbook of acculturation and health, 10, 15-28.

Berry, J. W., Phinney, J. S., Sam, D. L., & Vedder, P. (2006). Immigrant youth: Acculturation, identity, and adaptation. Applied psychology, 55(3), 303-332.

Bhatt, G., & Hackney, L.-D. (2014). Khan Academy.

Bronfenbrenner, U. (2000). Ecological systems theory. American Psychological Association.

Bürgin, D., Anagnostopoulos, D., Vitiello, B., Sukale, T., Schmid, M., & Fegert, J. M. (2022). Impact of war and forced displacement on children's mental health—multilevel, needs-oriented, and trauma-informed approaches. European child & adolescent psychiatry, 31(6), 845-853.

Buriel, R. (1993). Acculturation, respect for cultural differences, and biculturalism among three generations of Mexican American and Euro American school children. The Journal of genetic psychology, 154(4), 531-543.

Copping, A., Shakespeare-Finch, J., & Paton, D. (2010). Towards a culturally appropriate mental health system: Sudanese-Australians' experiences with trauma. Journal of Pacific Rim Psychology, 4(01), 53-60.

Cunningham, M., & Cunningham, J. D. (1997). Patterns of symptomatology and patterns of torture and trauma experiences in resettled refugees. Australian and New Zealand Journal of Psychiatry, 31(4), 555-565.

De Haas, H., Castles, S., & Miller, M. J. (2019). The age of migration: International population movements in the modern world. Bloomsbury Publishing.

Deng, F. (2009). Customary Law in the Modern World : The Crossfire of Sudan's War of Identities (1 ed.). Taylor and Francis. http://VU.eblib.com.au/patron/FullRecord.aspx?p=460300

Deng, F. M. (1972). Dinka of the Sudan. ed. Holt, Reinhart, and Winston. In: Inc. Prospect Heights, IL: Waveland Press.

Deng, S. A. (2013B). New Settlers' Family Resilience – Positive Parenting Programme [Training Booklet]. Auckland South Sudanese Community Inc.

Deng, S. A. (2016a). Fitting the jigsaw: South Sudanese family dynamics and parenting practices in Australia Victoria University].

Deng, S. A. (2016b). South Sudanese youth acculturation and intergenerational challenges. Annual Conference,

Deng, S. A., & Marlowe, J. (2013). Refugee Resettlement and Parenting in a Different Context. Journal of Immigrant & Refugee Studies. http://www.tandfonline.com

Deng, S. A., & Marlowe, J. M. (2013). Refugee Resettlement and Parenting in a Different Context. Journal of Immigrant & Refugee Studies, 11(4), 416-430.

Deng, S. A., & Pienaar, F. (2011). Positive parenting: Integrating sudanese traditions and New Zealand styles of parenting. An evaluation of strategies with Kids-Information for Parents (SKIP). Australasian Review of African Studies, The, 32(2), 160.

Dunlavy, A. C. (2010). The Impact of Acculturation, Trauma, and Post-Migration Stressors on the Mental Health of African Immigrants and Refugees in Sweden University of Pittsburgh].

Earnest, J., Housen, T., & Gillieatt, S. (2007). Adolescent and young refugee perspectives on psychosocial well-being. ISBN, 1(74067), 5193.

Fisher, P. (2007). Experiential knowledge challenges 'normality' and individualized citizenship: towards 'another way of being'. Disability & society, 22(3), 283-298.

Gamble, D. N., & Weil, M. (2010). Community practice skills: Local to global perspectives. Columbia University Press.

Grossman, M., & Sharples, J. (2010). Don't Go There: Young People's Perspectives on Community Safety and Policing: a Collaborative Reseach Project with Victoria Police, Region 2 (Westgate). Victoria University.

Harris, V., & Marlowe, J. (2011). Hard Yards and High Hopes: The Educational Challenges of African Refugee University Students in Australia. International Journal of Teaching and Learning in Higher Education, 23(2), 186-196.

Hinkley, T., Brown, H., Carson, V., & Teychenne, M. (2018). Cross sectional associations of screen time and outdoor play with social skills in preschool children. PloS one, 13(4), e0193700.

Johnson, D. H. (2016). The Root Causes of Sudan's Civil Wars: Old Wars & New Wars (Vol. 38). Boydell & Brewer.

Joshi, L. H. (2015). New Old-Fashioned Parenting: A Guide to Help You Find the Balance between Traditional and Modern Parenting. Summersdale Publishers LTD-ROW.

Lansford, J. E., Chang, L., Dodge, K. A., Malone, P. S., Oburu, P., Palmérus, K., Bacchini, D., Pastorelli, C., Bombi, A. S., & Zelli, A. (2005). Physical discipline and children's adjustment: Cultural normativeness as a moderator. Child development, 76(6), 1234-1246.

Losoncz, I. (2011). Blocked opportunity and threatened identity: Understanding experiences of disrespect in South Sudanese Australians. Australasian Review of African Studies, The, 32(2), 118.

Losoncz, I. (2012). "We are thinking they are helping us, but they are destroying us."–Repairing the legitimacy of Australian government authorities among South Sudanese families.

Maher, S., Deng, S. A., & Kindersley, N. (2018). South Sudanese Australians: constantly negotiating belonging and identity. Sudan Studies, 58, 53-65.

Mansouri, F., Ben-Moshe, D., & Johns., A. (2015). Intergenerational Relationsh in New-Arrived Communities in Victoria: A Pilot Study Report.

Marlowe, J., Harris, A., & Lyons, T. (2014). South Sudanese diaspora in Australia and New Zealand: Reconciling the past with the present. Cambridge Scholars Publishing.

Marlowe, J. M. (2009). Conceptualising refugee resettlement in contested landscapes.

Marlowe, J. M. (2010). Beyond the discourse of trauma: shifting the focus on Sudanese refugees. Journal of refugee studies, 23(2), 183-198.

Mathers, M., Canterford, L., Olds, T., Hesketh, K., Ridley, K., & Wake, M. (2009). Electronic media use and adolescent health and well-being: cross-sectional community study. Academic pediatrics, 9(5), 307-314.

McDonald-Wilmsen, B., & Gifford, S. M. (2009). NEW ISSUES IN REFUGEE RESEARCH.

McMichael, C., Gifford, S., & Correa-Velez, I. (2011). Negotiating family, navigating resettlement: family connectedness amongst resettled youth with refugee backgrounds living in Melbourne, Australia. Journal of Youth Studies, 14(2), 179-195.

MenjÅvar, C., & Menjívar, C. (2000). Fragmented ties: Salvadoran immigrant networks in America. Univ of California Press.

Milner, K., & Khawaja, N. G. (2010). Sudanese refugees in Australia the impact of acculturation stress. Journal of Pacific Rim Psychology, 4(1), 19-29.

Ochocka, J., & Janzen, R. (2008). Immigrant parenting: A new framework of understanding. Journal of Immigrant & Refugee Studies, 6(1), 85-111.

Papadopoulos, R. K. (2007). Refugees, trauma and adversity-activated development. European Journal of Psychotherapy and Counselling, 9(3), 301-312.

Pittaway, T., & Dantas, J. A. (2024). African youth gangs: The marginalization of South Sudanese young people in Melbourne, Australia. Journal of Immigrant & Refugee Studies, 22(1), 178-194.

Potocky-Tripodi, M. (2002). Best practices for social work with refugees and immigrants. Columbia University Press.

Pouch, G. (2006). Intergenerational conflict, changes and resolutions within the Sudanese community: Parents vs. young people. International Consortium for Intergenerational Programs Conference, Melbourne, Australia,

Renzaho, A., McCabe, M., & Sainsbury, W. (2011). Parenting, role reversals and the preservation of cultural values among Arabic speaking migrant families in Melbourne, Australia. International journal of intercultural relations, 35(4), 416-424.

Rex, J., Joly, D., & Wilpert, C. (1987). Immigrant associations in Europe.

Richman, N. (1998). In the Midst of the Whirlwind: A Manual for Helping Refugee Children. ERIC.

Richtel, M. (2010). Growing up digital, wired for distraction. The New York Times, 1.

Sanders, M. R. (1999). Triple P-Positive Parenting Program: Towards an empirically validated multilevel parenting and family support strategy for the prevention of behavior and emotional problems in children. Clinical child and family psychology review, 2(2), 71-90.

Schweitzer, R., Melville, F., Steel, Z., & Lacherez, P. (2006). Trauma, post-migration living difficulties, and social support as predictors of psychological adjustment in resettled Sudanese refugees. Australian and New Zealand Journal of Psychiatry, 40(2), 179-188.

Searle, W., Prouse, E., L'Ami, E., Gray, A., & Gruner, A. (2012). New land, new life: Long-term settlement of refugees in New Zealand–main report. Quota Refugees Ten Years on. Department of Labour. Wellington.

Serraglio, D. A., & Adaawen, S. (2023). International Organization for Migration (IOM).".

Shortt, M., Tilak, S., Kuznetcova, I., Martens, B., & Akinkuolie, B. (2023). Gamification in mobile-assisted language learning: A systematic review of Duolingo literature from public release of 2012 to early 2020. Computer Assisted Language Learning, 36(3), 517-554.

SKIP. (2011). Strategies with Kids – Information for Parents (SKIP). Conscious Parenting. Supporters of Parents, Module One New Zealand Ministry of Social Development. . Retrieved 3 Sept from http://www.skip.org.nz/documents/resources/research-and-training/training-moduleconscious-parenting.pdf

Song, L. (2012). Raising network resources while raising children? Access to social capital by parenthood status, gender, and marital status. Social Networks, 34(2), 241-252.

Stansfeld, S. A., Marmot, M., & Wilkinson, R. (2006). Social support and social cohesion. Social determinants of health, 2, 148-171.

Straker, L., Beynon, A., Smith, S., Johnson, D., Wyeth, D., Sefton Green, J., & Kervin, L. evidence-based decision making regarding digital technology use with, by and for children.

Straus, M. A. (1991). Discipline and deviance: Physical punishment of children and violence and other crime in adulthood. Social problems, 133-154.

Tribe, R. (1999). Therapeutic work with refugees living in exile: observations on clinical practice. Counselling Psychology Quarterly, 12(3), 233-243.

Westoby, P. (2008). Developing a community-development approach through engaging resettling Southern Sudanese refugees within Australia. Community development journal, 43(4), 483-495.

Yenika-Agbaw, V., & Mhando, L. (2014). African Youth in Contemporary Literature and Popular Culture.

www.ingramcontent.com/pod-product-compliance
Lightning Source LLC
Chambersburg PA
CBHW011521070526
44585CB00022B/2488